The School Tradition
of the
Old Testament

The School Tradition of the Old Testament

THE BAMPTON LECTURES FOR 1994

E. W. HEATON

OXFORD UNIVERSITY PRESS
1994

Oxford University Press, Walton Street, Oxford OX2 6DP
Oxford New York Toronto
Delhi Bombay Calcutta Madras Karachi
Kuala Lumpur Singapore Hong Kong Tokyo
Nairobi Dar es Salaam Cape Town
Melbourne Auckland Madrid
and associated companies in
Berlin Ibadan

Oxford is a trade mark of Oxford University Press

Published in the United States
by Oxford University Press Inc., New York

British Library Cataloguing in Publication Data
Data available

Library of Congress Cataloging in Publication Data
The school tradition of the Old Testament: the Bampton lectures
for 1994/E. W. Heaton.
Includes bibliographical references and indexes.
1. Education in the Bible. 2. Bible. O.T.—Authorship.
3. Wisdom—Biblical teaching. 4. Education, Ancient. 5. Wisdom
literature—Criticism, interpretation, etc. I. Title.
BS1199.E38H43 1994 221.6'7—dc20 94–5918
ISBN 0–19–826362–7

1 3 5 7 9 10 8 6 4 2

Typeset by Cambrian Typesetters, Frimley, Surrey
Printed in Great Britain on acid-free paper by
Biddles Ltd., Guildford and King's Lynn

For our grandchildren
ALEXANDRA
DAVID, EMILY
GEORGINA, HARRIET, WILLIAM

PREFACE

I have good reason to be more than usually grateful to have been invited (quite out of the blue) to be the Bampton Lecturer for 1994. After my retirement two years ago relieved me of pressing duties, my former colleagues generously recalled that I was due to give the Bamptons in 1980, when a change of Deaneries from Durham to Christ Church suddenly demanded all my attention and forced me, with great reluctance, to withdraw. It is very pleasing, after fourteen years, to be given this second chance.

The period during which I have been mulling over the theme of these lectures goes back even further. I discover, somewhat to my surprise, that the school tradition of the Old Testament emerges, inchoately at first and quite explicitly later, in almost everything I have written. My first (and very modest) academic articles nearly fifty years ago were about Egypt and the Story of Joseph. The commentary on *Daniel*, which was published in 1956, placed special emphasis on its origin in a learned circle of teachers, and in *The Old Testament Prophets* (1958, 1977) I argued that the great independent figures of the eighth and seventh centuries were educated laymen. *The Hebrew Kingdoms* (1968) provided a further opportunity of developing the theme that 'men of learning made an immense, if anonymous, contribution to the presentation and growth of Israel's distinctive heritage'. *Solomon's New Men* (1974), as this somewhat trendy title was intended to suggest, explored the emergence of Israel as a bureaucratic state 'like all the nations' (and, in particular, Egypt), with school-trained officials to run it. I have given this outline to indicate that the present study has a certain claim to independence; it is, at least, the result of following a scent detected long ago and not of allowing fashions in scholarship to lead me by the nose.

I am, nevertheless, deeply indebted to many Old Testament scholars, as I hope my bibliographical notes adequately acknowledge, and there are three, in particular, to whom I owe a great deal. I have profited immensely from the work of R. N. Whybray, even though his academic caution disallowed my main contention about the importance of schools in Old Testament times. However, in his seminal study, *The Intellectual Tradition in the Old Testament* (1974), it enabled him to demolish a lot of jerry-building thrown up by 'wisdom studies' and so clear the ground for fresh constructions with more reliable foundations. Secondly, the important monograph of André Lemaire, *Les Écoles et la formation de la Bible dans l'ancien Israël* (1981), followed by his paper, *Sagesse et écoles* (1984), with their extensive reviews of current scholarship, provided a welcome support to the conclusions being presented in this study. Above all, however, I wish to express my gratitude to my friend, John Barton, now most appropriately established in Oxford's Oriel Chair of the Interpretation of Holy Scripture, for the inspiring freshness and clarity of his published work, especially on the post-exilic understanding of prophecy (*Oracles of God*, 1986) and the ethical teaching of the Old Testament.

These eight lectures were delivered in the University Church of St Mary the Virgin, Oxford, on Sunday mornings during the Hilary and Trinity Terms, 1994, in a somewhat abbreviated version of the present text. It has been a great pleasure to renew my dealings with Oxford University Press.

Finally, I must affectionately salute my wife and family for being so marvellously tolerant of my disappearances into the study, especially during our summer stay in Arkadia.

E. W. HEATON

Arkadia, Greece

ACKNOWLEDGEMENT

The biblical quotations are taken (except as otherwise noted) from *The Revised English Bible with the Apocrypha*, first published in 1989 by Oxford and Cambridge University Presses. However, the practice of the translators in using capital letters for the divine name ('LORD') has not been followed.

CONTENTS

List of Abbreviations   xii

    I.   A Jerusalem School Inspected   1

    II.   Schools and Libraries   24
          Excursus: The Art of Speaking

    III.   School-Books from Egypt   45

    IV.   Education in Wisdom   65

    V.   Prophets and Teachers   93

    VI.   Story-Writers   115

    VII.   Honest Doubters   137

    VIII.   Belief and Behaviour   159

    IX.   Retrospect   183

Chronological Tables   191

Index of Biblical References   195

Index of Subjects   204

ABBREVIATIONS

ANET	*Ancient Near Eastern Texts relating to the Old Testament*, J. B. Pritchard (ed.), 1955
BA	*Biblical Archaeologist*
BAR	J. H. Breasted, *Ancient Records of Egypt*, 5 vols., 1906–7
BASOR	*Bulletin of the American Schools of Oriental Research*
BJRL	*Bulletin of the John Rylands Library*
BZAW	*Beihefte zur Zeitschrift für die Alttestamentliche Wissenschaft*
Caminos	R. A. Caminos, *Late Egyptian Miscellanies*, 1954
CBQ	*Catholic Biblical Quarterly*
CE	*Chronique d'Égypte*
CJTh	*Canadian Journal of Theology*
DOTT	*Documents from Old Testament Times*, D. Winton Thomas (ed.), 1958
Erman, AE	*The Ancient Egyptians: A Sourcebook of their Writings*, A. Erman, trans. A. M. Blackman, with new introduction by W. K. Simpson, 1966
ET	*Expository Times*
HUCA	*Hebrew Union College Annual*
JAOS	*Journal of the American Oriental Society*
JBL	*Journal of Biblical Literature*
JCS	*Journal of Cuneiform Studies*
JEA	*Journal of Egyptian Archaeology*
JNES	*Journal of Near Eastern Studies*
JSOT	*Journal for the Study of the Old Testament*
JSS	*Journal of Semitic Studies*
JTS	*Journal of Theological Studies*, New Series
LAE	*The Literature of Ancient Egypt*, William Kelly Simpson (ed.), New Edition, 1973

Lambert	*Babylonian Wisdom Literature*, W. G. Lambert (ed.), 1960
NEB	*New English Bible*, 1970
RB	*Revue Biblique*
VT	*Vetus Testamentum*
ZAW	*Zeitschrift für die Alttestamentliche Wissenschaft*

I

A JERUSALEM SCHOOL
INSPECTED

1. *Hypotheses*

'Scepticism is always respectable in a scholar; it is thought better to disbelieve something that may turn out to be true than to believe something that may turn out to be false.'[1] This sharp observation by a former Oxford tutor in classics is amply confirmed by the many respectable Old Testament scholars who are still sceptical about the existence of schools in ancient Israel, which is, of course, the presupposition upon which our whole enquiry rests. Their doubt is nurtured by the fact that there is no unambiguous reference to a school in Israel until Ben Sira's 'house of instruction', which flourished in Jerusalem during the early years of the second century BC. For them, absence of evidence is evidence of absence.[2]

It will emerge as we proceed that, in fact, the evidence for schools from the pre-exilic period onwards is weighty and diverse, but it is worth pausing to notice how little importance is to be attached to the absence of *the kind of evidence* which the sceptical scholars look for and fail to find. If we are to draw conclusions, by the same criteria, from the silence of the Old Testament authors, the armed forces of Israel lacked any efficient organization until the troops began to get regular pay in the second century BC;[3] there were no

---

[1] M. L. West, *Early Greek Philosophy and the Orient* (1971), 170.
[2] Ecclus. 51: 23; for example, R. N. Whybray: 'The evidence for the existence of schools with professional teachers in Israel, at any rate until late times, is, then, not conclusive.' *The Intellectual Tradition in the Old Testament* (1974), 43.
[3] 1 Macc. 14: 32; F. C. Grant and H. H. Rowley (eds.), *Dictionary of the Bible*, 2nd edn. (1963): 'Army' (5), 56.

reliable courts or judicial procedures;[4] medical treatment was not available before the second century BC;[5] there were no leather-workers to make harness and writing-scrolls;[6] there were no brick-makers for ordinary house-building;[7] the preparation of oil from olives was an unknown skill;[8] nobody ever went hunting or fishing;[9] nobody ever played games or enjoyed any kind of recreation;[10] there were no wedding ceremonies or celebrations;[11] and weaving cannot have been much practised, since the only loom mentioned in the Old Testament is the one in which Delilah trapped the seven loose locks of Samson's hair.[12] If the Old Testament were a reference book like *Whitaker's Almanack*, silence on these matters of everyday life would be significant; but this is not the case. So much for the absence of evidence.

Most of our sceptical scholars, who like to be on the safe side, still ascribe the most obviously academic of the Old Testament writings to a specific class of men who, it is claimed, were known as 'the wise'. This theory of authorship was primarily invented to account for the books of Job and Ecclesiastes, both of which are dominated by intellectual discussion and use the terms 'wise' and 'wisdom' more often than the rest of the Old Testament put together.[13] The isolation of these two eccentric works, written some time after the Exile, was somewhat reduced when Ecclesiasticus was acknowledged as a late 'wisdom' book and Proverbs as an early one.

Unfortunately, no scholar has been able to *locate* these literary 'wise men' in any recognizable structure or corner of Israelite society; their activity has never been pinned down as a coherent historical phenomenon. It is true that the Old Testament writers use 'the wise' to describe foreign court officials,[14] but they never use the term (with one possible

---

[4] *Dictionary of the Bible*, 'Justice', 543–4.
[5] Ibid., 'Medicine' (1), 637–8; (4), 640.
[6] Ibid., 'Arts and Crafts', (5), 59; 'Writing' (8), 1048.
[7] Ibid., 'Arts and Crafts', (4), 58.   [8] Ibid., 'Oil', 710.
[9] Ibid., 'Hunting', 407; Fishing, see 'Food' (6), 302.
[10] Ibid., 'Games', 315.   [11] Ibid., 'Marriage', (5)(2), 625–6.
[12] Judg. 16: 13, 14; *Dictionary*, 'Spinning and Weaving' (3), 933.
[13] Whybray, *Intellectual Tradition*, 76–120.
[14] Gen. 41: 8; Exod. 7: 11; Jer. 50: 35; 51: 57; Esther 1: 13; cf. Isa. 19: 11, 12.

exception)[15] for any of the officers or courtiers in the royal entourage of Israel.[16]

The identity of the 'wise men' and the historical context of their 'wisdom tradition' have been made even more obscure in recent scholarship by the extension of the category of 'wisdom' to bring under its umbrella a wide variety of literary genres (stories, prophetic oracles, psalms, poems, and expositions of the law) judged (often plausibly) to possess a style and intellectual stance akin to the four basic wisdom books.[17] This development has led to confident talk of a 'Wisdom Movement' from which 'Wisdom Influence' had emanated and spread, it seems, like some cultural virus. This inflated 'Wisdom Movement' is even more elusive than the more modest 'wisdom tradition' from which it sprang and, being more inclusive, is less coherent. The famous speech of Theseus in the final act of *A Midsummer Night's Dream* irresistibly springs to mind:

> More strange than true, I never may believe
> These antique fables, nor these fairy toys . . .
> Such shaping fantasies, that apprehend
> More than cool reason ever comprehends . . .
> And as imagination bodies forth
> The forms of things unknown, the poet's pen
> Turns them to shapes, and gives to airy nothing
> A local habitation and a name.
> Such tricks hath strong imagination.

Some of those who recognize that the enthusiastic proponents of the 'Wisdom Movement' have simply given to 'airy nothing a local habitation and a name' suggest that, in order to extricate scholarship from the present methodological confusion, we must distinguish different kinds of wisdom—such as instruction for everyday life, wisdom literature, philosophical and theological reflection—and

---

[15] Jer. 18: 18; see Whybray, *Intellectual Tradition*, 24–31.

[16] Ibid. 15–31; 'wise' in Isa. 5: 21; 29: 14; Jer. 8: 8; 9: 23 appears to have a quite general meaning.

[17] Donn F. Morgan, *Wisdom in the Old Testament Traditions* (1981); J. L. Crenshaw, 'Method in Determining Wisdom Influence upon "Historical" Literature', *JBL* 88 (1969), 129–42; J. L. Crenshaw (ed.), *Studies in Ancient Israelite Wisdom* (1976), 3–13; J. A. Emerton, 'Wisdom', in G. W. Anderson (ed.), *Tradition and Interpretation* (1979), 221–7.

relate each to its own specific *Sitz im Leben*. Easier said, one might think, than done.[18] Another escape from the impasse is to consider the literature now covered by the 'Wisdom Movement' as deriving from an informal 'Intellectual Tradition' cultivated—without professional or institutional support—by a succession of educated and prosperous farmers of the kind depicted in the Prologue to the book of Job.[19]

The idea of the landed gentry writing books for each other's enjoyment has a certain conservative charm, but it is no less nebulous than the hypothesis it seeks to replace. The 'Intellectual Tradition' is essentially a residual concept— what is left (like the grin of the Cheshire Cat) when all other interpretations have been made to vanish on linguistic grounds. The term 'wise', it is claimed, is adjectival rather than specific and vocational and is not used to designate any kind of professional class—whether court officials, writers of books, or school teachers.[20] But these educated and prosperous farmers are no more than fictitious characters, invented, after the elimination of all the more familiar candidates, in order to account for Proverbs, Job, and Ecclesiastes along with those parts of the Old Testament literature which share their outlook and idiom. The hypothesis of an informal and unstructured 'Intellectual Tradition' is not a very serviceable tool for those wishing to engage in further investigations. Since it is not related to any identifiable Israelite institution about which we have some knowledge and can ask further questions, it makes no contribution to our understanding of the complex traditions which underlie the Old Testament. Most obviously, it fails to explain how the Israelite authors came into contact with the school literature of Egypt and how their tradition and their writings were transmitted through all the vicissitudes of Israel's history.

In view of the confusion and loss of confidence among those engaged in the 'wisdom research' industry, our modest proposal is to experiment with the hypothesis that the

---

[18] Crenshaw, *Studies in Ancient Israelite Wisdom*, 3–5, 22; A. Lemaire, *Les Écoles et la formation de la Bible dans l'ancien Israël* (1981), 45; A. Lemaire, 'Sagesse et écoles', *VT* XXXIV/3 (1984), 271.

[19] Whybray, *Intellectual Tradition*, 65–70.   [20] Ibid. 15–54.

literature which has been at the centre of the discussion was the product of Israel's schools. It was the authors' education which gave their writings a distinctive identity. It is, of course, true that all the books of the Old Testament without exception were written by schoolmen (in the minimal sense that their authors were taught at school to read and write) and it might be thought that this all-inclusiveness makes it impossible to fashion any significant definition of the school tradition, since (as a wise friend of Isaak Walton put it) 'that which is everybody's business is nobody's business'.[21]

It seems feasible, however, to make distinctions clear enough for our present purpose, which is to explore the influence of the schools. We have only to consult our own experience of schools and colleges to recognize that those of their members who subsequently put pen to paper do so in varied capacities and in correspondingly varied genres. You have physicists as well as novelists, accountants as well as poets, scholars as well as comedians, archaeologists as well as political commentators, chemists as well as writers on cookery. It would, perhaps, be invidious, but certainly not very difficult, to single out those publications in this diverse literary output which reflected most clearly their authors' educational background. By analogy, it ought to be possible to make some progress in identifying a core of Old Testament writings, which by their subject-matter, their literary form, and, above all, their delight in language, reveal what their authors encountered at school. Our working hypothesis is that it will be illuminating to review these writings against their school background, in the expectation that our attention will be drawn to features in them often overlooked and that we shall become more aware of the impressive continuity of Israel's school tradition.

Notwithstanding its wide ramifications, the school tradition will be found to have its distinctive features. It is distinct from popular religion and that view of divine–human relations which was embodied in the cult. Characteristically, it is engaged in the teaching of a moral and reasonable faith,

---

[21] Izaak Walton, *The Compleat Angler; or the Contemplative Man's Recreation*, ch. 2.

which is detached (or, at least, semi-detached) from national triumphalism. In addition, it provides the vital clue to the activity in Israel of a less parochial brand of theologian; it helps explain the obscure transmission of Israel's literature through the centuries; and it illuminates the way in which the received tradition was reshaped and reinterpreted by a succession of scholarly editors.

Our exploration of the school tradition will move from the known to the relatively unknown and that means taking as our starting point the school of Ben Sira in Jerusalem.

2. Ben Sira

Joshua ben Sira, or, if you prefer it, Jesus son of Sirach—Ben Sira for short—ran a school in Jerusalem at the beginning of the second century BC and the substance of what he taught has been preserved (albeit in a written-up form) in the book Ecclesiasticus:

> I, Jesus son of Sirach Eleazar, of Jerusalem,
> whose mind became a fountain of wisdom,
> have provided in this book
> instruction in good sense and understanding.
> Happy the man who occupies himself with these things,
> who lays them to heart and becomes wise![22]

It is no coincidence that this confident colophon adopts the regular convention of the books of Instruction compiled by the scribal teachers of Egypt, as we may judge from the colophon at the end of *The Instruction of Amen-em-opet* (dated about 1100 BC):

> See thou these thirty chapters:
> They entertain; they instruct;
> They are the foremost of all books;
> They make the ignorant to know . . .
> Fill thyself with them; put them in thy heart
> And be a man who can interpret them,
> Who will interpret them as a teacher.[23]

But prefaces are usually more interesting than colophons, since they enjoy the advantage of hindsight and afford, in

---

[22] Ecclus. 50: 27–9.   [23] *ANET* 424b; *LAE* 265.

consequence, the best clue to an author's purpose. In the case of Ben Sira's book, it is singularly fortunate that his grandson wrote a most perceptive and delightful piece, when (some time after 132 BC) he translated Ecclesiasticus into Greek for the benefit of the Jews in Dispersion in Egypt:

It is the duty of those who study the scriptures not only to become experts themselves, but also to use their scholarship for the benefit of the world outside through both the spoken and the written word. For that reason my grandfather Jesus, who had applied himself diligently to the study of the law, the prophets, and the other writings of our ancestors, and had gained a considerable proficiency in them, was moved to compile a book of his own on the themes of learning and wisdom, in order that, with this further help, scholars might make greater progress in their studies by living as the law directs.

You are asked, then, to read with sympathetic attention, and to make allowances wherever you think that ... some of the expressions I have used are inadequate. For what is said in Hebrew does not have the same force when translated into another tongue.

Thanks to the discovery of manuscripts in the storeroom of an ancient synagogue in Cairo, in Cave II at Qumran, and in the excavations at Masada, we may now read about two-thirds of Ecclesiasticus in Hebrew, but whether or not these texts are closer to the original than the Greek translation is still the subject of learned debate.[24] Fortunately, and despite his grandson's scholarly caveats, we may be reasonably confident that the Greek version of Ben Sira's book gives us authentic access to his mind, especially since, being both voluminous and repetitive, his teaching depends little on textual minutiae.

Only perhaps the old-style classics tutor, with files full of diverse and well-thumbed pieces for translation into Greek and Latin, would readily recognize Ben Sira's compilation as the stock-in-trade of a practising schoolmaster. It embraces an astonishing variety of literary genres: blocks of direct instruction and didactic sentences, poems about wisdom and

---

[24] Emil Schurer, *The History of the Jewish People in the Age of Jesus Christ*, rev. edn. by Geza Vermes, Fergus Millar, Martin Goodman, vol. iii, part 1 (1986), 202–5.

creation, hymns, prayers, eulogies, numerical sayings—all jostling each other with the minimum of organization.

The range of Ben Sira's literary genres is paralleled by the range of his curriculum: family relations and friendship, justice and generosity, honour and shame, reticence and self-control, the cultivation of wise speech, wine, women and social etiquette, work and money, physical and mental health, not forgetting gratitude to God the bountiful Creator. As we shall see later, these were the standard topics taught in both Israelite and Egyptian schools, reflecting an awareness that morality and religious belief were as much a part of education for life as professional and technical expertise.

Ben Sira's moral teaching was explicitly an appeal to the native intelligence and capacity of men as beings made in God's image:

> The Lord created human beings from the earth
> and to it he turns them back again.
> He set a fixed span of life for mortals
> and gave them authority over everything on earth.
> He clothed them with power like his own
> and made them in his own image.
> He put the fear of them into all creatures
> and granted them lordship over beasts and birds.
> He fashioned tongues, eyes, and ears for them,
> and gave them minds with which to think.
> He filled them with understanding and knowledge
> and showed them good and evil.[25]

Ben Sira was a rational man. He urges his pupils to use their brains.[26] He speaks approvingly of the 'mind solidly backed by intelligent thought'[27] and disparagingly of the 'small mind'[28] and the 'shallow mind'.[29] Solomon's son and successor is dismissed summarily as 'a man of weak mind, the fool of the nation'.[30] It is not surprising that any form of irrationality, such as finding significance in dreams and divination, earns his most vigorous (and perceptive) condemnation:

---

[25] Ecclus. 17: 1–7; cf. Gen. 1: 26–31.
[26] Ecclus. 14: 20.   [27] Ecclus. 22: 17.
[28] Ecclus. 16: 23.   [29] Ecclus. 19: 4.   [30] Ecclus. 47: 23.

Vain hopes delude the senseless,
and dreams give wings to a fool's fancy.
Paying heed to dreams
is like clutching a shadow or chasing the wind.
What you see in a dream is nothing but a reflection,
The image of a face in a mirror.
Truth can no more come from illusion
than purity can come from impurity.
Divination, omens, and dreams are all futile . . .[31]

For this no-nonsense tutor, it was not paranormal experience, but the hard slog of study which gave a young man access to knowledge:

If it is your wish, my son, you will be instructed;
if you give your mind to it, you will become clever;
if you are content to listen, you will learn;
if you are attentive, you will grow wise.[32]

Do not neglect the discourse of the wise,
but apply yourself to their maxims;
from these you will gain instruction
and learn how to serve the great.
Attend to the discourse of your elders.
for they themselves learned from their fathers.[33]

Ben Sira described himself as the last in a long succession—

I, last of all, kept watch.
I was like a gleaner following the grape-pickers—[34]

and his conservative ideal of education, devoted to keeping alive the wisdom of the past, illustrates how (and explains why) the school tradition of the Ancient Near East had changed so little in two thousand years. As early as 2100 BC, the Egyptian king Merikare received this advice from his father: 'Copy thy fathers and thy ancestors . . . Behold, their words remain in writing. Open, that thou mayest read and copy (their) wisdom. (Thus) the skilled man becomes learned.'[35]

---

[31] Ecclus. 34: 1–5.   [32] Ecclus. 6: 32, 33.
[33] Ecclus. 8: 8, 9.   [34] Ecclus. 33: 16.
[35] ANET 415a; LAE 182; cf. The Instruction of Ptahhotep: 'he converses in the same way to his children, by renewing the instruction of his father', ANET 414b; LAE 174. The New Kingdom encomium of learned Egyptian scribes of the past

Ben Sira included in his book a glowing description of the man of learning (partly, perhaps, a reflection in his own mirror) and, while it confirms the conservatism of the school tradition, its reference to practical experience indicates that the professional teacher was expected to be more than 'merely academic':

> How different it is with one who devotes himself
> to reflecting on the law of the Most High,
> who explores all the wisdom of the past
> and occupies himself with the study of prophecies!
> He preserves the sayings of the famous
> and penetrates the subtleties of parables.
> He explores the hidden meaning of proverbs
> and knows his way among enigmatic parables.
> The great avail themselves of his services,
> and he appears in the presence of rulers.
> He travels in foreign countries,
> learning at first hand human good and human evil.[36]

Learning at first hand, by travel in foreign countries, is something to which Ben Sira lays claim in one of his explicitly autobiographical passages:

> He who is well travelled knows much,
> and a person of experience knows what he is talking about.
> He who has little experience knows little,
> but travel increases a person's resources.
> In the course of my own journeyings I have seen much
> and understand more than I can put into words.
> I have often been in deadly danger
> but escaped, thanks to the experience I had gained.[37]

Keen observation was a distinctive feature of the literature most intimately associated with the school tradition and one of Ben Sira's boasts was that 'many such things have I seen with my own eyes'.[38] It is hardly coincidental that the word

---

illustrates the conservatism of the school tradition and the importance attached to the established classics: 'As for those learned scribes from the time of the successors of the gods . . . their names will endure for ever . . . they made heirs for themselves of the writings and books of instruction they made . . . More profitable is a book than a graven tablet', *Papyrus Chester Beatty IV, LAE* 1; *ANET* 431–2.

[36] Ecclus. 39: 1–4.
[37] Ecclus. 34: 9–12.
[38] Ecclus. 16: 5; cf. 19: 29, 30; 26: 9; 45: 6–14.

for 'beautiful' is virtually monopolized by these school writings and Ben Sira uses it more than any other author. 'The eye likes to look on grace and beauty',[39] he writes, and (with some reluctance) he recognizes the beauty of women.[40] But he reserves his highest praise for the 'marvellous . . . handiwork of the Most High' in the natural order:

> Look at the rainbow and praise its Maker;
> it shines with a surpassing beauty . . .
> He scatters the snowflakes like birds alighting;
> they settle like a swarm of locusts.
> The eye is dazzled by their beautiful whiteness,
> and the mind is entranced as they fall.[41]

Aesthetic appreciation was closely linked, in the school tradition, with a fastidious attention to language. Although, presumably, Ben Sira's pupils were well grounded in the basic skills of reading and writing and, indeed, some of the splendid 'set-pieces' of his book probably originated as models for exercises in composition, the kind of education which emerges most clearly is training for public affairs, and, for this, the key was the spoken rather than the written word:

> Never remain silent when a word might put things right,
> and do not hide your wisdom,
> for it is by the spoken word that wisdom is known,
> and learning finds expression in speech.[42]

Wisdom, Ben Sira claims, will find words for her devotees when they speak in the assembly[43] and one of the basic types of the happy man is 'the speaker who has an attentive audience'.[44] While it is true (as students of this school literature quickly discover) that 'they who are trained in learning . . . pour forth apt proverbs',[45] more than mere rhetoric is needed; you must know where you stand and be able to argue for it:

> Shake a sieve, and the rubbish remains;
> start an argument, and a man's faults show up.

[39] Ecclus. 40: 22.   [40] Ecclus. 9: 8; 26: 16, 17.
[41] Ecclus. 43: 11, 17, 18; cf. 42: 22.   [42] Ecclus. 4: 23, 24.
[43] Ecclus. 15: 5.   [44] Ecclus. 25: 9.   [45] Ecclus. 18: 29.

As the work of a potter is tested in the kiln,
so a man is tried in debate.[46]

Stand firmly by what you know,
and be consistent in what you say.
Be quick to listen,
but over your answer take time.
Give an answer if you know what to say,
but if not, hold your tongue.
Through speaking come both honour and dishonour,
and the tongue can be its owner's downfall.[47]

What Bishop Butler in a famous sermon was to call 'Guardianship of the tongue' was so crucial to Ben Sira's concept of the educated man engaged in public life that in one passage he breaks into a fervent prayer about it:

O for a sentry to guard my mouth
and a seal of discretion to close my lips,
to prevent them from being my downfall,
to keep my tongue from causing my ruin!
Lord, Father, and Ruler of my life,
do not abandon me to the tongue's control
or allow it to bring about my downfall.[48]

Few features of Ben Sira's outlook so clearly demonstrate his continuity with the international school tradition as this conviction about the critical significance of speech. From Egypt, for example, in the third millennium, we have the counsel of the Vizier Ptahhotep: 'If you are a trusted man who sits in the council of his lord, set your heart on excellence. If you are quiet, it will be more profitable than *tftf*-plants; speak (only) when you know you can clarify the issue. It is the expert who speaks in the council, for speech is more difficult than any craft.'[49] To this we may add a later Assyrian proverb: 'The scribal art is the mother of orators and the father of scholars.'[50]

There is an apparent paradox in the school tradition between the cultivation of speech and the cultivation of

---

[46] Ecclus. 27: 4, 5.   [47] Ecclus. 5: 10–13; cf. 20: 18.
[48] Ecclus. 22: 27–23: 1; cf. the Babylonian collection of sayings, *Counsels of Wisdom*: 'Let your mouth be controlled and your speech guarded'; 'Beware of careless talk, guard your lips', Lambert, 101, 105.
[49] *LAE* 168; *ANET* 414a.   [50] Lambert, 259.

silence, but it is resolved by their common origin in the cultivation of a rigorous intellectual discipline:

> Fools speak before they think
> but the wise think before they speak.[51]

Silence does not result from having nothing to say but from deciding that what you have it in mind to say is better left unsaid. As Ben Sira put it:

> There is the person who is silent, at a loss for an answer;
> another is silent, biding his time.
> The wise are silent until the right moment,
> but a swaggering fool is always speaking out of turn.[52]

Garrulity, gossip, and that kind of compulsive blabbing sometimes praised as candour betray a lack of that mental and moral discipline which it was the primary aim of the schools to teach. In condemning them, Ben Sira was continuing a tradition well established in the schools of Egypt. 'Do not tell what is in your mind to all comers',[53] he writes, echoing *The Instruction of Ani*: 'Thou shouldst not express thy (whole) heart to the stranger' and *The Instruction of Amen-em-opet*:

> Empty not thy belly to everybody . . .
> Better is a man whose talk (remains) in his belly
> Than he who speaks it out injuriously.[54]

The scribal ideal of the discreet, cautious, tight-lipped, silent man is readily intelligible in schools founded to train candidates for the Civil Service, but its influence far exceeded the vocational needs of the bureaucracies of the Ancient Near East and came to colour the whole ethos of educated society. It was a society which cared for good breeding and good manners:

> An ill-mannered man is like an ill-timed story
> continually on the lips of the ill-bred.[55]

> A fool guffaws,
> but a clever man smiles quietly, if at all.

[51] Ecclus. 21: 26. [52] Ecclus. 20: 6, 7; cf. 20: 20; 32: 4.
[53] Ecclus. 8: 19; cf. 9: 18; 19: 6–12; 21: 28.
[54] *ANET* 420b, 424a; *LAE* 260. [55] Ecclus. 20: 19.

> A fool rushes into a house,
> while someone of experience hangs back politely.
> A boor peers into a house from the doorstep,
> while a well-bred person stands outside.[56]

In a revealing 'homes-and-gardens' figure of speech, Ben Sira gives us a glimpse of an unrelaxed middle-class urban society, in which a man looking for promotion was well advised to watch his step:

> As you enclose your garden with a thorn hedge,
> and as you tie up securely your silver and gold,
> so weigh your words and measure them,
> and make for your mouth a door that locks.
> Take care you are not tripped by your tongue
> to fall before a waiting enemy.[57]

The pupils at Ben Sira's school came from a social class which employed servants,[58] enjoyed ready access to a doctor,[59] had property to dispose of,[60] and could afford 'fine clothes',[61] but they were clearly not the idle rich of Jerusalem. All of them were being trained for jobs:

> To be employed and to be one's own master, both are sweet . . .[62]

> Stand by your contract and give your mind to it;
> grow old at your work.
> Do not envy the wicked their achievements;
> trust the Lord and stick to your job.[63]

Although Ben Sira used a version of the famous Egyptian school text known as *The Satire on the Trades* in drawing a sharp contrast between the educated professional and the working man,[64] he so far parts company with its white-kilt snobbery as actually to commend getting your hands dirty:

> Do not resent manual labour;
> work on the land was ordained by the Most High.[65]

[56] Ecclus. 21: 20, 22, 23.
[57] Ecclus. 28: 24–6; see Robert Gordis, 'The Social Background of Wisdom Literature', *HUCA* 18 (1943–4), 77–118.
[58] Ecclus. 4: 30; 6: 11; 33: 30, 31.   [59] Ecclus. 18: 19; 38: 1–15.
[60] Ecclus. 33: 19–23.   [61] Ecclus. 11: 4.
[62] Ecclus. 40: 18.   [63] Ecclus. 11: 20, 21.
[64] Ecclus. 38: 24–34; see p. 54.   [65] Ecclus. 7: 15.

And he warns his pupils against 'dropping out':

> Do not be too clever to do a day's work
> or give yourself airs when you have nothing to live on.[66]

When he depicts the humiliation of having to cadge a bed for the night, he illustrates that visual imagination and eye for telling detail which made the schoolmen masters of the short story:

> Do not become known for living on hospitality.
> It is a miserable life going from house to house,
> keeping your mouth shut because you are a visitor.
> Without thanks you play the host and hand round the drinks,
> and into the bargain must listen to things that rankle:
> 'Come here, you stranger, and lay the table;
> whatever you have there, hand it to me.'
> 'Be off, stranger! Make way for a more important guest;
> my brother has come to stay, and I need the guest room.'[67]

Climbing the rungs of the social ladder was a delicate balancing act demanding the greatest circumspection. And so, as school teachers had been doing for two thousand years, Ben Sira advised his young men to be cautious in making friends above their station,[68] on how to behave at official banquets,[69] and what to do when they were asked to dine with, perhaps, a prospective employer:

> If a great man invites you, be slow to accept,
> and he will be the more pressing in his invitation.
> Do not push yourself forward, for fear of a rebuff,
> but do not keep aloof, or you may be forgotten.
> Do not presume to converse with him as an equal,
> and put no trust in his effusive speeches;
> the more he speaks, the more he is testing you,
> weighing you up even while he smiles.[70]

It is not surprising that the educated mobile middle class, which was nurtured and perpetuated by the school tradition, became obsessed by public recognition and public disgrace. Ben Sira reflects this preoccupation:

---

[66] Ecclus. 10: 26. [67] Ecclus. 29: 23–7. [68] Ecclus. 13: 2.
[69] Ecclus. 31: 12–32: 13. [70] Ecclus. 13: 9–11.

> He who educates his son makes his enemy envious
> and will boast of him among friends.[71]

> Do not commit an offence against the community
> and so incur a public disgrace.[72]

Such criteria are used even for the heroes of Israel's past:

> Abraham was the great father of a host of nations;
> no one has been found to equal him in fame;[73]

and Moses, we are told, 'won favour in the eyes of all'.[74] In a society which attaches paramount importance to keeping up appearances and is regulated not by the clear stipulations of a recognized moral code but by the diffuse and more ambiguous response of public opinion, shame is the besetting neurosis.[75] Although there is a danger of our being too simplistic in identifying 'shame cultures', there can be no doubt that sensitivity about honour and dishonour had always characterized Israel's school tradition. The fact that Ben Sira shared this notion of social accountability and cared deeply about what the neighbours thought makes his attitude to the Law of Moses somewhat problematic.

It is sometimes said that he effected a momentous change in Israel's intellectual tradition by subordinating the pursuit of wisdom to obedience to the Law, so that the integrity and autonomy of a rational and empirical approach to life, shared by educated men throughout the Ancient Near East, were shattered by the weight of a legalism which was at once nationalistic and authoritarian. There is no denying that Ben Sira's work often asserts the primacy of the Law:

> If you long for wisdom, keep the commandments,
> and the Lord will give it you without stint.[76]

> A sensible person puts his trust in the law,
> finding it reliable like the oracle of God.[77]

---

[71] Ecclus. 30: 3.   [72] Ecclus. 7: 7.
[73] Ecclus. 44: 19.   [74] Ecclus. 45: 1.
[75] David Daube, 'The Culture of Deuteronomy,' ORITA, University of Ibadan, vol. iii, no. 1 (1969), 27–52; David Daube, 'Shame Culture in Luke', in M. D. Hooker and S. G. Wilson (eds.), Paul and Paulinism (1982), 355–72.
[76] Ecclus. 1: 26.   [77] Ecclus. 33: 3.

> Better to lack brains and be godfearing
> than to have great intelligence and transgress the law.[78]

Despite assertions like these, it is obvious that Ben Sira, while clearly attaching value to the Law and wanting to relate it to his own school tradition, talked about it to his pupils so little that it is impossible to identify in all his fifty-one chapters a single specific commandment. It is also noticeable that his references to the Law sometimes occur quite unexpectedly and bear so little relation to their context as to suggest that he is hedging his bets by clumsy second thoughts:

> Take the measure of your neighbours as best you can,
> and accept advice from those who are wise.
> Let your discussion be with intelligent men
> *and all your talk about the law of the Most High.*[79]

The most obvious example of this editorial clumsiness occurs at the end of the great hymn on Wisdom in chapter 24, which was almost certainly modelled on an Egyptian Isis aretalogy of the kind current in the Hellenistic world and (as established by the Oxyrhynchus Papyri) known in Palestine. Isis, the goddess of many names, was regarded as the Creator of the Cosmos and the sovereign principle of Moral Order among men, so that her role was congruous with the concept of wisdom in the school tradition as being fundamental alike to the natural order and human society.[80] However, neither Isis nor Wisdom could congruously be identified with a written Code of Law, as the beginning of the next section following the hymn suddenly asserts:

> All this is the book of the covenant of God Most High,
> the law laid on us by Moses.[81]

It is probably best to conclude that the over-simple identification of Law and Wisdom in Ecclesiasticus reflects unresolved problems in Ben Sira's own thinking. He taught in an age

---

[78] Ecclus. 19: 24.
[79] Ecclus. 9: 14, 15; cf. 21: 11; 23: 22, 23.
[80] A. D. Nock, *Conversion* (1933), 48–9; M. Hengel, *Judaism and Hellenism* (1974), i. 158–61.
[81] Ecclus. 24: 23; cf. 15: 1; Gerard von Rad, *Wisdom in Israel* (1972), 244–7; Joseph Blenkinsopp, *Wisdom and Law in the Old Testament* (1983), 141–4.

when the integrity and identity of Judaism were severely threatened by the powerful forces of Hellenism[82] and his work was compiled only a few years before the book of Daniel—that extraordinarily courageous response by another schoolman to the attempt of Antiochus Epiphanes in 167 BC to obliterate the Jewish religion.[83] It is probable that Ben Sira's roll-call of the heroes of Israel's past in chapters 44–9, a genre for which there was no precedent in Jewish literature, was intended to raise national morale and stiffen opposition to the Greeks, like the comparable roll-call—from Abraham to Daniel—ascribed to Mattathias at the beginning of the revolt against Antiochus.[84]

Thus a conservative academic, whose only desire was to live a quiet life as a conscientious tutor, was caught up in a crisis with which (for all his wisdom) he found it difficult to cope. His set of mind was benevolently paternalistic rather than authoritarian and his allegiance to the religious establishment, as is often the way with dons, was probably traditional and ceremonial rather than deeply committed. Even under the pressures of his age, there can be no doubt what it was which continued to make him tick—the inherited wisdom of the school tradition (including its uncomplicated piety) and the nurturing of a capacity for intelligent moral choice:

> Rely rather on a godfearing person whom you know to be a
>   keeper of the commandments,
> one who is with you heart and soul
> and will show you sympathy if you have a setback.
> But trust your own judgement also,
> for you have no more reliable counsellor.
> One's own mind has sometimes a way of bringing word
> better than seven watchmen posted on a tower.
> But above all pray to the Most High
> to guide you on the path of truth.[85]

---

[82] Ecclus. 2: 10–14; 3: 21–4; 11: 34; 41: 8; see Alexander A. Di Lella, 'Conservative and Progressive Theology: Sirach and Wisdom', *CBQ* 38 (1966), 139–54.

[83] E. W. Heaton, *The Book of Daniel* (1956), 19–24, 68–79. Ben Sira reflects the crisis most clearly in the prayer for national deliverance in Ecclus. 36: 1–17.

[84] 1 Macc. 2: 49–68.   [85] Ecclus. 37: 12–15; cf. 32: 23.

Ben Sira was no doubt influenced by the Hellenism which he found it necessary to oppose, but the degree of his indebtedness is more difficult to assess than once was thought.[86] The growing recognition of an intellectual tradition among the schoolmen of the Ancient Near East, which antedated Plato and itself contributed to Greek philosophical thinking, prevents our following those earlier scholars who ascribed each and every element of rational or speculative thought in Ecclesiasticus to the influence of Hellenism. For example, Ben Sira had to counter the view that the transcendent Lord of Creation was indifferent to the mundane existence of mere individuals:

> Do not say, 'I am hidden from the Lord;
> who is there up above to give a thought to me?
> Among so many I shall not be noticed;
> what am I in the immensity of creation?' . . .
> These are the thoughts of a small mind,
> the absurdities of a senseless and misguided person.[87]

But such thoughts were not the monopoly of the Epicureans, as the debate of the book of Job clearly testifies,[88] and, before that, a controversy in which the prophet Isaiah was involved:

> Woe betide those who seek to hide their plans
> too deep for the Lord to see!
> When their deeds are done in the dark
> they say, 'Who sees us? Who knows of us?'[89]

Such scepticism was, as we shall see later, a recurrent topic in the school literature of Egypt and Mesopotamia, where, incidentally, the debating formula which Ben Sira uses—'Do not say . . .'—appears to have been well established.[90] Like his predecessors in the schools, he found himself having to argue the case for God's just government of the world. In

---

[86] Jack T. Sanders, *Ben Sira and Demotic Wisdom* (1983), 27–59; Hengel, *Judaism and Hellenism*, i. 146–9; West, *Early Greek Philosophy, passim*.

[87] Ecclus. 16: 17–23; cf. 15: 19; 17: 15–20; 23: 18; 39: 19.

[88] Job 34: 21, 22.   [89] Isa. 29: 15; cf. 5: 19; Zeph. 1: 12.

[90] Ecclus. 5: 1–6; 11: 23, 24; 15: 11, 12; Prov. 24: 29; *The Instruction of Amen-em-opet*, ANET 423b; LAE 258; *The Instruction of Ani*, ANET 420b; see J. L. Crenshaw, 'The Problem of Theodicy', *JBL* 94/1(1975), 47–64.

three great didactic poems,[91] he is content simply to reaffirm the wonder and harmony of the Order of Creation and assure his pupils that 'in due time' (a favourite phrase of the schoolmen),[92] all their doubts and questions would be answered:

> Let these be your words of thanksgiving:
> 'All that the Lord has done is excellent;
> all that he commands will in due time take place.'
> Let no one ask, 'What is this?' or 'Why is that?'
> In due time all such questions will be answered . . .
> The deeds of all mankind lie plain before him,
> and there is no hiding from his eyes.
> From the beginning to the end of time he keeps watch;
> nothing is too marvellous or too difficult for him.
> Let no one ask, 'What is this?' or 'Why is that?'
> for everything has been created for its own purpose.[93]

This confidence in the sovereignty of reason in the world is no less Oriental than Greek,[94] but it is to the Greeks that Ben Sira is indebted for a feature quite new to the school tradition. This is the idea that the harmony of the universe arises from its complementarity, that is to say, its structure in 'opposites':

> Look at all the works of the Most High—
> they are in pairs, one the counterpart of the other.[95]

> His works endure, all of them active for ever
> and all responsive to their several functions.
> All things go in pairs, one the counterpart of the other;
> he has made nothing incomplete.
> One thing supplements the virtues of another.
> Of his glory who can ever see too much?[96]

Although, as Dr Needham has taught us, the idea of opposites (known as Yin and Yang) was familiar to the Chinese as early as the fourth century BC,[97] it was from an

[91] Ecclus. 16: 24–17: 14; 39: 16–35; 42: 15–43: 33. On the idea of cosmic order in these passages, see James D. Martin, 'Ben Sira—A Child of his Time', in James D. Martin and Philip R. Davies (eds.), *A Word in Season* (1986), 148–51.
[92] Ecclus. 1: 23, 24; 10: 4; 20: 7; 39: 17.
[93] Ecclus. 39: 16–21; cf. 3: 21–4.
[94] West, *Early Greek Philosophy*, 177.
[95] Ecclus. 33: 15.   [96] Ecclus. 42: 23–5.
[97] J. Needham, *Science and Civilization in China*, vol. ii (1956), 273–8.

even earlier philosophical tradition that Ben Sira borrowed. Aristotle, in reporting on the Pythagoreans, also uses the formula 'most human affairs go in pairs'.[98] The concept first clearly appears in Anaximander (early sixth century BC), where the basic opposites are heat and cold (dryness and wetness), as in Ben Sira's revised version of the choice offered in Deuteronomy:

> He has set before you fire and water:
> reach out and make your choice.[99]

Heraclitus, later in the sixth century BC, is more fundamentally illuminating. For him, the actual and desirable state of the world is differentiation arising from correct apportionment and it is to be seen in terms of opposites. Behind all these opposites there is unity, which, according to one fragment, is God.[100] Against this background, it is possible to see that Ben Sira, as he tries to justify the diverse fortunes of men, was writing not simply as a pragmatic traditionalist, but doing his best to exploit elements of Greek philosophy:

> Why is one day more important than another,
> when every day of the year has its light from the sun?
> It was by the Lord's decision that they were distinguished;
> he appointed the various seasons and festivals:
> some days he made high and holy,
> and others he assigned to the common run of days.
> All mankind comes from the ground—
> Adam himself was created out of earth—
> yet in his great wisdom the Lord distinguished them
> and made them go their various ways:
> some he blessed and lifted high,
> some he hallowed and brought near to himself,
> others he cursed and humbled
> and removed from their place.
> As clay is in the potter's hands
> to be moulded just as he chooses,
> so are human beings in the hands of their Maker
> to be dealt with as he decides.

[98] G. S. Kirk, J. E. Raven, and M. Schofield, *The Presocratic Philosophers*, 2nd edn. (1983), 337–8.

[99] Ecclus. 15: 16; Deut. 30: 15, 19; Kirk, Raven, and Schofield, *Presocratic Philosophers*, 119–20.

[100] Ibid. 190–1; West, *Early Greek Philosophy*, 140.

> Good is the opposite of evil, and life of death;
> so the sinner is the opposite of the godly.
> Look at all the works of the Most High—
> they are in pairs, one the counterpart of the other.[101]

Of the four different kinds of connection between evident opposites in the thought of Heraclitus, two in particular throw light on Ben Sira's remarkably serene confidence. The first is that good things are seen to be possible only if we recognize their opposites; as Heraclitus puts it: 'Disease makes health pleasant and good, hunger satiety, weariness rest.' The second is that opposite effects are produced by one and the same thing; thus Heraclitus writes: 'Sea is the most pure and most polluted water; for fishes it is drinkable and salutary, but for men it is undrinkable and deleterious.'[102] It is this kind of thinking which underlies Ben Sira's attempts to justify the ways of God to man.

It is mistaken, he teaches, to be resentful about the inevitability of death, as though it were an unmitigated tragedy, since it means different things to different people:

> How bitter the thought of you, O Death,
> to anyone at ease among his possessions,
> free from cares, prosperous in all things,
> and still vigorous enough to enjoy a good meal!
> How welcome your sentence, O Death,
> to a destitute person whose strength is failing,
> who is worn down by age and endless anxiety,
> resentful and at the end of his patience!
> Do not fear death's sentence;
> remember those before you and those coming after.
> This is the Lord's decree for all mortals;
> why try to argue with the will of the Most High?[103]

There are a few other indications that Ben Sira was in touch with the Greek world. He made, for example, direct

[101] Ecclus. 33: 7–15; see G. E. R. Lloyd, *Polarity and Analogy* (1966); 18: 'Although pairs of opposites are by no means the only elements or principles which we find used by the Presocratic philosophers, and although they appear in very different roles in different types of theory, most major philosophers from Anaximander down to, and perhaps including, the Atomists may be said to have referred to opposites in one context or another in their general cosmological doctrines or in their explanations of particular natural phenomena.'
[102] Kirk, Raven, and Schofield, *Presocratic Philosophers*, 188–9.
[103] Ecclus. 41: 1–4; cf. 39: 26, 27.

and conscious borrowings from the work of Theognis, an aristocratic writer of the sixth century BC, whose reputation rests on an elegiac poem giving practical advice to a young friend in the manner of the school tradition.[104] Another scrap of evidence which has attracted the attention of scholarly detectives is the remarkably abstract conclusion to one of the poems celebrating the wonders of Creation:

> However much we say, our words will always fall short;
> the end of the matter is: God is all.[105]

Before the Hebrew text of Ecclesiasticus was discovered, 'God is all' was dismissed as a Stoicizing gloss; now *hakkōl* merits recognition as indicating Ben Sira's own knowledge of Stoicism.

This contribution of Hellenism is, however, no more than a drop in the ocean compared to Ben Sira's indebtedness to Israel's own school tradition. The core curriculum which he presented to his well-favoured pupils was simply a more sophisticated version of the teaching given in earlier and less grand schools, as will emerge in our study of the book of Proverbs.

[104] Sanders, *Ben Sira*, 29–38.
[105] Ecclus. 43: 27; see Sanders, *Ben Sira*, 51–2.

II

SCHOOLS AND LIBRARIES

The writings of the Old Testament present a rich and varied feast of about half a million words. To deny the existence and importance of schools in Israel is rather like refusing to recognize the practice of cattle-breeding in the middle of a meal of roast beef. Since it is the end-product which provides the evidence, the method of our investigation will be to see how the diverse literary skills of Israel's authors, in both poetry and prose, bear witness to their educational background. Their knowledge of the school-books of Egypt and their use of traditional didactic language and literary forms are explicable only in terms of their training in academic institutions which were *professional, established, and stable.*

Although, notoriously, there is little specific factual data about Israel's schools *as institutions*,[1] a great volume of suggestive evidence has been supplied by archaeologists digging beyond her borders—in Mesopotamia, Egypt, and Syria. It would, indeed, be strange if Israel had administered her state, conducted her business, and produced her literature without the skills which her neighbours had found necessary and had been systematically teaching in their schools for some two thousand years.

New evidence is regularly being unearthed of the great importance attached to reading and writing in the Fertile Crescent. The most recent discovery on a spectacular scale was made in 1974 and 1975 at Tell Mardikh, the site of the ancient city of Ebla in north Syria, when over 10,000

---

[1] A. Lemaire, *Les Écoles et la formation de la Bible dans l'ancien Israël* (1981), 7–71.

cuneiform clay tablets from about 2500 BC were brought to light.[2] They are mostly in Sumerian, but about a fifth of the words are in a hitherto unknown Semitic language, which, it seems, was the local vernacular.

The bulk of these texts are administrative, dealing with agriculture, the textile industry, and trade in metals, but there is, in addition, a considerable quantity of school texts, such as bilingual vocabularies in Sumerian and Eblaite—the first of their kind known to history— and word-lists, not unlike the later *onomastica*, of which, significantly, some are identical with texts excavated at sites in Sumer. The discovery of a number of stories, hymns, and proverbs shows that the schooling of Ebla's scribes embraced literature as well as language, to which, on the evidence of a text written by a visiting professor from the Sumerian school at Kish, we may add mathematics. Those Old Testament scholars who imply that Israel lived in a cultural vacuum should ponder this early evidence of come-and-go between the scribal schools of the Ancient Near East.

The period of the Ebla discoveries corresponds to the heyday of the schools of Sumer, whose activity is reflected in tens of thousands of clay tablets used for administrative purposes in the last half of the third millennium BC.[3] Direct evidence of Sumerian school life comes later—from the period 2000–1500 BC—and consists not only of hundreds of tablets used for school exercises, but of a number of revealing essays (also intended for instruction in the class-room) about teachers and their pupils. Of the latter, the most popular was the text published in 1949 by S. N. Kramer, who gave it the title *Schooldays*. Presented as an Old Boy's recollections of his daily school routine, it immediately provides a *Sitz im Leben* for the exercise tablets:

I recited my tablet, ate my lunch, prepared my [new] tablet, wrote it, finished it; then my model tablets were brought to me; and in the afternoon my exercise tablets were brought to me. When the school was dismissed, I went home, entered the house, and found my

[2] Giovanni Pettinato, 'The Royal Archives of Tell Mardikh-Ebla', *BA* 39/2 (May 1976).
[3] C. B. F. Walker, *Cuneiform* (1987), 33–9.

father sitting there. I explained (?) my exercise tablets to my father, (?) recited my tablet to him, and he was delighted . . .[4]

Another illuminating text further illustrates how socially ambitious fathers pressurized their sons. In this case, the father is himself a scribe and his son is kicking over the traces:

'Go to school,' he urges, 'stand before your "school-father", recite your assignment, open your schoolbag, write your tablet, let your "big brother" write your new tablet for you. After you have finished your assignment and reported to your monitor, come to me and do not wander about in the street . . . Night and day, you waste in pleasures. You have accumulated much wealth, have expanded wide, have become fat, big, broad, powerful and puffed.'[5]

This early yuppie was clearly a mature student. We lack the evidence to be able to trace the stages by which the Sumerian pupil-scribe graduated from elementary exercises in reading and writing to more advanced studies, but an oral examination satirically described in a text from the period 1720–1600 BC indicates that the course was long and the curriculum wide. The scene is the courtyard of the 'tablet-house', where a teacher is testing his pupil before the assembled staff: 'Come, my son, sit at my feet. I will talk to you, and you will give me information! From your childhood to your adult age you have been staying in the tablet-house. Do you know the scribal art that you have learned?'

There follows a highly various and inconsequential list of topics: the secret meaning of Sumerian words; translation from Sumerian to Akkadian and *vice versa*; the occult language of all classes of priests and members of other professions; how to draw up, cover, and seal a document; all categories of songs and how to conduct a choir; the technical jargon of silversmiths and jewellers . . . mathematics, division of fields, allotting of rations; the use and technique of various musical instruments. True to form, the examiner has the last word:

What have you done, what good came of your sitting here? You are already a ripe man and close to being aged! Like an old ass you are

[4] S. N. Kramer, *The Sumerians* (1963), 237–8; cf. C. J. Gadd, *Teachers and Students in the Oldest Schools* (1956). [5] Kramer, *Sumerians*, 244–45.

not teachable any more . . . but, it is still not too late! If you study night and day and work all the time modestly and without arrogance, if you listen to your colleagues and teachers, you can still become a scribe! Then you can share the scribal craft, which is good fortune for its owner, a good angel leading you, a bright eye possessed by you, *and it is what the palace needs*.[6]

The scribal student certainly kept his bright eye on the needs of the palace, for it was the palace which provided the jobs and the purpose of his training was essentially vocational. Nevertheless, as is splendidly demonstrated by the collection of texts in the library of Ashurbanipal, the last of the great kings of Assyria (669–632 BC), the schools of Mesopotamia produced a large volume of literature. One need only recall works like *The Creation Epic* and *The Epic of Gilgamesh* from the second millennium BC, didactic writings such as *The Babylonian Theodicy* from the eleventh century BC, and detailed historical annals like *The Babylonian Chronicle* from the seventh century BC.[7]

The evidence suggests that the reading public for these books was extremely confined. Scribes were recruited from the prosperous and aspiring middle class and they became members of an élite social group trained to serve a largely illiterate population. The schools did not aim to provide a general education for the aristocracy or the priesthood, nor, until the Cassite period (1500–1200 BC, dubbed 'the Babylonian Middle Ages'), were they attached to temples. They were lay institutions—highly professional and, it would appear, terribly earnest.

Time would fail us if we attempted to explore all the archaeological evidence for schools in the Ancient Near East, but even a simple roll-call of the principal archives is impressive. *Sippar*, on the Euphrates, produced, along with some 60,000 items of temple business, a collection of exercise tablets for its temple school from the period 2004–1595 BC.[8] *Mari*, also on the Euphrates, rewarded its French excavators

---

[6] C. H. Kraeling and R. M. Adams (eds.), *City Invincible* (1960), 100–1; J. P. J. Olivier, 'Schools and Wisdom Literature', *Journal of Northwest Semitic Languages*, (1975) 49–60.
[7] *ANET* 60–99; Lambert, 63–91; *ANET* 301–5; *DOTT* 75–83.
[8] Ernst Posner, *Archives in the Ancient World* (1972), 46.

with an archive of clay tablets from the period 1813–1759 BC, which included the name of the scribal graduate who looked after it.[9] That remarkable file of letters discovered at *El Amarna* in Egypt, which, for the most part, were addressed to the Pharaoh between 1387 and 1362 BC by his eastern allies and Syrian vassals, clearly establishes that the scribes of the Levant were well versed in Akkadian—the international language of diplomacy—and, of course, this skill presupposes schools in the city-states of Syria.[10] The archive excavated at *Ugarit* from about 1400 BC is renowned for the disclosure of its own hitherto unknown Semitic language, for the ability of its scribes to cope with another half-dozen languages, and for a number of literary texts of great importance for Old Testament studies. The library of the high priest was identified and its cache of exercise tablets suggests that it also served as the scribal school.[11]

It was, however, the scribal education of Egypt which exercised the most direct influence on the schools of Israel.[12] In the Ramesside period (1320–1085 BC), which best illuminates the Egyptian context of Israel's emergence as a nation, schools were attached to the principal state institutions—the Temples, the Treasury, and the Army—and large deposits of writing exercises on ostraca (that is, potsherds and limestone flakes) probably indicate the use of regular school buildings.

Egypt was a bureaucrat's paradise, full of jobs for every grade of office-worker, as a letter of this period sent by one scribe to another amply illustrates: 'When my letter reaches you, you shall cause the great dyke to be made . . . Mark the multitude of subordinates you have here. To let you know everyone by his name. Catalogue of jobs of men, plebeians, and craftsmen; the totality of all performers of tasks who are

[9] Ibid. 29–31; J. M. Sasson, 'Some Comments on Archive Keeping at Mari', *Iraq*, (1972), 55–6.

[10] *ANET* 483–90; *DOTT* 38–45.

[11] Posner, *Archives*, 31–5; A. F. Rainey, 'The Scribe at Ugarit, his Position and Influence', *Proceedings of the Israel Academy of Sciences and Humanities*, iii/4 (1968), 126–47.

[12] R. J. Williams, 'Scribal Training in Ancient Egypt', *JAOS* 92/2 (1972), 214–21; Olivier, 'Schools and Wisdom Literature', 55–6; James L. Crenshaw, 'Education in Ancient Israel', *JBL* 104 (1985), 601–15; A. Lemaire, 'Sagesse et écoles', *VT* xxxiv 3 (1984), 270–81.

capable with their hands, performers of manual labour and office jobs, magistrates commanding administrators, chief major-domo, mayor, headmen of villages, quartermaster . . . chief of departments, scribe of the offering table, controllers, retainer, messenger of administrators, brewer, baker, butcher, servant, confectioner, baker of cakes, butler tasting the wine, chief of works, overseer of carpenters, chief-craftsman, deputy, draughtsman, sculptor, miner, quarryman, demolisher, stone-worker . . . barber, basket maker.'[13] It is not surprising that the scribal schools, unlike those of Mesopotamia, were far from being élitist. Even the craftsmen of Deir el-Medina, working on the Theban necropolis, were taught to read and write, and the student for whom *The Instruction of Ani* is said to have been written was the son of a modest temple-scribe and it was his own mother who prepared his school lunch.[14]

After learning to read and write, by the slavish copying of extracts from the traditional 'classical' texts,[15] students in Egypt moved on to vocational studies, such as a very elementary form of mathematics for careers in building, surveying, tax-collecting and all kinds of book-keeping, or geography, which was designed to equip the diplomat and the provincial administrator. For specialized training, scribes were apprenticed to senior officials and sometimes, it seems, as in Mesopotamia, remained on the books for years on end. As a distinguished Egyptologist once observed: 'The Pharaonic writers held the laudable view that a man is never too old to learn, together with the perhaps less laudable view that one is never too old to teach.' Provision must have been made at some later point in a young man's education for

---

[13] Caminos, 497–8.
[14] *ANET* 420–1; Erman, *AE* 234–42; cf. William C. Hayes, *Cambridge Ancient History*, vol. ii, part 1, 3rd edn. (1973), 43.
[15] A recent study has established that the normal procedure in the scribal schools was copying directly from a written text and not from dictation. 'Some works which originated in the Middle Kingdom are preserved only in copies made during the New Kingdom, by which time Middle Egyptian was archaic. As a result, much of what the pupils wrote they evidently did not understand; and this fact, together with the carelessness and incompetence typical of schoolboys, all too frequently led to well-nigh hopeless corruptions', R. J. Williams, 'The Sages of Ancient Egypt in the Light of Recent Scholarship', in Jack M. Sasson (ed.), *Oriental Wisdom, JAOS* 101/1 (1981), 5.

training in the art of speaking. This is a constant theme of the school tradition, not only in Egypt and Israel, but also (and pre-eminently) in Athens. Isocrates, 'that Old man eloquent' of Milton's tenth sonnet, founded his famous school about two hundred years before Ben Sira, but they were kindred spirits (see Excursus, at the end of this chapter).

It is also remarkable how the ethos of these scribal schools remained so constant. The Egyptian student who had started to play the fool is rebuked in the same terms as his counterpart in Sumer more than a thousand years earlier: 'I am told that you have given up books and are reeling in pleasures. You go from street to street, with the smell of beer every time you withdraw . . . You have been found scaling a wall, after having broken the stocks . . . If only you knew that wine is taboo.'[16] Constant also are the oleaginous blandishments to persevere with the scribal profession: 'Be a scribe, that your limbs may be smooth and your hands languid, that you may go out dressed in white, being exalted so that the courtiers salute you . . . [One who is skilled] arises step by step until he reaches (the position of) an official, in favour corresponding to his talents.'[17] No less remarkable than the common ground between these schoolmen of different ages and different national cultures is the common ground between them and ourselves. They display so many basic human motives and responses as to be intelligible to an unexpected degree and this should give us confidence in interpreting the work of the schoolmen of Israel.[18]

When we turn to Israel, it is not surprising to find that the contribution of Palestinian archaeology to our enquiry is extremely modest. It goes without saying that no structure which could be identified as a school building has been unearthed, since no distinctive traces could be expected to have survived the deposits of two-and-a-half thousand years. It is worth remembering that the present-day visitor to Jerusalem will be disappointed if he expects to find any evidence of so renowned a building as Solomon's Temple.

Documents of any importance would have been written on

---

[16] Williams, 'Scribal Training', 218.
[17] Ibid.
[18] A. Demsky, in *Encyclopaedia Judaica*, vi (1971), cols. 382–98.

papyrus or leather, both of which are short-lived in the humid climate of Palestine. Ironically, we have the imprint of the fibres of papyrus on scores of clay seals, which were intended to guarantee the security of the documents which have now perished. The preservation of the books of the Old Testament, also written on papyrus or leather, indicates that they received special care and attention.

Most of the writing which has survived in Palestine for the spade of the archaeologist is inscribed on bits of pottery and is, inevitably, fragmentary and difficult to interpret. The minimalist view is that these inscriptions reveal no more than an elementary level of literacy for which no school training need be postulated. The most speculative view is that some of these finds were beginners' exercises in writing and should be interpreted as evidence for the activity of schools in the locality in which they were discovered. Scholars who—with good reason—stress the importance of schools in ancient Israel are in danger of being misled into attaching too much significance to the fact of mere literacy and in straining what is no more than ambiguous data. A good case does not need, and is not strengthened by, supplementary arguments of doubtful validity.

However, recent finds in two southern military outposts on the edge of the Judaean desert may provide reliable evidence from the eighth century BC not only of literacy, but of some kind of school. At Kuntilat-Ajrud, three fragments of the Hebrew alphabet, written on the shoulder of a large earthenware jar, two executed expertly and one clumsily, suggest a teacher and a pupil engaged in a school exercise. On two other jars, there was inscribed a conventional formula for introducing a letter or a message. Their similarity to inscriptions attested in Egypt and Mesopotamia suggests that they, too, may have been school training material.[19] At the neighbouring fortress of Qadesh-Barnea, some 50 km. to the north, six paleo-Hebrew ostraca from roughly the same period include a fragment of an abecedary written in ink and two ostraca with tables of weights and measures in Egyptian hieratic. The most recently discovered of the ostraca, with

---

[19] Lemaire, *Les Écoles*, 25–33.

model writing on one side and what amounts to muddle on the reverse, strengthens the case for detecting here the work of elementary schoolboys.[20]

However, the only incontrovertible archaeological evidence for schools in the Hebrew kingdoms is provided by the Siloam Tunnel inscription and the Lachish Letters. The Siloam Tunnel inscription, celebrating the completion of Hezekiah's amazing engineering feat in quarrying a tunnel nearly two thousand feet long, is written in regular Hebrew prose of the kind it is improbable you could learn at home. It records the triumphant moment when the two gangs, who had been working in the dark from opposite ends, finally met face to face: 'And when the tunnel was driven through, the quarrymen hewed (the rock), each man towards his fellow, axe against axe.'[21] The Lachish Letters give us further examples of classical Hebrew prose. Discovered in the ashes of a guard-room at the gate of Lachish, they were written on the eve of the Babylonian siege of Jerusalem by the junior officer in charge of a military outpost. In one of the letters, he indignantly spurns the suggestion that he should seek the help of a scribe: 'And now thou hast sent a letter . . . And as for what my lord said, "Dost thou not understand?—call a scribe!", as Yahweh liveth no one hath ever undertaken to call a scribe for me . . .'[22] This is an interesting witness both to his own ability to read and write and to the availability of professionals.

Indications from archaeological evidence that literacy in Israel was not confined to professional scribes are supported by a considerable number of scattered references to reading and writing in the books of the Old Testament. A diligent scholar has reported that 'while, for instance, in the *Iliad* writing is referred to only once, and in the *Odyssey* not even once, in the Bible we find as many as 429 references to writing or written documents'.[23] There is a passage in Isaiah which specifically distinguishes the literate from the illiterate:

[20] Ibid. 20–5; A. Lemaire and Pascal Vernus, 'L'Ostracon paléo-Hébreu No. 6 de Tell Qudeirat (Qadesh Barnea)', in M. Görg (ed.), *Fontes atque Pontes*, Festgabe H. Brunner (1983), 302–26.   [21] *ANET* 321b; *DOTT* 209–11.
[22] *ANET* 321–2; *DOTT* 212–17.
[23] David Diringer, in P. R. Ackroyd and C. F. Evans, *Cambridge History of the Bible* (1970), i. 13.

'The prophetic vision of it all has become for you like the words in a sealed book. If you hand such a book to one who can read and say, "Pray read this," he will answer, "I cannot; it is sealed." Give it to one who cannot read and say, "Pray read this"; and he will answer, "I cannot read".'[24] Ezekiel is told to write on two leaves of a wooden tablet 'for all to see'[25] and Habakkuk is given a similar instruction: 'Write down a vision, inscribe it clearly on tablets, so that it may be read at a glance.'[26] In a literate society a written document could be addressed to the general public and that is what Job wanted from the Almighty:

> If my accuser had written out his indictment,
> I should not keep silence and remain indoors.
> No! I should flaunt it on my shoulder
> and wear it like a crown on my head.[27]

As a final example, we recall that Jeremiah is represented as 'having written on a scroll a full description of the disaster which would befall Babylon' and Seraiah, the king's quartermaster, is told, 'When you have finished reading the scroll, tie a stone to it and throw it into the middle of the Euphrates with the words, "So will Babylon sink . . ." '[28]

The Old Testament writers appear to take a degree of general literacy for granted,[29] but this reference to the king's quartermaster is a reminder that nothing less than a fully professional scribal training was needed for many of Israel's royal officials. We are given formal lists of them for the reigns of David and Solomon[30] and later references show that some of the posts survived to the end of the monarchy. Much scholarly ingenuity has been expended on the translation of their Hebrew titles, although a few moments' reflection on the British offices of 'Speaker' and 'Home Secretary' (not to mention those members of the Royal Household entitled the 'Clerk of the Closet' and the 'Ladies of the Bedchamber') will suggest that what an official is called may throw very little light on what he (or she) actually does.

---

[24] Isa. 29: 11, 12.   [25] Ezek. 37: 15–20.
[26] Hab. 2: 2.   [27] Job 31: 35, 36.   [28] Jer. 51: 60–4.
[29] A. R. Millard, 'The Practice of Writing in Ancient Israel', *BA* 35 (1972), 98–111; M. Haran, 'On the Diffusion of Literacy and Schools in Ancient Israel', *VT*, Supp xl (1988), 81–95.   [30] 2 Sam. 8: 15–18; 20: 23–6; 1 Kgs. 4. 1–6.

The three principal lay offices were those of Secretary of State, Royal Herald, and High Steward. The fact that they were all taken over from the administrative structure of Egypt (whether directly or mediated through the Canaanite tradition of Jerusalem) provides a clue to their respective functions.[31] The Secretary of State was the first officer of the kingdom, responsible, we may surmise, for state correspondence and the royal annals; the Royal Herald was the equivalent of the high-ranking Egyptian officer who acted as the Pharaoh's personal representative and chief of court protocol; and the High Steward was modelled on the officer who managed the vast personal estates of the Pharaoh. In addition, there were twelve district governors (with their own Superintendent), whose job it was to collect the taxes in kind from the twelve administrative regions into which (following Egyptian practice) Solomon had divided the country, and (again following Egyptian practice) there was a Superintendent of the Forced Levy. A vivid little narrative recounting a plea made by the principal officers of King Hezekiah to the commander of the Assyrian army confirms what we might have guessed: 'Please speak to us in Aramaic, for we understand it; do not speak Hebrew to us within earshot of the people of the city wall.'[32] Royal officials were educated men.

The influence of Egypt, whether in matters of government and administration or in the realm of education and literature, is readily accounted for. During the Nineteenth and Twentieth Dynasties (c.1320–1070 BC), the Pharaohs changed their imperial policy in Palestine, and instead of simply exploiting the country economically and sending in troops to put down the occasional rebellion, they now became an occupying power with large numbers of resident soldiers and administrators. More archaeological material has been found disclosing the presence of Egyptians in Palestine at this time than for any comparable period during the entire Bronze Age.[33]

[31] E. W. Heaton, *Solomon's New Men* (1974), 47–60.
[32] 2 Kgs. 18: 17–37; see v. 26.
[33] James M. Weinstein, 'The Egyptian Empire in Palestine: A Re-Assessment', *BASOR* 241 (1981), 1–28; R. J. Williams, 'A People Come Out of Egypt', *VT*, Supp.

This saturation of Palestine with things Egyptian involved cultural exchange as well as political domination. The Pharaohs made a practice of recruiting and training foreigners, as is suggested by the chauvinistic claim in *The Instruction of Ani*: 'Negroes are taught to speak Egyptian, and Syrians, and all strangers likewise.'[34] Even the arrogant prince of Byblos, in his encounter with the unfortunate Wenamun, was prepared to acknowledge Egypt's cultural leadership: 'Now when Amon founded all lands, in founding them he founded first the land of Egypt . . . for craftsmanship came out of it, to reach the place where I am, and learning came out of it . . .'[35]

Although the Egyptian empire collapsed a century before the foundation of the Hebrew monarchy, contacts with Palestine continued. From the time of Solomon, who, we are casually informed, 'allied himself to Pharaoh king of Egypt by marrying his daughter',[36] to the end of the monarchy, communications with Egypt remained open—to the despair of prophets like Isaiah:

> Woe betide the rebellious children! says the Lord,
> who make plans, but not of my devising,
> who weave schemes, but not inspired by me,
> so piling sin on sin.
> Without consulting me they hurry down to Egypt
> to seek shelter under Pharaoh's protection,
> to take refuge under Egypt's shadow.[37]

A recent statistical analysis of general archaeological data on settlement, public works, and luxury goods in Palestine suggests that it was in the eighth century BC that Israel's schools really began to flourish and that they were (not surprisingly) concentrated in Jerusalem, with Lachish as a possible second centre.[38] To get an idea of the activity of schoolmen in Jerusalem a century later, one could hardly do

---

xxviii (1975), 238–52; R. J. Williams, in J. R. Harris (ed.), *The Legacy of Egypt* (1971), 257–90.

[34] Erman, *AE*, 241; J. M. A. Janssen, 'Fonctionnaires sémites au service de l'Égypte', *CE* 26 (1951), 50–62; R. de Vaux, *Ancient Israel* (1961), 98, 284–6; *BAR* ii, para. 467; *ANET* 239a, 486 n. 11.

[35] *ANET* 27b; *LAE* 149.   [36] I Kgs. 3: 1.

[37] Isa. 30: 1, 2; 31: 1; cf. Hos. 7: 11; 8: 13; 9: 3–6; 2 Kgs. 18: 24; 25: 26.

[38] David W. Jamieson-Drake, *Scribes and Schools in Monarchic Judah* (1991), 154–7; Thomas L. Thompson, *Early History of the Israelite People* (1992), 332–3.

better than reflect on the drama of the scroll in the thirty-sixth chapter of the book of Jeremiah, itself an admirably controlled and accomplished literary composition. We meet Baruch, to whom Jeremiah dictates his oracles (and whose brother, incidentally, is the king's quartermaster), along with the son and grandson of Shaphan, Josiah's Secretary of State. As the action develops and the scene shifts from a scribal office in the Temple precincts to the cabinet room in the palace, we are left with a strong impression of the close relationship of those involved in the king's administration and, above all, of its very modest scale.[39] The destruction of Baruch's scroll is presented in a vivid domestic scene: 'Since it was the ninth month of the year, the king was sitting in his winter apartments with a fire burning in a brazier in front of him. Every time Jehudi read three or four columns of the scroll, the king cut them off with a penknife and threw them into the fire in the brazier. He went on doing so until the entire scroll had been destroyed on the fire.'[40] The sequel raises a general issue of some significance: 'Then Jeremiah took another scroll and gave it to the scribe Baruch son of Neraiah, who wrote on it at Jeremiah's dictation all the words of the book which Jehoiakim king of Judah had burnt in the fire; and much else was added to the same effect.'[41] The question is: what happened to *this* scroll? In other words (and generalizing our enquiry), how, where, and by whom were the writings which eventually made up the Old Testament collected, preserved, and transmitted from generation to generation?

Once again we are faced with the absence of any direct biblical or archaeological evidence and once again we must affirm that absence of evidence is not evidence of absence. The only certainty is that the books of the Old Testament were in fact preserved and so we are challenged to explain how this came about by making what we can of oblique indications in our texts and of analogies from neighbouring cultures. Speculation is often a necessary adjunct to scholarship rather than a low-grade substitute for it.

---

[39] J. Muilenburg, 'Baruch the Scribe', in J. I. Durham and J. R. Porter (eds.), *Proclamation and Presence* (1970), 224–5.

[40] Jer. 36: 22, 23.　　　　　　　　　　　　　　　　[41] Jer. 36: 32.

Texts, like that of Jeremiah, were written on scrolls of papyrus or leather and stored in jars (like the Dead Sea Scrolls), or baskets, or boxes and deposited in buildings where they could be consulted. In Egypt, documents were stored and copied in what was called the 'House of Life'.[42] The general accessibility of books in Israel is presupposed by frequent editorial references to supplementary sources: 'David raised this lament over Saul and Jonathan his son; and he ordered that this dirge over them should be taught to the people of Judah. It was written down and may be found in the Book of Jashar.'[43] In the same vein, we find: 'The other events of Jeroboam's reign, in war and peace, are recorded in the annals of the kings of Israel.'[44] Such footnotes would be meaningless if the documents were not readily available. One of the psalmists (or, perhaps, an annotator) was even more explicit:

> This will be written down for future generations,
> that people yet unborn may praise the Lord;

and the Chronicler refers to laments which 'have become traditional in Israel, and they are found in the written collections'.[45]

It would increase our confidence in the establishment of libraries in Israel, which must, in any case, be presupposed, if we could trust a statement in a letter at the beginning of the Second Book of the Maccabees: 'These same facts are set out in the official records and in the memoirs of Nehemiah. Just as Nehemiah collected the chronicles of the kings, the writings of prophets, the works of David, and royal letters about sacred offerings, *to found his library*, in the same way Judas has collected for us all the documents that had been dispersed as a result of the recent conflict.'[46] Unfortunately, this letter, it seems, is a forgery from the first century BC, although the writer had the right ideas about the preservation and transmission of literature.[47]

Libraries of considerable size have been unearthed

---

[42] A. H. Gardiner, 'The House of Life', *JEA* 24, (1938), 157–79.
[43] 2 Sam. 1: 17, 18.   [44] I Kgs. 14: 19; cf. 14: 29; 16: 14.
[45] Ps. 102: 18; 2 Chron. 35: 25.   [46] 2 Macc. 2: 13, 14.
[47] O. Eissfeldt, *The Old Testament*, trans. Peter R. Ackroyd (1965), 580–1.

throughout the Ancient Near East and the most famous of
these—at Nineveh—was deliberately initiated by Ashurbanipal (669–632 BC), to bring together a complete set of
ancient Mesopotamian texts. The library catalogue has now
been partially recovered and it reveals a high degree of critical
scholarship in ascribing the works listed—hitherto anonymous—to named authors.[48] Only a few years earlier, 'the
men of Hezekiah', we are told, were transcribing 'more
proverbs of Solomon' in Jerusalem.[49] But that is all we are
told and so we are left to speculate about the character of this
centre, where, under royal patronage, literature was collected
and edited. We can, however, reconstruct an outline catalogue
for the Jerusalem library at the beginning of the second
century BC, by discovering from Ecclesiasticus which scrolls
Ben Sira had read or had a nodding acquaintance with. It
turns out to be impressively extensive and omits from the
biblical list familiar to us only a few minor (or later) works.[50]
On this evidence, Ben Sira's grandson was justified in
claiming that he 'had applied himself diligently to the study
of the law, the prophets and the other writings of our
ancestors'.

Libraries in Jerusalem, we may reasonably assume, were an
integral part of the capital's educational establishment.
Indeed, the schools were the only institutions which provided
the stability, continuity, and scholarship which were necessary
for the production of the Old Testament as we know it.[51]
There can be no doubt, for example, that the oracles of Amos
and Isaiah entered the stream of written tradition in the
eighth century BC and were safely transmitted through the
fall of Jerusalem in 587 BC and the succeeding Exile. During
their long period in the libraries of Jerusalem, the scrolls, of
course, underwent change at the hands of their scholarly
guardians.

[48] W. G. Lambert, 'A Catalogue of Texts and Authors', *JCS* 16 (1962), 59–77.
[49] Prov. 25: 1.
[50] Alexander A. Di Lella, *The Wisdom of Ben Sira* (1987), 41.
[51] W. McKane, reviewing R. N. Whybray, *The Intellectual Tradition in the Old Testament* (1974), commented: 'Can we envisage that the process by which the Old Testament became canonical scriptures and was transmitted in connection with Herculean labours was either initiated or continued without a class of learned men?', *JSS* 20/2 (1975), 247.   [52] Isa. 16: 13, 14.

Perhaps the greatest achievement of biblical scholarship has been to demonstrate that the Old Testament is, as a whole and in its several parts, stratified like an archaeological site, each successive community having made its own particular additions and modifications. Students have been diligent in trying to identify the circumstances and outlook of the communities responsible for these changes, but they have shown a surprising lack of curiosity about the 'how' and the 'where' of this whole complex literary process. Editing is achieved not (as the scholarly literature sometimes seems to suggest) by a kind of literary osmosis (let us say) from the northern kingdom to the south, but only by *a particular person on a particular day using a writing instrument at a particular desk in a particular building*. It was in such buildings that writings were collected, catalogued, studied, used for teaching, edited, transcribed, treasured, and transmitted. It was in this setting that law books were expanded and updated, histories revised (and some virtually rewritten), prophetic oracles amplified and reinterpreted, collections of proverbs compiled, and so on. The so-called book of Isaiah, for example, is essentially a prophetic anthology made by the schoolmen of Jerusalem, who put together oracles culled from diverse sources over a period of three or more centuries (and that is a long time for the completion of any literary work). At one point, an honest editor acknowledges that an earlier oracle against Moab had not in fact been fulfilled and he attempts to make good the failure: 'These are the words which the Lord spoke long ago about Moab; *and now he says*: "In three years, as a hired labourer counts them off exactly, the vast population in which Moab glories will be brought into contempt; those who are left will be few and feeble and bereft of all honour." '[52] This revised version illustrates what has been identified as an extensive process of 'inner-biblical exegesis'. The use of editorial conventions and techniques which are in line with the established scribal tradition of the Ancient Near East helps us identify some of the corrections, amplifications, elucidations, and reinterpretations which the texts have received during the long process of their transmission through the schools.[53]

[53] Michael Fishbane, *Biblical Interpretation in Ancient Israel* (1985).

The most striking feature of this literary activity is that the changes were effected not by deletion but by addition. As far as we can judge, the schoolmen were reluctant to use waste-paper baskets. When a new code of law was received into the tradition, the old ones were not discarded; when the books of Chronicles were produced to give a new slant to the history covered by Samuel and Kings, the older version was retained in tandem. This process of accommodation and accumulation explains why Holy Scripture is a notoriously complex and often confusing literary patchwork.

To speak of 'Holy Scripture' is immediately to raise a question about the bearing of this editorial process on the schoolmen's understanding of authority. They felt free, it seems, to make changes, because they supposed that, in doing so, they were rejuvenating and so upholding the received tradition. They also felt free to make additions to the tradition, because, although it was authoritative, there was no sense of its being exclusively so. Recently it has been convincingly argued that the notion of a canon of Scripture did not emerge until the Christian era and that in Old Testament times nobody entertained the idea of a finite selection of books designed to be exclusive and finally authoritative.[54] What was exclusive and finally authoritative (certainly after the Exile) was the Law of Moses and to this all other received writings were secondary. A similar view prevailed in Mesopotamia, where it was held that 'the sum of revealed knowledge was given once for all by the antediluvian sages' and so there was no conscious attempt to make anything like a 'canon' from the literature current in the schools.[55] In Israel, comparably, the writings outside the Pentateuch were not thought of as being 'canonical', but as belonging to a general category of subordinate authority called 'the Prophets', as in the familiar New Testament description of the Scriptures as 'the Law and the Prophets'.[56] The longer writings were copied and transmitted in the schools of Jerusalem, the more they gained in authority, in

---

[54] James Barr, *Holy Scripture: Canon, Authority, Criticism* (1983), 49–74; John Barton, *Oracles of God* (1986), 35–95.

[55] W. G. Lambert, 'Ancestors, Authors, and Canonicity', *JCS* 11 (1957), 9.

[56] Matt. 5: 17; 7: 12; Acts 13: 15; cf. 2 Macc. 15: 9.

line with the widespread notion that wisdom belonged to the past. The cut-off point for authentic revelation was the period of Ezra in the fourth century BC, which is why all the books written later are supplied with impeccably ancient credentials: Ruth lived in the days of the Judges; David wrote the Psalms: Solomon was the author of Ecclesiastes and the Song of Songs; Tobit was a contemporary of Isaiah and Daniel a contemporary of Ezekiel, and so on.

It is generally agreed that Ezra initiated profound changes in the school tradition of Jerusalem. He was a 'scribe, expert in the Law of Moses', who had 'devoted himself to the study and observance of the law of the Lord and to teaching statute and ordinance in Israel'.[57] With the help of the Levites (a somewhat obscure body of perpetual curates who now begin to enjoy the limelight),[58] Ezra developed a Seminary for the interpretation and teaching of the Law, which came to dominate the religious and intellectual life of Judaism. It is impossible to determine how many other schools were active in Jerusalem in the post-exilic period and how they may have overlapped in function and membership. Although it seems probable that the old priestly school attached to the Temple declined in importance,[59] there is incontrovertible evidence that, alongside Ezra's Seminary for 'the Law', a parallel school was still faithfully preserving, teaching, producing, and reproducing 'the Prophets'. This was the tradition which nurtured both conservative scholars like Ben Sira and radical thinkers like the authors of Job and Ecclesiastes.

EXCURSUS

The Art of Speaking

Since our knowledge of the content of the teaching in Egyptian schools is mainly derived from literary compositions which were used in the class-room, it might be suspected that

[57] Ezra 7: 6, 10.
[58] Neh. 8: 7–12; 2 Chron. 17: 7–9; 34: 12, 13; 35: 3.
[59] 2 Chron. 29: 34.

our view of it is unbalanced and attaches too much importance to the liberal arts. However, an emphasis on the cultivation of the art of speaking is surprisingly explicit from the earliest period. Thus we have from *The Instruction of Ptahhotep* (*c.*2350 BC):

Here begin the maxims of good speech spoken by . . . the Vizier Ptahhotep . . . Wait on the speech of a sage and listen, for you desire that you may be established in the mouths of the listeners when you speak. Enter into the condition of an expert and speak to perfection, and every plan of yours will be in order;[60]

from *The Instruction for Merikare* (*c.*2100 BC):

Be skillful in speech, that you may be strong . . .
words are braver than all fighting;[61]

and from *The Prophecy of Neferti* (*c.*1990 BC):

Come, Neferti my friend, say some fine words to me, choice phrases at hearing which My Majesty will be entertained . . . Thereupon he stretched out his hand to a box of writing materials and took out a papyrus-roll and a palette, and he put into writing what the Lector Neferti said.[62]

Against a comparable background of training men for leadership in public affairs, the school tradition of the Old Testament similarly stresses the importance of expert and persuasive speech:

Someone may live by the fruit of his tongue;
his lips may earn him a livelihood.
The tongue has power of life and death;
make friends with it and enjoy its fruits.[63]

(Wisdom) will advance him above his neighbours
and find words for him when he speaks in the assembly.[64]

Wisdom is too lofty for a fool to grasp;
he remains tongue-tied in the public assembly.[65]

That speaking was an art for experts is recognized both by Moses—'I have never been a man of ready speech'—and by

---

[60] *LAE* 160, 175.   [61] *LAE* 181: *ANET* 415a.
[62] *LAE* 235–6.   [63] Prov. 18: 20, 21; cf. 16: 23; 22: 17, 18.
[64] Ecclus. 15: 5; cf. 4: 24; 21: 17.   [65] Prov. 24: 7; cf. 5: 13, 14.

Jeremiah: 'I am not skilled in speaking; I am too young.'[66] Ben Sira describes the various public platforms for which his pupils were trained, in the course of pointing out that these were not open to uneducated craftsmen:

> All those rely on their hands,
> and each is skilful at his own craft . . .
> Yet they are not in demand at public discussions,
> nor do they attain to high office in the assembly.
> They do not sit on the judge's bench
> or understand the decisions of the courts.
> They cannot expound moral or legal principles
> and are not ready with maxims.[67]

It is of considerable interest to note that Ben Sira's aims and outlook as a teacher correspond closely to those of Isocrates, who founded his Athenian school for training orators some two hundred years earlier (c.392 BC). Unlike other Sophists, he moved away from the kind of rhetoric required for argument in the courts and developed an interest in speeches on large political themes, couched in meticulously crafted prose. In a work entitled *On the Antidosis*,[68] written when he was 82, Isocrates vigorously defended his innovations as a teacher: 'All men take as much pleasure in listening to this kind of prose as in listening to poetry, and many desire to take lessons in it, believing that those who excel in this field are wiser and better and of more use to the world than men who speak well in court.' Here speaks a liberal-minded tutor who wished to educate well-rounded men for leadership in the Greek cities.

The same work includes a famous exposition of Isocrates' concept of 'the art of discourse', which gives us further insight into his civilized convictions:

---

[66] Exod. 4: 10; Jer. 1: 6.

[67] Ecclus. 38: 31, 33; cf. 23: 24; 41: 18.

[68] See George A. Kennedy, *Classical Rhetoric and its Christian and Secular Tradition from Ancient to Modern Times* (1980), 32–3: '[The Antidosis] takes the form of a judicial defense in an antidosis trial, a trial in which the defendant is challenged to undertake an expensive public service or else exchange property with another citizen who has been assigned the obligation to pay for the service in question . . . Here the claim is imagined that Isocrates has made great sums from his school, but the charge is extended into one of corrupting the young by teaching them to speak and thus to gain an advantage in contests contrary to justice.'

We ought to think of the art of discourse just as we think of the other arts, nor show ourselves intolerant towards that power which, of all the faculties which belong to the nature of man, is the source of most of our blessings. For in the other powers which we possess, we are in no respect superior to other living creatures . . . but, because there has been implanted in us the power to persuade each other and to make clear to each other whatever we desire, not only have we escaped the life of wild beasts, but we have come together and founded cities and made laws and invented arts; and, generally speaking, there is no institution devised by man which the power of speech has not helped us to establish. For this it is which has laid down laws concerning things just and unjust, and things honourable and base; and if it were not for these ordinances we should not be able to live with one another. It is by this that we confute the bad and extol the good. Through this we educate the ignorant and appraise the wise; for the power to speak well is taken as the surest index of a sound understanding, and discourse which is true and lawful and just is the outward image of a good and faithful soul. With this faculty we both contend against others on matters which are open to dispute and seek light for ourselves on things which are unknown; for the same arguments which we use in persuading others when we speak in public, we employ also when we deliberate in our thoughts; and, while we call eloquent those who are able to speak before a crowd, we regard as sage those who most skilfully debate their problems in their own minds. And, if there is need to speak in brief summary of this power, we shall find that none of the things which are done with intelligence take place without the help of speech, but that in all our actions as well as in all our thoughts speech is our guide, and is most employed by those who have the most wisdom.[69]

Although, as far as we know, Isocrates had no connection with the school tradition of the Ancient Near East, his splendidly reflective analysis helps us to penetrate it more imaginatively. It illuminates not only the importance it attached to persuasive speech, but also how this art was part of an education in the humanities, including the promotion of literature and guidance in morality.

[69] See Donald Lemen Clark, *Rhetoric in Greco-Roman Education* (1957), 51–8, from which the quotations are taken.

III

SCHOOL-BOOKS FROM EGYPT

Contrary to the general impression of familiarity which has been created by spectacular exhibitions and beautifully illustrated books, our knowledge of ancient Egypt is thin and patchy. Egyptologists are emphatic about the scantiness of their evidence and lament the fact that the Egyptian scribes, unlike their counterparts in Mesopotamia, wrote on their home-produced papyrus and not on clay. Papyrus, of course, is fragile and cannot long withstand damp, with the consequence that only those writings which originated in the arid zones of Egypt, safe from the annual inundation of the Nile, have survived.[1] To this totally fortuitous selection of papyri, all there is to add are the potsherds and limestone flakes used by schoolboys for their class-room exercises; these cost little and were thrown away in heaps. From these meagre remains, it is reckoned that altogether we have evidence for some seventy different works, but of these only fifteen are more or less complete. In these circumstances, it is astonishing that we can identify so many connections and so much common ground between the school literature of Egypt and the school literature of Israel; we can only speculate about how much greater Israel's indebtedness actually was.[2]

One of the writings which has survived intact is not only among the earliest, but is also, perhaps, the most representative of its distinctive genre—the didactic 'Instruction'.[3]

---

[1] W. Edgerton, in C. H. Kraeling and R. M. Adams (eds.), *City Invincible* (1960), 143–4; Keith C. Seele, ibid. 116.

[2] G. Posener, in J. R. Harris (ed.), *The Legacy of Egypt* (1971), 223. See Chronological Table.

[3] The Egyptian word used for this kind of composition, meaning 'teaching' or 'instruction', is not confined to it. 'It is attested as a heading for didactic treatises, propaganda tractates, laments, tomb autobiographies, onomastica, calendars of

Characteristically, this took the form of a series of exhortatory paragraphs addressed by a senior official to his son and successor, with the purpose of training him for office according to the guidance provided by traditional teaching and past experience. In this case, the author was the City Governor and Vizier Ptahhotep and the four-thousand-word document he produced about the year 2350 BC survived by being copied century after century in the school class-room.[4]

The Instruction of Ptahhotep is full of humane good sense and it established a basic pattern of teaching which we find reflected in the core curriculum of Israel's schools over a thousand years later. Even for Ptahhotep, what he had to teach his son was already hallowed by tradition. As the king says, in responding to his Vizier's proposal: 'Teach him what has been said in the past; then he will set a good example to the children of the magistrates, and judgment and all exactitude shall enter into him. Speak to him, for there is none born wise.'[5] The key to wisdom was education.

The young man preparing for high office should cultivate a stable and civilized style of life. He is counselled to love his wife and make her happy,[6] to avoid improper sexual liaisons,[7] to keep on good terms with friends and to be patient with difficult ones.[8] Avarice is to be avoided like the plague, since it destroys all human relationships: 'greater is the claim of the gentle man than that of the strong.'[9] Success and wealth, however, are to be enjoyed, but discreetly: 'If you have become great after your poverty and achieved property ... do not boast of what has accrued to you in the past, do not trust in your riches, which have accrued to you by the gift of God.'[10]

It is obvious that the generalized character of this teaching was intended for a larger audience than the Vizier's son and this is particularly clear in the advice about showing

---

lucky and unlucky days, schoolboy exercises and a satire on the trades', R. J. Williams, 'The Sages of Ancient Egypt in the Light of Recent Scholarship', in Jack M. Sasson (ed.), *Oriental Wisdom, JAOS* 101/1 (1981), 7.

[4] *LAE* 159–76; *ANET* 412–14. See J. Leclant, 'Documents nouveaux et points de vue récents sur les Sagesses de l'Égypte ancienne', in *Les Sagesses du Proche-Orient Ancien*, Bibliothèque des Centres d'Études supérieures spécialisés (1963), 5–26.
[5] *LAE* 160.   [6] *LAE* 167.   [7] *LAE* 166, 171.
[8] *LAE* 168, 171, 172.   [9] *LAE* 166–7.   [10] *LAE* 170; cf. 163–4.

deference to superiors, whether it be in dispute,[11] or at dinner. Here we have the earliest evidence of that extraordinarily persistent international tradition, so beloved of the schoolmen, about how to behave when you are asked to dine: 'If you are one of the guests at the table of one who is greater than you, accept what he gives when it is set before you . . . Do not speak to him until he calls, for no one knows what may be displeasing; speak when he addresses you.'[12] Two thousand years later, Ben Sira was giving much the same advice:

> If a great man invites you, be slow to accept,
> and he will be the more pressing in his invitation . . .
> Do not presume to converse with him as an equal,
> and put no trust in his effusive speeches.[13]

An admirable combination of shrewd perception and moral sensitivity informs Ptahhotep's teaching. It goes without saying, of course, that an official sitting in judgement should be impartial and avoid raking up old scores,[14] but Ptahhotep's insight and human sympathy take him further: 'If you are a leader, be pleased when you hear the speech of a petitioner; do not rebuff him until his belly is emptied of what he has planned to tell you; the victim of wrong prefers the venting of his feelings to the performance of that for which he has come . . . a kindly hearing is a soothing of the heart.'[15] On the other hand, an official must never vent his feelings, especially on a man of lowly status: 'If you find a disputant arguing, a humble man who is not your equal, do not be aggressive against him in proportion as he is humble; let him alone, that he may confute himself. Do not question him in order to relieve your feelings . . . for wretched is he who would destroy him who is poor of understanding.'[16]

Perhaps Ptahhotep's strongest claim to have provided the basic model for future teachers is this emphasis on disciplined self-control. 'Great respect', he says, 'is given to the quiet man.'[17] In dealing with an argumentative person, it is better not to answer back: 'it means that he will be dubbed an

[11] *LAE* 161.   [12] *LAE* 162–3.   [13] Ecclus. 13: 9–11.
[14] *LAE* 170.   [15] *LAE* 166.
[16] *LAE* 161.   [17] *LAE* 163.

ignoramus when your self-control has matched his pro-
lixity.'[18] The theme is recurrent; 'Angry speech spoken by
anyone, great or small, should not be repeated'; 'Do not
repeat slander . . . for it is the result of hot temper'; 'Suppress
your desires, control your mouth; so will your counsel be
heard among the magistrates'; 'Plan to live in peace.'[19]

Undergirding this quietism is a firm belief in divine
sovereignty: 'it is God who advances position, and those who
elbow in do not succeed';[20] 'No terror of man has ever been
effective; it is only the ordinance of God which is effective.'[21]
In this last saying, we have what is perhaps the earliest
expression of a maxim often repeated in the school tradition,
including a contributor to the book of Proverbs:

> The human mind may be full of schemes,
> but it is the Lord's purpose that will prevail.[22]

The related idea of not trying to organize tomorrow but
being content to wait and see what it brings is found in a
whole series of Egyptian and Israelite texts. Ptahhotep writes:
'No one knows what may happen when he perceives
tomorrow and the straightforward character who is content
with it is a (real) character.'[23] In *The Tale of the Eloquent
Peasant*, written, perhaps, some two hundred years later, we
have: 'Do not prepare for the morrow before it has come, for
none knows the trouble in it.'[24] At least a thousand years
later still, we have in the book of Proverbs:

> Do not praise yourself for tomorrow's success;
> you never know what a day may bring forth.[25]

And, finally, the maxim found its way into the Sermon on the
Mount: 'So do not be anxious about tomorrow; tomorrow
will look after itself.'[26]

The confidence of Ptahhotep is no longer to be found in the
educational manuals of the New Kingdom (1540–1070 BC),
largely, it seems, because they derive from more modest
members of a society which had itself become less assured.

[18] *LAE* 161.   [19] *LAE* 163, 168, 175, 162.   [20] *LAE* 165.
[21] *LAE* 162.   [22] Prov. 19: 21.   [23] *LAE* 168.
[24] *LAE* 41; cf. *The Instruction of Amen-em-opet*, *LAE* 258, 260.
[25] Prov. 27: 1; cf. Ecclus. 11: 19.   [26] Matt. 6: 34.

The author of *The Instruction of Ani*[27] represents himself as a temple-scribe writing for his son, and his teaching reflects the hopes and fears of aspirants to middle-class status; its atmosphere of suburban domesticity is far removed from the court and its corridors of power: 'I shall let thee know upon earth about the man who seeks to found his household. Make thou a garden-plot. Enclose thou (a bed of) cucumbers in front of thy plow-land. Plant thou trees inside (so that) they may be a shelter in every section of thy home. And fill thy hand (with) every flower which thy eye may behold. One feels the need of them all.'[28]

The Instruction is addressed to schoolboys from homes where the mother of the family nurses her own babies, provides her school-children's lunch, does all the housework, and is said to deserve a husband who will give her a helping hand.[29] With a view to their career as scribes, the boys from this background must learn to keep things to themselves ('Do not talk a lot. Be silent, and thou wilt be happy'[30]), to be careful about the friends they make, to avoid strange women and strong drink, to be respectful to superiors and not answer them back, to keep on good terms with the police and not get mixed up in demonstrations, and, above all, to grasp the golden opportunities afforded by a scribal education: 'Devote thyself to the writings, and put them in thine heart, and then all that thou sayest is excellent. To whatsoever office the scribe is appointed, he consulteth the writings.'[31]

Ani is punctilious in his religious observance and acknowledges a transcendent power which governs all things and should never be questioned: 'When thy messenger comes to take thee . . . Do not say: "I am (too) young for thee to take," for thou knowest not thy death. When death comes, he steals away the infant which is on its mother's lap like him who has reached old age.'[32] This austere concept is tempered, however, by a new awareness of a personal god who actually cares: 'Pray thou with a loving heart, all the words of which are hidden, and he will do what thou needest, he will hear what thou sayest, and he will accept thy offering.'[33]

---

[27] Erman, *AE* 234–42; extracts in *ANET* 420–1.
[28] *ANET* 420b.   [29] *ANET* 421a.   [30] *ANET* 420a.
[31] Erman, *AE* 238.   [32] *ANET* 420b.   [33] *ANET* 420a.

The explicitly religious basis of scribal education in the New Kingdom is further illustrated by *The Instruction of Amen-em-opet*,[34] written some time before 1000 BC by an administrator in the Ministry of Agriculture. It follows the convention of a father's advice to his son and makes large and varied claims in its preface:

> The beginning of the instruction about life,
>   The guide for well-being,
> All the principles of official procedure,
>   The duties of courtiers;
> To know how to refute the accusation of one who made it,
>   And to send back a reply to the one who wrote;
> To set one straight on the paths of life,
>   And make him prosper on earth.[35]

For this teacher also, wisdom consists in the calm acceptance of what has been divinely ordained. It is useless for a man to join the rat-race,[36] since everything has already been determined.[37] Success comes by committing oneself silently into God's hands and leaving the issue to be decided according to his 'plan':

> Indeed, you cannot know the plans of God;
>   You cannot perceive tomorrow.
> Sit yourself at the hands of God:
>   Your tranquillity will cause them to open.[38]

Equally, God is the sole ground of morality—'it is locked up with his seal'.[39] He 'sets straight the boundaries of the arable land',[40] upholds honesty in buying and selling,[41] abominates false talk and false records,[42] and brings retribution to all who flout his will.[43] He is man's creator and that is the fundamental reason for acting with compassion towards the needy:

> Do not jeer at a blind man nor tease a dwarf,
>   neither interfere with the condition of a cripple;

---

[34] *LAE* 241–65; extracts in *ANET* 421–4 and *DOTT* 172–86.
[35] *LAE* 242.   [36] *LAE* 249.
[37] *LAE* 249.   [38] *LAE* 260; cf. *LAE* 259.
[39] *LAE* 258.   [40] *LAE* 248; cf. *LAE* 247; Prov. 22: 28.
[41] *LAE* 256–7.   [42] *LAE* 254, 255–6.   [43] *LAE* 256–7.

> Do not taunt a man who is in the hand of God (i.e. insane),
>   Nor scowl at him if he errs.
> Man is clay and straw,
>   And God is his potter.[44]

Such was the religious and moral context in which Amen-em-opet sought to train a candidate for a career in the Civil Service.[45] He should aim to become 'The truly temperate man'[46]—reticent,[47] tactful,[48] imperturbable,[49] unambitious,[50] self-effacing,[51] reliable,[52] just,[53] and scrupulously honest is both word and deed.[54] He should avoid currying favour with the great[55] and be content with that station in life to which it had pleased God to call him.[56]

The Instruction of Amen-em-opet is particularly interesting as the principal source of a section of the book of Proverbs, in which the Israelite teacher has sometimes adopted the Egyptian text verbatim.[57] When he wrote

> You see an artisan skilful at his craft:
>   He will serve kings, not common men,[58]

he had in mind the final flourish of Amen-em-opet's book:

> Mark for your self these thirty chapters:
>   They please, they instruct,
> They are the foremost of all books;
>   They teach the ignorant.
> If they are read to an ignorant man,
>   He will be purified through them.
> Seize them; put them in your mind
>   And have men interpret them, explaining as a teacher.
> As a scribe who is experienced in his position,
>   He will find himself worthy of being a courtier.[59]

---

[44] *LAE* 262; cf. *LAE* 244–5; Ecclus. 33: 13; Rom. 9: 21.
[45] *LAE* 242, 265.   [46] *LAE* 246, 247, 250.
[47] *LAE* 244, 245, 260, 261.   [48] *LAE* 261, 263.   [49] *LAE* 258.
[50] *LAE* 249–50.   [51] *LAE* 251.   [52] *LAE* 262.
[53] *LAE* 259.   [54] *LAE* 246–7, 248, 254, 256, 259.
[55] *LAE* 263.   [56] *LAE* 249–50.
[57] Prov. 22: 17–23: 14; see R. J. Williams, 'The Alleged Semitic Original of the *Wisdom of Amenemope*', *JEA* 47 (1961), 100–6; B. Couroyer, 'L'Origine égyptienne de la Sagesse d'Amenemopé', *RB* 70 (1963), 208–24.
[58] Prov. 22: 29.   [59] Ch. 30; *LAE* 265.

Four wooden tablets provide evidence that this Instruction, like the others, was copied in the class-room and no doubt the same purpose was served by the book of Proverbs.

The last major manual, *The Instruction of Onchsheshonqy*, written about 400 BC and unknown until its publication in 1955, comes from the popular fringe of the Egyptian school tradition.[60] It is an artless anthology of sayings running to about two-thirds the length of the biblical book of Proverbs and reflects, not the urban and official ethos of scribal education, but the ordinary down-to-earth life of a rural community, in which school work had to be fitted in with work on the farm: 'Let your son learn to write, to plough, to fowl and to trap according to the season of the year.'[61] The 550 sayings cover many of the themes which, as we shall see, were common to the school tradition of Egypt and Israel: caution in speech ('Do not say the first thing that comes into your head'[62]) caution in making friends ('Do not be too trusting lest you become poor'[63]), caution in relations with superiors ('Do not sit down beside your better. Do not talk too much in the presence of your master?'[64]) and, above all, caution in relations with women, about whom there are no less than fifty sayings, most of them lamentably crude.

The theological stance of the *Instruction* is summed up in the saying 'nothing happens except what God ordains',[65] and this belief in a 'Disposer Supreme' finds expression in the conventional antithesis 'Man proposes, but God disposes', which goes back in Egyptian tradition at least two thousand years:

---

[60] S. R. K. Glanville, 'The Instructions of Onchsheshonqy', *Catalogue of Demotic Papyri in the British Museum*, vol. ii (1955); B. Gemser, 'The Instructions of Onchsheshonqy and Biblical Wisdom Literature', *VT* Supp. VII (1960), 102–28; William McKane, *Proverbs* (1970), 117–50. A late Egyptian demotic work of religious and moral instruction, generally known as the 'Papyrus Insinger' after one of the manuscripts by which it has come down to us, is now judged to have originated about the time of Ben Sira (190 BC) and there can be little doubt that he made direct borrowings from it. See Jack T. Sanders, *Ben Sira and Demotic Wisdom* (1983), 69–103.

[61] Onch. 17. 23; Gemser, 'Instructions', 116.

[62] Onch. 7. 24; Gemser, 'Instructions', 112.

[63] Onch. 16. 21, 22; Gemser, 'Instructions', 121; cf. Ecclus. 6: 7.

[64] Onch. 13. 23; 17. 25; Gemser, 'Instructions', 119.

[65] Onch. 22. 25; Gemser, 'Instructions', 114.

> The designs of the god are one thing;
> the thoughts of men are another.[66]

For the student of the biblical tradition, the most illuminating feature of this work is the style of its sayings. Some are epigrammatic statements, such as this saying on motherhood as an 'honourable estate':

The mother is the one who produces; precept only reproduces;[67]

there are antithetical sayings, such as we find in the Old Testament on the wise man and the fool:

A wise man is he who desires a friend (?); a fool is he who desires an enemy;[68]

and there are instructions which have a distinctly proverbial flavour:

Do not say 'young man' to one who is grown up.[69]

Most interesting of all are the colloquial proverbs. Unlike the sayings which have undergone literary elaboration and polishing and have in the process been tied down to a clearly defined meaning, colloquial proverbs do not invite us to take them at their face value, but, rather, to use our wits in exploring how they fit a great variety of situations. There is a general point lurking in the background, but it is expressed in highly specific terms:

When a crocodile surfaces, its length is measured.[70]

When a crocodile wants a donkey, it puts on a wig.[71]

He who has been bitten by the bite of a snake is afraid (even) of a coil of rope.[72]

It is probable that pithy sayings of this unsophisticated kind, which evidently attracted the attention of compilers and

[66] Onch. 26. 14; cf. *The Instruction of Ptahhotep*, *LAE* 162; *The Instruction of Amen-em-opet*, *LAE* 258; Prov. 16: 9; 19: 21; 20: 24; 21: 31; 29: 26; see R. J. Williams, in J. R. Harris (ed.), *The Legacy of Egypt* (1971), 280.
[67] Onch. 12. 8; McKane, *Proverbs*, 126–7.
[68] Onch. 12. 2; McKane, *Proverbs*, 126.
[69] Onch. 7. 2; McKane, *Proverbs*, 147.
[70] Onch. 10. 4; McKane, *Proverbs*, 129.
[71] Onch. 24. 8; Gemser, 'Instructions', 112.
[72] Onch. 14. 14; Gemser, 'Instructions', 116.

editors, provided some of the raw material for the fashioning of didactic sentences in the book of Proverbs.

In addition to these conventional instructions, five oddly assorted works, to judge by the quantity of unearthed ostraca, were particular favourites in the Egyptian schools. The first of these was called *Kemyt* (meaning 'The Whole'), of which no less than four hundred fragmentary copies survive.[73] It was a manual giving standard conventions for letter-writing, with advice on practising self-control and working hard at one's books, in order to become a top civil servant. Having started its extraordinary career about 2000 BC, it remained a basic school text for at least a thousand years.

A second favourite was *The Instruction of Khety, son of Dauf*, written about 1960 BC, and often referred to as *The Satire on the Trades*.[74] The school provenance of the work (established by a number of papyri, writing-boards, and no less than 247 ostraca) is confirmed by its conventional form—that of an Instruction given by a father to his son, in this case as he sails up the Nile for the young man's enrolment in the scribal school at Memphis. The writing ends with a section of general advice of the kind which had become traditional for scribes in training—caution about disputes, discretion in dealing with officials, reserve in talking, reliability as a messenger, diligence as a student, and so on, but the body of the document is a lively set-piece satirizing the sorry plight of manual workers. The caricature of the bricklayer at work may serve to illustrate its style:

I shall also describe to you the bricklayer. His kidneys are painful. When he must be outside in the wind, he lays bricks without a garment. His belt is a cord for his back, a string for his buttocks. His strength has vanished through fatigue and stiffness, kneading all his excrement. He eats bread with his fingers, although he washes himself but once a day.[75]

A mocking paragraph is devoted to no less than eighteen jobs in which you get your hands dirty, until, finally, the catalogue

[73] G. Posener, in J. R. Harris (ed.), *The Legacy of Egypt* (1971), 224, 230; G. Posener, *Littérature et politique dans l'Égypte de la XIIᵉ dynastie* (1956), 4–7; a quotation from *Kemyt* occurs at the beginning of *The Satire on the Trades*, ANET 432b n. 2.   [74] LAE 329–36; ANET 432–4.   [75] LAE 332.

reaches its inevitable conclusion: 'Behold, there is no pro-fession free of a boss—except for the scribe: he is the boss. But if thou knowest writing, then it will go better with thee . . .'[76] This work inspired many imitators and for centuries schoolboys learnt to read and write by copying out dire warnings about forsaking the white-kilt profession of a scribe.[77] As late as 190 BC, Ben Sira was familiar with a version of the theme:

> A scholar's wisdom comes of ample leisure;
> to be wise he must be relieved of other tasks.
> How can one become wise who follows the plough . . .?
> So it is with the smith, sitting by his anvil,
> intent on his ironwork.
> The fiery vapours shrivel his flesh
> as he wrestles in the heat of the furnace.[78]

Khety, the author of *The Satire*, is said to have written two more of the five most popular school texts—*The Instruction of Amenemhet* and the *Hymn to the Nile*. It is not immediately obvious why the former won such popularity as is suggested by its having been read and copied continuously for some fourteen to seventeen centuries.[79] The 'instruction' form is no more than a convention borrowed from the school tradition, since the work, in fact, is a piece of political propaganda. It was written to support the succession to the throne of Sesostris I (1971–1928 BC), after the assassination of his father, King Amenemhet.[80] The dead king is represented as warning his son against repeating his cardinal error of trusting people: 'trust no brother, know no friend, make no intimates, for there is no profit in it . . . I gave to the poor man, I cherished the orphan, I caused him who had nothing

[76] *ANET* 434a; *LAE* 334.
[77] Caminos, 371–428; E. W. Heaton, *Solomon's New Men* (1974), 105–8; B. van de Walle, 'Le Thème de la Satire des Métiers dans la littérature égyptienne', *CE* 22 (1947), 50–72. [78] Ecclus. 38: 24–34.
[79] 'The text of Amenemhet . . . is preserved at least in part on six papyri (one still unpublished), one unpublished leather roll, three writing boards and 194 ostraca (five of which are still unpublished) . . . All of which means that from the time of its composition during the early part of the reign of Senwosret I this work was read and copied continuously for a period of some fourteen to seventeen centuries', Williams, 'Sages of Ancient Egypt', 10.
[80] *LAE* 193–7; *ANET* 418–19; see Posener, *Littérature et politique*, 61–86.

to attain (to wealth) . . . but it was he who ate my bread who raised levies . . .'[81] Comparable disillusion and caution were echoed much later in the writings of Israel's schoolmen.[82] If the unusually human portrayal of the Pharaoh contributed to the popular appeal of this work, we must also take into account the writer's literary talent. His description of the entry of the conspirators achieves its dramatic effect with splendid simplicity:

It was after supper, and night had fallen. I took an hour of recreation lying on my bed, for I was weary and I began to doze, when weapons were brandished and men argued about me. I acted like the snake of the desert, for I awoke at the fighting and I was by myself, and I found that it was a combat with the guard. If I had made haste with weapons in my hand, I would have made the cowards retreat in confusion, but no man is brave at night, and no one can fight alone.[83]

Such narrative skill was a significant element in Israel's indebtedness to the Egyptian scribal tradition.

The third work attributed to Khety, the *Hymn to the Nile*,[84] from about 1960 BC, is a composition of some sophistication, celebrating the annual miracle of the river's inundation, in a kind of nature mysticism detached from any connection with the cult:

> No one knows the place he's in,
> His cavern is not found in books.
> He has no shrines, no portions,
> No service of his choice;
> But youths, his children, hail him,
> One greets him like a king.
> Lawful, timely, he comes forth,
> Filling Egypt, South and North;
> As one drinks, all eyes are on him,
> Who makes his bounty overflow.[85]

Although no direct echo of this particular hymn has been identified in the Old Testament, Israel's psalmists were certainly inspired by Egyptian models. The most outstanding example of this legacy is the similarity between the hymn to

---

[81] *LAE* 194.   [82] See pp. 79–80.
[83] *LAE* 194–5.   [84] *ANET* 372–3.
[85] M. Lichtheim, *Ancient Egyptian Literature*, vol. i (1973), 207.

the sun-disk Aten, composed for the radical religious reformer, King Akhenaten, in the middle of the fourteenth century BC, and Psalm 104.[86] The Egyptian hymn celebrates the wonders of day and night, the joyful energy of men and animals, the secret nurture of embryos in the womb and in the egg, the remarkable differentiation of the races of mankind in speech and colour, including the thoughtful provision of 'a Nile in the sky' (that is, our usual wet weather) as a means of irrigation for those fated to live in foreign lands:

> How plentiful it is, what you have made,
> although they are hidden from view,
> sole god, without another beside you;
> you created the earth as you wished,
> when you were by yourself, (before)
> mankind, all cattle and kine,
> all beings on land, who fare upon their feet,
> and all beings in the air, who fly with their wings.[87]

Similarly, Psalm 104 is a joyful celebration of the majesty and splendour of God's works in Creation—the heavens, the earth and the seas, the provision of food for birds, beasts, and men, the regularity of sun and moon, day and night—all bearing witness to the Creator's life-giving care:

> Countless are the things you have made, Lord;
> by your wisdom you have made them all;
> the earth is full of your creatures.[88]

The last of the five favourite class-room texts, *The Story of Sinuhe*, has been described as the 'Robinson Crusoe' of Egyptian schoolboys.[89] It takes the form of an autobiographical narrative (of the kind Egyptians delighted to have inscribed on their tombs) and recounts the adventures of a high-ranking palace official who fled the country on hearing of the assassination of the king, Amenemhet I. Eventually, Sinuhe settled in Palestine, where he rapidly rose to a position of leadership, but advancing years made him yearn for the land of his birth, to which he was urged to return by the new

---

[86] *LAE* 289–95; *ANET* 369–71; *DOTT* 142–50; see A. Barucq, *L'Expression de la louange divine et de la prière dans la Bible et en Égypte* (1962), 303, 316–21.
[87] *LAE* 292.   [88] Ps. 104: 24.   [89] *LAE* 57–74; *ANET* 18–22.

king, Sesostris I. After a right royal and rapturous homecoming, he was accorded unprecedented privileges and lived
happily ever after.

The *Story of Sinuhe* has all the ingredients of a best-seller—
adventure, swashbuckling bravery, patriotism, psychological interest, foreign local colour, and an ending fit for
a hero. Generations of schoolmasters must have responded
to its liveliness as literature and even more to its explicit
propaganda for their system of training. For Sinuhe is the
very model of an educated and successful official. He is
always in command of the situation. He marries the native
ruler's eldest daughter, becomes the chief of one of the
country's most attractive regions, directs the local armed
forces, accumulates vast wealth, and, on his return to Egypt,
is created a Companion among the Nobles and granted a
grace-and-favour residence. The narrative includes a vivid
account of a fight between Sinuhe and the champion warrior
of Palestine, which some think was the prototype of the tale
of David and Goliath,[90] and the hero's success story as a
whole invites comparison with the success story of Joseph in
Genesis. As we shall see later, after their didactic Instructions,
the most conspicuous and influential achievement of Egypt's
schoolmen was the development of the short story as a
literary form and this, without doubt, contributed to the
narrative art of the schoolmen of Israel.

One specific feature which *The Story of Sinuhe* and the
story of Joseph have in common is an application to narrative
of the 'Man proposes/God disposes' theme. Both writers
recognize two levels of interpretation of the events they
recount, arising from autonomous human action on the one
hand and divine control on the other. Joseph says to his
brothers: 'It is clear that it was not you who sent me here, but
God, and he has made me Pharaoh's chief counsellor.'[91]
Similarly, Sinuhe tells the Palestinian ruler: 'I do not know
what brought me to this land. It was like the plan of a
God.'[92] Later in the narrative, this convenient interpretation
becomes more explicit: 'This flight which your servant made,

---

[90] *LAE* 64–5; 1 Sam. 17: 4–51.
[91] Gen. 45: 8; cf. 50: 20.   [92] *LAE* 61.

it was not premeditated. It was not in my mind. I did not prepare it. I cannot say what separated me from my place. It was like a dream . . . with the God who decreed this flight drawing me on.'[93] Sinuhe goes so far as to speak of his exile as a divine punishment and interprets its successful outcome as evidence of divine mercy: 'I became rich in treasure, a great proprietor of cattle. God acts in such a way to be merciful to one whom he had blamed, one whom He causes to go astray to another land. For today His heart is appeased.'[94] What moral the schoolboys derived from this kind of theological whitewash is anybody's guess.

The chance discovery in 1891 of an unknown work in a jar near El-Hiba has made a fascinating addition to our evidence of the Egyptian scribes' delight in story-telling. As the format of the papyrus indicates, the document, now known as *The Story of Wenamun*,[95] is a genuine report of an official mission by an envoy of the Theban High Priest, but it has been written up as a tale of adventure illustrating with sardonic humour the decline in Egypt's prestige at the end of the New Kingdom (about 1070 BC). Wenamun, the wretched envoy, was sent on a voyage north to obtain pinewood for the ceremonial barge of Amun and was given an unexpectedly rough reception by the Prince of Byblos. The narrative is full of sharp dialogue and well-observed detail. Wenamun's first meeting with the Prince is introduced with a splendid touch: 'I found him sitting in his loft, having turned his back to a window so that it was to the rear of his head that the waves of the great Syrian sea were breaking.'[96] The story ends with his attempted murder in Cyprus, recounted with sang-froid and comic detail: 'The winds wafted me to the land of Alasiya (Cyprus), and the townsmen came out against me to kill me. And so I picked my way through them to the place where Hatiba, the princess of the town, was. I met her after she had left from one house of hers and as she was about to enter her other one. I saluted her and said to the people who were standing around her: Surely there is one among you who understands Egyptian. And one of them said: I

---

[93] *LAE* 69–70.   [94] *LAE* 65.
[95] *LAE* 142–55; *ANET* 25–9.   [96] *LAE* 146–7.

understand.'[97] Writing of this quality was being produced by
the Egyptian scribes in the century before King David. David
himself was later described by a schoolman of Israel in
comparably limpid prose: 'David remained in Jerusalem, and
one evening, as he got up from his couch and walked about
on the roof of the palace, he saw from there a woman
bathing, and she was very beautiful.'[98]

Another frequently copied text was a piece of political
propaganda known as *The Prophecy of Neferti*,[99] written in
support of King Amenemhet I, who usurped the throne in
1991 BC. In order to give it the appearance of authority, the
message is cast in the form of a prediction represented as
having been made in the distant past, asserting that the land
would be overwhelmed by chaos: 'I show you the land in
calamity, for what had never happened has now happened.
Men will take weapons of war and the land will live in
confusion. Men will make arrows of bronze . . . and a man's
heart will think of himself alone . . . and a man sits quiet,
turning his back, while one man kills another.'[100] And then,
as if by divine intervention, with the coming of the new (and
present) king, 'Right will come to its place (again) and Wrong
will be thrust outside.'[101] It is of some interest to observe that
the idea of a Messianic Age with the advent of a king
validated by ancient prediction emerged in ancient Egypt
over a thousand years before it was taken up by the school
tradition of the Old Testament and that the device of
disguising present happenings as events predicted in the past
was well established before it was used in the book of
Daniel.[102]

Among the later New Kingdom school texts, the most
entertaining and, therefore, the most frequently copied, was a
compilation running to about twenty-eight pages known as
The Satirical Letter of the Scribe Hori.[103] It takes the form of
a reply by Hori, a 'teacher of apprentices in the Office of
Writings', to a pompous letter from a military scribe on

[97] *LAE* 154–5.   [98] 2 Sam. 11: 2.
[99] *LAE* 234–40; *ANET* 444–6.
[100] *LAE* 237–8.   [101] *LAE* 240.
[102] See E. W. Heaton, *The Book of Daniel* (1956), 56–8.
[103] *ANET* 475–9; Erman, *AE* 214–34.

active service in Syria and Palestine. Among other things, he boasts of his deep learning: 'I am more profound as a scribe than heaven or earth or the underworld. I know the mountains in *deben* and *hin* (that is, weights and measures)!'[104] It is worth pausing to note that it is this piece of school idiom which the prophet Second Isaiah used to describe the supremacy of God as Creator:

> Who has measured the waters of the sea in the hollow of his hand,
> or with its span gauged the heavens?
> Who has held all the soil of the earth in a bushel,
> or weighed the mountains on a balance,
> the hills on a pair of scales?[105]

As Hori points out, the pretensions of the scribe cannot conceal his incompetence, which the muddle of his letter only too clearly reveals: 'Thy statements mix up this with that; all thy words are upside-down; they are not connected.'[106] On this peg, Hori in his reply hangs a number of model lessons for his students—in letter-writing, arithmetic, and geography. The last section of the text includes a sarcastic grilling of his pupil on the geography of the region from northern Syria to the Egyptian frontier: 'Let me tell thee of another strange city, named Byblos. What is it like? And its goddess? Once again—thou hast not trodden it. Pray instruct me about Beirut, about Sidon and Sarepta. Where is the stream of the Litani? What is Uzu like?'[107] And so it goes on, relentlessly. Hori is probably caricaturing a method of viva voce teaching used in the schools. Something very much like it was familiar to the writer of that blistering interrogation which was designed to humiliate Job, when he rejected the Comforters' specious answers to his doubts. It is strange that many interpreters admire it as God's decisive speech from the whirlwind and the key to the meaning of the drama:

> Brace yourself and stand up like a man;
> I shall put questions to you, and you must answer.[108]

---

[104] *ANET* 476b.   [105] Isa 40: 12.
[106] *ANET* 475b.   [107] *ANET* 477a.
[108] Job 38: 3; see pp. 144–5.

When they were not being bullied by their teachers, the young literati of the schools of this period (1320–1070 BC) found time to write love poems. Some four dozen poems in four major collections have survived, so that we have a fair sample of what Egyptian audiences used to enjoy.[109] Under the heading, 'Beginning of the Songs of Entertainment', one collection includes a piece which every reader of the biblical Song of Songs will find familiar; in it, the woman associates her charms with those of a garden—good for walking in, like Eden, in the cool of the day:

> I am your best girl:
> I belong to you like an acre of land
> which I have planted
> with flowers and every sweet-smelling grass.
>
> Pleasant is the channel through it
> which your hand dug out
> for refreshing ourselves with the breeze,
> a happy place for walking
> with your hand in my hand.
>
> my body is excited, my heart joyful,
> at our traveling together.
>
> Hearing your voice is pomegranate wine,
> for I live to hear it,
> and every glance which rests on me
> means more to me than eating and drinking.[110]

Another collection, with the title, 'The Beginning of the Songs of Extreme Happiness', presents a cycle of stanzas (spoken alternately by the man and the woman), which so appealed to Ezra Pound that he published his own translation. They portray affection and sensual delight in allusive and far-fetched language, which may well have been drawn from a common stock on which later the Song of Songs also drew. The first stanza, in which the man praises what he calls his 'lady love without a duplicate', conveys the general flavour:

> One, the lady love without a duplicate,
> more perfect than the world,

[109] *LAE* 296–325; *ANET* 467–9; Erman, *AE* 242–51; *DOTT* 187–91.
[110] *LAE* 308–9; cf. S. of S. 4: 12–5: 1; 6: 2, 3, 11, 12; Gen. 3: 8; see p. 122.

see, she is like the star rising
at the start of an auspicious year.

She whose excellence shines, whose body glistens,
glorious her eyes when she stares,
sweet her lips when she converses,
she says not a word too much.

High her neck and glistening her nipples,
of true lapis her hair,
her arms finer than gold,
her fingers like lotus flowers unfolding.[111]

The Egyptian lyrics and the Song of Songs share the same
rustic scenery, which coruscates with exotic fauna and
flora;[112] both refer to the woman as 'sister'[113] and use the
motif of 'the man at the door' and 'the mother in the
background';[114] and, not surprisingly, love-sickness is a
theme they have in common.[115] In *The Story of Wenamun*,
we are told that the Prince of Byblos retained an Egyptian
singer at his court and sent her (along with two jugs of wine
and a ram)[116] to cheer up his stranded visitor; this suggests
one way in which Egyptian love-songs may have been
disseminated and come to influence the poets of Palestine.
If 'many waters cannot quench love' in the Song of
Songs, even shark-infested waters cannot deter the Egyptian
suitor:

> The love of my sister is on yonder side
> Of the stream in the midst of the fish.
> A crocodile stands on the sandbank;
> Yet I go down into the water.
> I venture across the current;
> my courage is high upon the waters.
> It is thy love which gives me strength;
> For thou makest a water-spell for me.

---

[111] *LAE* 315–16; cf. S. of S. 6: 10; 5: 11, 14.

[112] *LAE* 322; cf. S. of S. 2: 9; 8: 14; 7: 3; *LAE* 299; cf. S. of S. 2: 1–6.

[113] *DOTT* 189–90; *LAE*, Introduction, 297; S. of S. 4: 9–12; 5: 1. This usage
was familiar in Sumerian love songs; see Roland E. Murphy, *The Song of Songs*
(1990), 46 n. 220.

[114] *LAE* 325; S. of S. 5: 2–7; *LAE* 317, 320; S. of S. 3: 4; 8: 1, 2.

[115] *LAE* 316, 320; S. of S. 2: 5; 5: 8.

[116] *ANET* 28b; *LAE* 154; cf. *ANET* 263b and 246 n. 30.

When I see my sister coming,
Then my heart rejoices.
My arms are open wide to embrace her.[117]

We are told that the hieratic writing of the ostracon on which this passionate lyric survived was unusually crude. One of the young men, no doubt, had been neglecting his studies.

[117] S. of S. 8: 7; *DOTT* 189; *ANET* 468; *LAE* 310.

IV

EDUCATION IN WISDOM

Education in wisdom means training in 'know-how'. This splendid expression, which has been current in the United States since the early nineteenth century, identifies the essentially practical quality which the Old Testament writers called wisdom.[1] The term always signifies superior ability—the ability to get on top of things, to achieve a goal, to become expert, to exercise mastery, and so on. The attenuated modern view of wisdom as analytic insight detached from executive power, such as the elderly are supposed to possess, was quite foreign to ancient Israel. At one end of the spectrum, wisdom was used to describe the skill of seamen[2] and snake-charmers,[3] designers[4] and embroiderers,[5] carpenters[6] and metalworkers,[7] like Hiram, whom Solomon hired: 'His father, a native of Tyre, had been a worker in bronze, and he himself was a man of great skill and ingenuity, versed in every kind of craftsmanship in bronze' (or, as the Revised Standard Version translates more literally, 'he was full of wisdom, understanding and skill, for making any work in bronze').[8] At the other end of the spectrum, it was by wisdom that in the beginning God created the world and got it to work:

> By wisdom the Lord laid the earth's foundations
> and by understanding he set the heavens in place;

---

[1] See R. M. Hare, *The Language of Morals* (1952), 158–9: 'Everything we are taught how to do must be . . . reducible to principles, though these may be "know-hows" hard to formulate in language and more easily taught by example.'

[2] Ezek. 27: 8, 9; Ps. 107: 26, 27; 1 Kgs. 9: 27.   [3] Ps. 58: 5.

[4] Exod. 31: 3–11; 35: 31–3.   [5] Exod. 28: 3; 35: 35; 36: 8.

[6] Isa. 40: 20.   [7] I Chron. 22: 15; Jer. 10: 9.   [8] 1 Kgs. 7: 14.

by his knowledge the springs of the deep burst forth
and the clouds dropped dew.[9]

The wisdom of the Creator is essentially no different from
the wisdom of the craftsman, since both demand the intelligence which can fashion a design and execute it.[10]

The kind of wisdom which dominates the book of
Proverbs, where the use of the term in its various forms
accounts for nearly a third of the occurrences in the whole of
the Old Testament, is neatly indicated by the legendary
reputation of Solomon, who, of course, was eventually
adopted as Patron of the school tradition: 'God gave
Solomon deep wisdom and insight, and understanding as
wide as the sand on the seashore, so that Solomon's wisdom
surpassed that of all the men of the east and of all Egypt . . .
He propounded three thousand proverbs, and his songs
numbered a thousand and five. He discoursed of trees, from
the cedar of Lebanon down to the marjoram that grows out
of the wall, of beasts and birds, of reptiles and fish. People of
all races came to listen to the wisdom of Solomon . . .'[11]
Wisdom could be articulated in a body of knowledge you
came to listen to; it was something which could be taught and
learnt:

> Lecture a wise person, and he will grow wiser still;
> teach a righteous one, and he will add to his learning.[12]

> Listen to advice and accept instruction,
> and in the end you will be wise.[13]

The only specialized, vocational form of wisdom in the book
of Proverbs is not, as we might have expected, instruction for
the scribal profession, but teaching appropriate to the
training of an official at court:

> Do not push yourself forward at court
> or take your stand where the great assemble;

---

[9] Prov. 3: 19–20; cf. Isa. 40: 13, 14, 28; Jer. 10: 12; 51: 15; Ps. 104: 24; Job 26: 12; 28: 23–8; 37: 16; 38: 36, 37.

[10] See Georg Fohrer, 'Sophia', in *Kittel's Theological Dictionary of the New Testament*, vii (1971), 476–96.

[11] 1 Kgs. 4: 29–34; cf. 1 Kgs. 11: 41; Prov. 25: 1; Eccles. 1: 1, 12, 13, 16; S. of S. 1: 1; Ecclus. 47: 14–17.   [12] Prov. 9: 9.

[13] Prov. 19: 20; cf. 5: 13; 8: 33; 22: 17; Job 33: 31–3.

for it is better to be told, 'Come up here,'
than to be moved down to make way for a nobleman.[14]

Material for the prospective courtier is, however, a relatively
minor element in the book and may merely reflect the
concern (perhaps superseded) of one of its diverse sources.
The purpose of the compilation as it now stands is the
education of both the young and adults in the received
tradition of behaviour and belief, as is evident from the
editor's grandiose preface, with its heaping up of synonymous
terms and its claim to a universal usefulness:

> The proverbs of Solomon son of David, king of Israel,
> by which mankind will come to wisdom and instruction,
> will understand words that bring understanding,
> and will attain to a well-instructed intelligence,
> righteousness, justice, and probity.
> The simple will be endowed with shrewdness
> and the young with knowledge and discretion.
> By listening to them the wise will increase their learning,
> those with understanding will acquire skill
> to understand proverbs and parables,
> the sayings and riddles of the wise.[15]

In his celebrated description of the man of learning, Ben
Sira repeated this formula:

> He preserves the sayings of the famous
> and penetrates the subtleties of parables,
> He explores the hidden meaning of proverbs.[16]

An investigation of his relationship to the book of Proverbs
holds the promise of illuminating both the content and
continuity of the school tradition.

A cursory reading may give the impression that the two
works differ too radically for any significant connection.
There is certainly a unity of style in Ecclesiasticus which the
editor of Proverbs has not attempted to impress on his
disparate sources, so that, despite the equally chaotic lack of

---

[14] Prov. 25: 6, 7; cf. 14: 35; 16: 10, 12–15; 18: 16; 19: 12; 20: 2, 8, 26, 28; 21:
1; 25: 4, 5, 15; 29: 4, 14; see W. Lee Humphreys, 'The Motif of the Wise Courtier in
the Book of Proverbs', in John G. Gammie, et al. (eds.), *Israelite Wisdom* (1978),
177–90.

[15] Prov. 1: 1–6.   [16] Ecclus. 39: 2, 3.

shape and structure in both compilations, it is more easily possible to read Ecclesiasticus *as a book*. Clearly, the received tradition has been reminted by a fairly sophisticated mind and related to the urbane society of Jerusalem in the early years of the second century BC. By contrast, the book of Proverbs reflects no specific historical setting, and, in addition, no interest in the historical, legal, and cultic traditions of Israel such as emerge in Ecclesiasticus.[17] Nevertheless, underlying Ben Sira's ambivalent espousal of the Law and the Temple, there is a simple and emphatic moral piety which we first find in the book of Proverbs. It affirms that the world is ordered by the benevolent providence of the Creator,[18] to whose bounty men should respond in quiet faith[19] and humble piety.[20] The issue of all things is in the hands of God[21] and he is the judge of right and wrong.[22] Such are the theological foundations of the moral and practical wisdom of Israel's school tradition.

Although it is arguably true, as Ben Sira observed, that there is no fool like an old fool,[23] there is a range of advice common to the book of Proverbs and Ecclesiasticus which appears to be primarily directed to young men. Not surprisingly, sexual discipline is a prominent theme. Ben Sira's basic instruction on the subject is packed into a single passage:

> Do not go near a loose woman,
> or you may fall into her snares.
> Do not keep company with a dancing-girl
> or you may be caught by her advances . . .
> Never surrender yourself to prostitutes,
> for fear of losing all you possess.

[17] What matters is prayer rather than sacrifice: Prov. 15: 8, 29; 20: 25; 21: 3, 27; 28: 9; cf. *The Instruction for Merikare*: 'More acceptable is the character of one upright of heart than the ox of the evildoer', ANET 417b; LAE 191; see L. G. Perdue, *Wisdom and Cult* (1977), 142–65.

[18] Prov. 8: 22–31; 14: 31; 17: 5; Ecclus. 16: 24–30; 39: 12–21.

[19] Prov. 3: 5; 16: 3, 6, 20; 22: 19; 29: 25; Ecclus. 2: 10, 15–18; 34: 13–17.

[20] Prov. 15: 33; 18: 12; Ecclus. 22: 27–23: 6; see the Egyptian prayers in ANET 379–81.

[21] Prov. 16: 33; 19: 21; 20: 24; 29: 26; Ecclus. 10: 4, 5; 33: 10–13.

[22] Prov. 11: 1; 16: 2, 11; 17: 3; 20: 9, 10, 23; 21: 2.

[23] Ecclus. 25: 2.

> Do not gaze about you in the city streets
> or wander in its unfrequented areas . . .
> Never sit down with another man's wife
> or join her in a drinking party,
> for fear of succumbing to her charms
> and slipping into fatal disaster.[24]

The book of Proverbs provides numerous precedents for such direct counselling, including a particularly vivid description of the accosting of a foolish lad by a married woman, whose husband was away on business:

> He was passing along the street at her corner,
> stepping out in the direction of her house . . .
> at dusk as the night grew dark,
> and there a woman came to meet him.
> She was dressed like a prostitute, full of wiles
> flighty and inconstant . . .
> She caught hold of him and kissed him;
> brazenly she accosted him and said . . .
> 'I have spread coverings on my couch,
> coloured linen from Egypt.
> I have perfumed my bed
> with myrrh, aloes, and cassia.
> Come! Let us drown ourselves in pleasure,
> let us abandon ourselves to a night of love;
> for my husband is not at home.'
> He followed her, the simple fool,
> Like an ox on its way to be slaughtered.[25]

There can be no doubt that such warnings, couched in memorable and unambiguous language, formed a regular part of the instruction given in Israel's schools,[26] as they had been, centuries earlier, in the schools of Egypt. *The Instruction of Ptahhotep*, a text from about 2350 BC which became a model for school use, contains a firm section on the topic of 'approaching the women' of a household, which ends with the intimidating statement: 'As for him who fails by reason of lusting after them no plan at all will succeed in his hand.'[27]

[24] Ecclus. 9: 3–9; cf. 19: 2, 3; 23: 16–27; 26: 19–27 (mg.).
[25] Prov. 7: 6–27.
[26] Prov. 6: 20–35; 9: 13–18; 23: 26–8; 29: 3; 30: 20.
[27] *LAE* 166.

And *The Instruction of Ani*, from the New Kingdom (1540–
1070 BC), like the book of Proverbs, warns of the danger of 'a
woman who is far away from her husband'.[28]

Inevitably, the topic of drinking and drunkenness was an
associated item on the young men's syllabus. Ben Sira, the
benevolent tutor, takes a measured view of the matter:

> Do not use wine to prove your manhood,
> for wine has been the ruin of many . . .
> Wine puts life into anyone
> who drinks it in moderation.
> What is life to somebody deprived of wine?
> Was it not created to gladden the heart?
> Wine brings gaiety and high spirits
> if people know when to drink and when to stop;
> but wine in excess makes for bitter feelings
> and leads to offence and retaliation.[29]

Comparable advice had echoed down the centuries, as the
book of Proverbs illustrates:

> Listen, my son, and become wise;
> set your mind on the right course.
> Do not keep company with drunkards
> or those who are greedy for the fleshpots.
> the drunkard and the glutton will end in poverty;
> in a state of stupor they are reduced to rags.[30]

The advice is pressed home in a telling description of the
heavy drinker:

> Whose is the misery? Whose the remorse?
> Whose are the quarrels and the anxiety?
> Who gets the bruises without knowing why?
> Whose eyes are bloodshot?
> Those who linger late over their wine,
> those always sampling some new spiced liquor.
> Do not gulp down the wine, the strong red wine,
> when the droplets form on the side of the cup.
> It may flow smoothly
> but in the end it will bite like a snake
> and poison like a cobra.

---

[28] *ANET* 420a.   [29] Ecclus. 31: 25–9; cf. 19: 2.
[30] Prov. 23: 19–21; cf. 20: 1; 31: 4, 5.

Then your eyes will see strange sights,
your wits and your speech will be confused;
you become like a man tossing out at sea,
like one who clings to the top of the rigging;
you say, 'If I am struck down, what do I care?
If I am overcome, what of it?
As soon as I wake up,
I shall turn to the wine again.'[31]

Like many schoolmen, this teacher clearly had the makings of a novelist.

Indeed, the school tradition as a whole discloses an admirably perceptive insight into human character. There are many penetrating sayings on 'the heart' as the seat of a person's interior life:

The heart knows its own bitterness,
and in its joy a stranger has no part.[32]

It is the heart that changes the look on the face
either for better or for worse.[33]

A person's inner spirit, it was recognized, affected not only his appearance but also his physical condition. An awareness of psychosomatic factors is no modern discovery:

Peace of mind gives health of body,
but envy is a canker in the bones.[34]

Wakeful nights make the rich person lose weight,
when the cares of wealth drive sleep away;
sleepless worry keeps him wide awake;
just as serious illness banishes sleep.[35]

One of the more unexpected features of the core curriculum of the schools is its inclusion of advice about how to behave when dining with important people. However, the precedents in Egyptian school text-books make it clear that this was no trivial matter of etiquette, but an essential part of the training of anybody who was ambitious to make his way

[31] Prov. 23: 29–35.
[32] Prov. 14: 10; cf. 12: 25; 13: 12; 14: 13; 15: 13, 30.
[33] Ecclus. 13: 25.
[34] Prov. 14: 30; cf. 16: 24; 17: 22; 18: 14.
[35] Ecclus. 31: 1, 2; cf. 42: 9, 10.

in the world. In *The Instruction of Ptahhotep*, we find: 'If you are one of the guests at the table of one who is greater than you, accept what he gives when it is set before you. Look at what is set before you and do not pierce him with much staring . . .'[36] *The Instruction of Amen-em-opet* is even more cautious:

> Do not eat a meal in the presence of a magistrate . . .
> Look at the cup in front of you,
> And let it suffice your need.[37]

The book of Proverbs repeats this teaching in the section which draws on *The Instruction of Amen-em-opet*:

> When you sit down to dine with a ruler,
> give heed to what is before you.
> Cut down your appetite
> if you are a greedy person.
> Do not hanker after his dainties,
> for they are not what they seem.[38]

Ben Sira elaborated the theme with evident relish:

> When seated at a grand table
> do not smack your lips and exclaim, 'What a feast!'
> Remember, it is a bad thing to have a greedy eye . . .
> Do not reach for everything within sight,
> or jostle your fellow-guests at the dish . . .
> Eat what is set before you, but not like a beast;
> do not munch your food and make yourself objectionable.
> Be the first to stop for good manners' sake . . .
> A person of good upbringing is content with little,
> so when he goes to bed he is not short of breath.[39]

Just as young men must be cautious as they make their way in society, so they must resist the temptation to get rich quick. In Proverbs we are told:

> Someone of steady character will enjoy many blessings,
> but one in a hurry to get rich will not go unpunished;[40]

---

[36] *LAE* 162–3.   [37] *LAE* 261.
[38] Prov. 23: 1–3.
[39] Ecclus. 31: 12–21; cf. 13: 9–11.
[40] Prov. 28: 20; cf. 13: 11; 20: 21; 23: 4, 5.

and in Ecclesiasticus:

> My son, do not engage in too many transactions;
> attempting too much, you will come to grief.[41]

In particular, transactions which involve standing surety for a stranger should be avoided according to Proverbs,[42] and Ben Sira (like many academics since) had disparaging remarks to make about commerce:

> How rare it is for a merchant to keep clear of wrong
> or a shopkeeper to be acquitted of dishonesty!
> Many have cheated for gain;
> a money-grubber will always turn a blind eye.
> As a peg is fixed in the joint between stones,
> So dishonesty squeezes in between selling and buying.[43]

On the other hand, the pursuits of the countryman were socially acceptable. Ben Sira's later admonition not to resent manual labour or farm work[44] is in line with the attractive picture of the pastoral life in Proverbs:

> Be careful to know the state of your flock
> And take good care of your herds . . .
> The grass is cropped, new shoots are seen,
> and the green growth on the hills is gathered in;
> the lambs provide you with clothing,
> and the he-goats with the price of a field,
> while the goats' milk is food enough for your household
> and sustenance for your servant-girls.[45]

Obviously, most schoolmen, if not rich, lived comfortably and were taught to enjoy their possessions. The outlook is nicely summed up in Proverbs:

> Wisdom builds the house,
> good judgement makes it secure,
> knowledge fills the rooms
> with costly and pleasing furnishings.[46]

---

[41] Ecclus. 11: 10.
[42] Prov. 6: 1–5; cf. Prov. 11: 15; 17: 18; 20: 16; 22: 26, 27.
[43] Ecclus. 26: 29–27: 2.
[44] Ecclus. 7: 15; cf. 9: 17.
[45] Prov. 27: 22, 25–7.
[46] Prov. 24: 3, 4; cf. 21: 20; 10: 15; 18: 11.

Ben Sira, in a similar vein, although warning his pupils about revelling in great luxury,[47] has a very positive attitude to the use of money:

> My son, treat yourself well if you can afford it,
> and present worthy sacrifices to the Lord . . .
> Before you die, treat your friend well;
> reach out as far as you can to help him.
> Do not miss a day's enjoyment
> or forgo your share of innocent pleasure.
> Are you to leave to others all you have laboured for
> and let them draw lots for your hard-earned wealth?[48]

A more general recognition that you should 'reach out as far as you can to help' is firmly established in the social ethics of the school tradition and it has its precedents and, probably, its roots in the teaching of the Egyptian scribes.[49] *The Instruction for Merikare*, dated about 2100 BC, includes this admirable advice: 'Do justice, that you may live long upon earth. Calm the weeper, do not oppress the widow, do not oust a man from his father's property, do not degrade magnates from their seats. Beware of punishing wrongfully; do not kill, for it will not profit you.'[50] In *The Instruction of Amen-em-opet*, the scribe in training was taught to be generous in his treatment of the poor by adopting a device to be reflected later in St Luke's parable of the Unjust Steward:

> If you find a large debt against a poor man,
>   Make it into three parts;
> Release two of them and let one remain:
>   You will find it a path of life . . .
> Better it is to be praised as one loved by men
>   Than wealth in the storehouse[51];

and among the poor, it was the widow who was the most vulnerable:

> Do not expose a widow if you have caught her in the fields,
>   Nor fail to give way if she is accused.

---

[47] Ecclus. 18: 32.   [48] Ecclus. 14: 11–15; cf. 30: 23.
[49] F. C. Fensham, 'Widow, Orphan, and the Poor in Ancient Near Eastern Legal and Wisdom Literature', *JNES* 21 (1962), 129–39.
[50] *LAE* 183; *ANET*, 415b.
[51] Luke 16: 1–8; *LAE* 254–5; *ANET* 423b.

Do not turn a stranger away [from] your oil jar
   That it may be made double for your family.
God loves him who cares for the poor,
   More than him who respects the wealthy.[52]

Both Proverbs and Ben Sira repeatedly enjoin a similar generosity:

To oppress the poor is to insult the Creator;
   to be generous to the needy is to do him honour.[53]

My son, do not cheat a poor person of his livelihood
or keep him waiting with hungry eyes . . .
Do not reject the appeal of someone in distress
or turn your back on the poor;
when one begs for alms, do not look the other way,
so giving him cause to curse you,
for if he curses you in his bitterness,
his Creator will hear his prayer.[54]

These moral injunctions are grounded in the will and purpose of God the Creator. It is, therefore, *simply as human beings* that the poor have a claim on their fellow-men: 'To sneer at the poor is to insult the Creator';[55] conversely, 'He who is generous to the poor lends to the Lord',[56] which recalls the saying on caring for the needy in St Matthew's gospel: 'Truly I tell you: anything you did for one of my brothers here, however insignificant, you did for me.'[57]

It is fascinating to observe how the low status generally accorded to women in Israel, as, indeed in the rest of the ancient world, undergoes a quite radical change in the civilized tradition of the schools. Despite an occasional outbreak of crude male chauvinism, Ben Sira reflects a sensitive understanding of marriage and family relationships:

Do not miss the chance of a wise and good wife;
her attractions are worth more than gold . . .
Honour your father with all your heart

---

[52] *LAE* 264; *ANET* 424b.
[53] Prov. 14: 31; cf. 14: 21; 15: 25; 21: 13; 22: 9, 22, 23, 28; 23: 10, 11; 24: 11, 12; 31: 8, 9.
[54] Ecclus. 4: 1, 4–6; 7: 32; 29: 8, 9; 35: 14–16.
[55] Prov. 17: 5, cf. Ecclus. 7: 11.
[56] Prov. 19: 17.
[57] Matt. 25: 40.

76 EDUCATION IN WISDOM

and do not forget your mother's birth-pangs.
Remember that your parents brought you into the world;
how can you repay them for all that they have done?[58]

The book of Proverbs ends with an elaborate acrostic poem presenting a paragon of wifely competence and virtue,[59] and its repeated sayings about a 'nagging wife' may well be (at least, in part) a back-handed appreciation of peaceful domesticity.[60] A notable insistence on the recognition due to the mother as well as the father of a family remained current in the school tradition from Proverbs to Ecclesiasticus:

> Listen to your father, who gave you life,
> and do not despise your mother when she is old . . .
> Give your father and mother cause for delight;
> may she who bore you rejoice.[61]

The Lord has given the father honour in his children's eyes
and confirmed a mother's rights in the eyes of her sons.
Respect for a father atones for sins;
to honour your mother is like laying up treasure.[62]

Once again, the literature of Egypt affords a precedent. In *The Instruction of Ani*, one of the later school texts, the pupil is told to show due gratitude to both his mother and his wife: 'When thou art a young man and takest to thyself a wife and art settled in thy house, set thy eye on how thy mother gave birth to thee and all (her) bringing thee up as well . . . Thou shouldst not supervise (too closely) thy wife in her (own) house, when thou knowest that she is efficient. Do not say to her: "Where is it? Fetch (it) for us!" when she has put (it) in the (most) useful place. Let thy eye have regard, while thou art silent, that thou mayest recognize her abilities.'[63]

In one respect, it seems, the magnanimity of the school tradition in Proverbs outstrips that of Ecclesiasticus. Ben Sira enjoins good relations with slaves—

> Do not ill-treat a servant who works honestly
> or a hireling whose heart is in his work.

---

[58] Ecclus. 7: 19, 27, 28; cf. 25: 1; 26: 1–4, 13–18; 36: 21–6.
[59] Prov. 31: 10–31.
[60] Prov. 19: 13; 21: 9, 19; 25: 24; 27: 15.
[61] Prov. 23: 22, 25; cf. 15: 20; 19: 26; 30: 17.
[62] Ecclus. 3: 2, 3.   [63] *ANET* 421a.

> Regard a good servant with deep affection
> and do not withhold his freedom from him.[64]

—but, on four separate occasions, Proverbs goes so far as to enjoin the restoration of good relations with one's *enemies*:

> Do not say,
> 'I shall do to him as he has done to me;
> I am paying off an old score.'
>
> If your enemy is hungry, give him food;
> if he is thirsty, give him a drink of water;
> for so you will heap live coals on his head,
> and the Lord will reward you.[65]

It is possible that the live coals reflect a penitential rite practised in Egypt, but a more probable background is again to be found in a remarkable maxim in *The Instruction of Amen-em-opet*:

> Row that we may ferry the evil man away,
> For we will not act according to his evil nature;
> Lift him up, give him your hand,
> And leave him in the hands of God;
> Fill his gut with your own food
> That he may be sated and ashamed.[66]

There can be no doubt that the schools were admirable in teaching their young men to respect people as individuals with rights and needs which must be recognized, but this preoccupation with the individual also had its less attractive consequences. The tensions endemic in a social tradition which set so high a value on self-improvement and individual achievement go far to explain its unhappy obsession with the need for caution in making friends[67] and its neurotic fear of rumour and gossip.[68] The teaching of Ben Sira reflects a long-established tradition which attached the highest importance to public recognition—success, fame, honour, dignity, and social approval:

---

[64] Ecclus. 7: 20, 21.
[65] Prov. 24: 29; 25: 21, 22; cf. 20: 22; 24: 17, 18.
[66] LAE 245; ANET 422a.
[67] Prov. 14: 20; 19: 4, 6, 7; 20: 6; Ecclus. 6: 7–17; 22: 19–26; 37: 1–6.
[68] Prov. 16: 28; 26: 20–2; Ecclus. 27: 16, 17.

> Someone poor but wise can hold his head high
> and take his seat among the great.[69]

> Do not be ashamed to discipline the ignorant and foolish,
> or a greybeard on trial for fornication.
> You will be showing your sound upbringing
> and win universal approval.[70]

The reverse of this goal of public recognition was, of course, the fear of public disgrace—shame, humiliation, loss of face:

> Keep close watch over a headstrong daughter,
> or she may give your enemies cause to gloat,
> making you the talk of the town, a byword among the people,
> shaming you in the eyes of the world.[71]

This shame culture is more clearly reflected in the book of Proverbs than in any other Old Testament writing. For example, a principal motive for avoiding the embraces of an adulteress is that you would be brought to ruin in the public assembly.[72] On the contrary, to embrace wisdom, that is, to do well at school, is the way to enhance your reputation:

> Do not forsake her, and she will watch over you;
> love her and she will safeguard you;
> cherish her, and she will lift you high;
> if only you embrace her, she will bring you to honour.[73]

> My son, do not forget my teaching . . .
> So will you win favour and success
> in the sight of God and man.[74]

The idiom 'in the sight of God and man' is more than a casual figure of speech. Both in Ecclesiasticus and Proverbs, there emerges an unexpected emphasis on the all-seeing character of God—'from whom no secrets are hid'. In Proverbs we have:

> The eyes of the Lord are everywhere,
> surveying everyone, good and evil.[75]

---

[69] Ecclus. 11: 1; cf. 11: 12, 13; 15: 5, 6; 38: 3; 41: 14–42: 8.
[70] Ecclus. 42: 8.
[71] Ecclus. 42: 11; cf. 1: 30; 5: 13; 6: 9; 20: 22, 26; 23: 3; 31: 31.
[72] Prov. 5: 14; cf. 6: 32–5.
[73] Prov. 4: 6, 8.   [74] Prov. 3: 1, 4; 22: 1.
[75] Prov. 15: 3; cf. 5: 21; 15: 11; 20: 27; 24: 12.

and in Ecclesiasticus:

> For great is the wisdom of the Lord;
> he is mighty in power, all-seeing;
> his eyes are on those who fear him;
> no human action escapes his notice.[76]

The fact that this idiom is rarely used in the Old Testament and is confined otherwise to the book of Job and one or two psalms[77] is a further small piece of evidence indicating the particular affinity and continuity between these two writings.

Perhaps the most distinctive and unambiguous similarity between Ben Sira's teaching and that of the book of Proverbs is their very clearly depicted ideal of the man who has learnt wisdom. He is reserved, cautious, patient, detached, discriminating, discreet—with everything under complete control:

> A clever person conceals his knowledge . . .
>
> A clever person . . . conceals his feelings . . .
>
> Clever people do everything with understanding . . .[78]

The wise man exercises caution in all human relations—with friends ('When you make a friend . . . be in no hurry to give him your trust'),[79] with neighbours ('beware of becoming too deeply involved'),[80] and, of course, with dubious characters ('A shrewd person sees trouble coming and lies low')[81]—but the school tradition is particularly sensitive to the need for caution in *speech*. This goes further than the danger of gossip, which is roundly and repeatedly condemned;[82] it is an intellectual rather than a moral discipline:

> Keep a guard over your lips and tongue
> and keep yourself out of trouble.[83]

---

[76] Ecclus. 15: 18, 19; cf. 17: 15–20; 23: 19.
[77] Job 34: 21, 22; Pss. 33: 13–15; 139: 1–4.
[78] Prov. 12: 16, 23; 13: 16.
[79] Ecclus. 6: 7.
[80] Ecclus. 29: 20.
[81] Prov. 22: 3; cf. Ecclus. 11: 9.
[82] Prov. 11: 13; 16: 27, 28; 18: 8; 20: 19; 25: 8–10; Ecclus. 5: 14; 9: 18; 19: 5–17; 21: 28; 28: 13–26.
[83] Prov. 21: 23; cf. Ecclus. 20: 7.

> Experience uses few words;
> discernment keeps a cool head.[84]

> Do not let anyone's insolence bring you to your feet;
> he is but waiting to trap you with your own words.[85]

Pupils in Egyptian schools were familiar with this kind of teaching, as *The Instruction of Amen-em-opet* illustrates:

> Do not get into a quarrel with the argumentative man
>   Nor incite him with words;
> Proceed cautiously before an opponent,
>   And give way to an adversary;
> Sleep on it before speaking,
>   For a storm come forth like fire in hay is
> The hot-headed man in his appointed time.[86]

The educated man was a cool man, whose virtues are constantly contrasted with the weaknesses of the hot-headed fool:

> The stupid give free reign to their anger;
>   the wise wait for it to cool.[87]

Sayings using this antithesis of wise/fool (or such parallel terms as stupid, simpleton, and arrogant) are a dominant feature of the book of Proverbs and (with the exception of that self-consciously academic exercise we know as Ecclesiastes) they virtually monopolize the use of the words for 'fool' in the Old Testament.[88] They uphold the positive ideal of the man educated in wisdom by dismissing his opposite; thus, the fool is a shame to his parents, intemperate, quarrelsome, violent, garrulous, obstinate, unteachable, lazy,

---

[84] Prov. 17: 27; cf. 10: 19; 13: 3; Ecclus. 32: 8.
[85] Ecclus. 8: 11; cf. Prov. 16: 32.   [86] *LAE* 245–6.
[87] Prov. 29: 11; cf. 12: 16; 14: 17, 29; 20: 3; Ecclus. 6: 2; 8: 16; 28: 8.
[88] The word translated 'stupid' (*kesīl*) occurs 49 times in Proverbs, 18 times in Ecclesiastes, and only 3 times elsewhere in the Old Testament; the word translated 'fool' (*'ewīl*) occurs 19 times in Proverbs and 7 times elsewhere; the word translated 'simple' (*petī*) occurs 14 times in Proverbs and 4 times elsewhere; and the word translated 'arrogant' (*lēṣ*) occurs 14 times in Proverbs and twice elsewhere. See R. N. Whybray, *The Intellectual Tradition in the Old Testament* (1974), 146, 134, 136–7, 146–7. The contrast between the wise and the fool is found in Egyptian school literature as early as *The Instruction of Ptahhotep*: 'The wise man rises early in the morning to establish himself, (but) the fool rises early in the morning (only) to agitate himself', *ANET* 414b; *LAE* 174. See R. B. Y. Scott, 'Wise and Foolish, Righteous and Unrighteous', *VT*, Supp. xxiii (1972), 146–65.

self-willed, and self-satisfied. It is evident that the teachers who composed these sayings were determined to leave nobody in doubt about the value of the instruction they provided:

> The tongues of the wise spread knowledge;
> the stupid talk a lot of nonsense.[89]

> A proverb in the mouth of fools
> dangles helpless as the legs of the lame.[90]

> The foolish have no interest in seeking to understand,
> but only in expressing their own opinions.[91]

Perhaps these teachers do protest too much. Many of their antithetical sayings, instead of illuminating the positive goal of education, are simply dismissive and, it seems, intended to distance the social group made up of schoolmen from the boorish lower orders;

> Do not address yourself to a stupid person,
> for he will disown your words of wisdom.[92]

> Listening to a fool is like travelling with a heavy pack,
> but delight is to be found in learned conversation.[93]

We have met this snobbery before. The scribes of the Egyptian schools, who suffered the feeling of powerlessness endemic in the academic world, sought to boost their confidence (and perhaps their recruitment) by inflating their own importance and dismissing the working classes. To this quest for cultural solidarity, the mocking caricature of the 'cloth-cap' world of the manual worker, commonly called the *Satire on the Trades*, bears eloquent witness.[94] It was the most popular of all the Egyptian school text-books.

Comparable to the antithetical sayings contrasting the wise

[89] Prov. 15: 2.   [90] Prov. 26: 7.
[91] Prov. 18: 2; cf. 12: 15; Ecclus. 21: 13, 14; see *The Lamentations of Khakheperre-sonbe*, written about 1800 BC, on the breakdown of social order in Egypt: 'All a man wants is his own talk. Everyone is lying in crookedness. Precision in speech is abandoned', *LAE* 233.
[92] Prov. 23: 9; cf. 13: 16; see Brian W. Kovacs, 'Is there a Class-Ethic in Proverbs?', in J. L. Crenshaw and J. T. Willis (eds.), *Essays in Old Testament Ethics* (1974), 173–87.
[93] Ecclus. 21: 16; cf. 20: 13, 20; 22: 7, 8; 33: 5.
[94] See E. W. Heaton, *Solomon's New Men* (1974), 104–8.

and the fool, the book of Proverbs has a series of antithetical sayings contrasting the righteous and the wicked. It can hardly be claimed that they are invariably intellectually exciting or morally persuasive:

> The hope of the righteous blossoms;
> the expectation of the wicked withers away.[95]

> The house of the wicked will be torn down,
> but the dwelling of the upright will flourish.[96]

And sometimes they plumb the depths of banality:

> By uprightness the blameless keep their course,
> but the wicked are brought down by their own wickedness.[97]

If the wise/fool sayings were intended to separate the sheep from the goats intellectually and socially and help build up a kind of cultural solidarity, it is conceivable that the righteous/ wicked sayings were addressed to the wider community to encourage solidarity in the pursuit of high moral standards:

> The righteous are concerned for the claims of the helpless,
> but the wicked cannot understand such concern.[98]

> When the righteous are in power the people rejoice,
> but they groan when the wicked hold sway.[99]

The present arrangement of the sayings in the book of Proverbs is the end-product of so prolonged and obscure an editorial process (dare one say in the school library at Jerusalem?) that it is fruitless to ascribe any distinctive group of sayings to some hypothetical 'interest group', or to a particular phase in the speculative evolution of the school tradition. We cannot, for example, identify a period when the teaching was systematically given a theological interpretation. The stance of the Egyptian school literature confirms the evidence which suggests that education in Israel from the very beginning was undertaken in a context of religious belief and was not, as used to be thought, originally entirely secular:

[95] Prov. 10: 28; cf. 10: 3, 7, 24.
[96] Prov. 14: 11.   [97] Prov. 11: 5.
[98] Prov. 29: 7; cf. 21: 25, 26; 10: 11; 12: 10.
[99] Prov. 29: 2; cf. 11: 10, 11; 28: 12, 28; 29: 16.

> The fear of the Lord is the foundation of knowledge;
> it is fools who scorn wisdom and instruction.[100]

> The first step to wisdom is the fear of the Lord,
> and knowledge of the Most Holy One is understanding.[101]

> Wisdom is rooted in the fear of the Lord.[102]

There is little evidence to suggest, however, that religious instruction as such was ever included in that part of the school syllabus reflected in the book of Proverbs. The many references to 'the Lord' may simply indicate the religious allegiance of the school, but it seems clear that sometimes they are intended to change the older teaching. The educated man's know-how, some teachers wished to assert, would always be overridden by the Lord's final say-so. Instead of the pragmatic

> Schemes lightly made come to nothing,
> but with detailed planning they succeed,[103]

we are presented with the theological:

> The human mind may be full of schemes,
> but it is the Lord's purpose that will prevail.[104]

At least one pious editor went over the top in his religious zeal and swept aside the fundamental educational purpose of the proverb collection as it was expounded in the preface:

> Face to face with the Lord,
> wisdom, understanding, counsel avail nothing.[105]

It takes all kinds to make a school tradition.

The continuity of the school tradition from the book of Proverbs to Ecclesiasticus is confirmed by the similarity in their use of literary genres. The most characteristic of the forms they share is the proverbial saying, fashioned as a poetic couplet:

> Like a decaying tooth or a sprained ankle
> is a perfidious person relied on in the day of trouble.[106]

---

[100] Prov. 1: 7.   [101] Prov. 9: 10.
[102] Ecclus. 1: 11–20; cf. Prov. 14: 2; 15: 33; 16: 6; Ps. 111: 10; Job 1: 1, 8.
[103] Prov. 15: 22.   [104] Prov. 19: 21; cf. 16: 1, 3, 9, 33; 20: 24; 21: 31.
[105] Prov. 21: 30; cf. Ecclus. 19: 23–5.   [106] Prov. 25: 19.

> Bread got by fraud may taste good,
> but afterwards it turns to grit in the mouth.[107]

> Like glaze spread on earthenware
> is glib speech that covers a spiteful heart.[108]

Such sayings were deliberate and self-conscious literary creations and cultivated accordingly; as Ben Sira observed:

> The invention of proverbs involves wearisome thought.[109]

> They who are trained in learning prove wise themselves
> and pour forth apt proverbs.[110]

> If an instructed man hears a wise saying,
> he applauds it and improves on it.[111]

In the background of such well-polished gems, it is possible to detect a much more lively tradition of colloquial proverbs—short, sharp, and memorable—which the schoolmen took over and (often regrettably) 'improved' for use in their teaching.[112] Characteristically, colloquial proverbs pick out a couple of things and pithily indicate their relationship.

It can be *close*:

> Where there are no oxen, the barn is empty;
> the strength of an ox ensures rich crops;[113]

or, *contrasting*:

> The lash of a ship raises weals,
> but the lash of a tongue will break bones;[114]

or, *comparable*:

> Like cold water to the throat that is faint with thirst
> is good news from a distant land.[115]

[107] Prov. 20: 17. [108] Prov. 26: 23.
[109] Ecclus. 13: 26. [110] Ecclus. 18: 29.
[111] Ecclus. 21: 15; cf. Eccles. 12: 9, 10; see W. McKane, *Proverbs* (1970), 10–33; James L. Crenshaw (ed.), *Studies in Ancient Israelite Wisdom* (1976), 13–16.
[112] For 'improvements' to point the moral, cf. Prov. 25: 23; 26: 20; Ecclus. 13: 1; see R. B. Y. Scott, 'Folk Proverbs of the Ancient Near East', in Crenshaw (ed.), *Studies in Ancient Israelite Wisdom*, 417–26.
[113] Prov. 14: 4; cf. 14: 23; Ecclus. 19: 12.
[114] Ecclus. 28: 17; cf. Prov. 25: 15; 27: 7.
[115] Prov. 25: 25; cf. 25: 13.

The colloquial proverb can also pin-point particular human characteristics or experiences:

> Sand, salt, and a lump of iron
> are less of a burden than a stupid person;[116]

and give warning of the consequences:

> Whoever digs a pit will fall into it;
> if he rolls a stone, it will roll back upon him.[117]

> One person is silent, and is reckoned to be wise;
> another chatters, and is detested for it.[118]

This kind of proverb, with its allusive style, teases the mind to explore a whole range of possible applications, whereas the didactic proverb uses unambiguous imagery, which may, nevertheless, be colourful or exaggerated, to pin down its interpretation and so produce a definitive piece of instruction:

> It is better to be modest and earn one's living
> than to play the grandee on an empty stomach.[119]

> To offer a sacrifice from the possessions of the poor
> is like killing a son before his father's eyes.[120]

The book of Proverbs contains over five hundred such didactic sayings and so the problem for its successive editors (a problem, it must be said, they failed to solve) was to avoid the kind of unstructured chaos which Ben Sira attributes to the fool:

> To a fool, wisdom is like a derelict house;
> the knowledge of the stupid is a string of ill-digested sayings.[121]

Ben Sira himself goes further than his predecessors; he groups some of his sayings according to subject and develops themes in more sustained poetic structures. We may observe, for example, how in one poem he has combined three independent proverbs to make the point that the way to size up a man is to involve him in an argument:

---

[116] Ecclus. 22: 15; cf. Prov. 30: 18, 19.
[117] Prov. 26: 27.
[118] Ecclus. 20: 5.
[119] Prov. 12: 9. [120] Ecclus. 34: 20. [121] Ecclus. 21: 18.

> Shake a sieve, and the rubbish remains;
> start an argument, and a man's faults show up.
> As the work of a potter is tested in the kiln,
> so a man is tried in debate.
> As a tree's fruit reveals the skill of the grower,
> so the expression of a man's thoughts reveals his character.
> Do not praise a man till you hear him in argument,
> for that is the test.[122]

Generally speaking, however, proverbs were not designed to be arranged in thematic groups. Each proverb is a one-off creation, standing on its own, making its point independently and not like a piece of a jigsaw intelligible only as part of a larger whole. When collected by compilers, proverbs are like marbles in a bag, touching but unrelated. It is for this reason that contradictory proverbs may be not merely included in the same collection, but actually put next to each other:

> Do not answer a fool as his folly deserves,
> or you will grow like him yourself;
> answer a fool as his folly deserves,
> or he will think himself wise.[123]

We still demonstrate the autonomy of the proverb, when we say without any sense of incongruity, not only 'Many hands make light work', but also 'Too many cooks spoil the broth'.

Next in importance to the proverb in these two books is the literary genre we have come to call the 'instruction'. Whereas the proverb has the form of a statement using the indicative tense, the instruction is cast in the form of direct and authoritative address using the imperative:

> Listen, my sons, to a father's instruction;
> consider attentively how to gain understanding;
> it is sound learning I give you,
> so do not forsake my teaching.[124]

> Listen, my son: accept my opinion
> and do not reject my advice.
> Put your feet in wisdom's fetters
> and your neck into her collar.[125]

[122] Ecclus. 27: 4–7. [123] Prov. 26: 4, 5.
[124] Prov. 4: 1, 2. [125] Ecclus. 6: 23, 24.

The instruction form is used in a little over a third of the book of Proverbs and there can be little doubt that it was taken over from the schools of Egypt, where, as we have seen, Instructions, conventionally addressed by a father to his son and successor in office, were used as text-books for reading and writing.[126] An isolated (and possibly by origin non-Israelite) section of the book of Proverbs, with the title 'Sayings of King Lemuel of Massa, which his mother taught him', provides the most striking (albeit small-scale) parallel to the Egyptian prototype. It gives straightforward advice about sexual promiscuity, the proper use of wine, and the protection of the poor:

> Lemuel, it is not for kings, not for kings to drink wine,
> or for those who govern to crave strong liquor.
> If they drink, they will forget rights and customs
> and twist the law against all who are defenceless.
> Give strong drink to the despairing
> and wine to the embittered of heart;
> let them drink and forget their poverty
> and remember their trouble no more.
> Speak up for those who cannot speak for themselves;
> oppose any that go to law against them;
> speak out and pronounce just sentence
> and give judgement for the wretched and the poor.[127]

Although the instruction gives advice with authority, characteristically, it includes motivation clauses which seek to provide a rational, common-sense basis for the behaviour it is recommending. In Ben Sira's splendid instruction about being appreciative of the medical profession, after a single imperative in the opening sentence, the motivation, with its multiplicity of good reasons, takes over entirely:

> Value the services of a doctor
> for he has his place assigned him by the Lord.
> His skill comes from the Most High,
> and he is rewarded by kings . . .
> The Lord has created remedies from the earth,
> and a sensible man will not disparage them . . .

---

[126] Prov. 1: 1–9: 18; 22: 17–24: 22. For a survey of works of instruction in the Ancient Near East, see M. L. West, *Hesiod, Works and Days* (1978), 3–15.
[127] Prov. 31: 4–9.

> The Lord has imparted knowledge to mortals,
> that by their use of his marvels he may win praise;
> by means of them the doctor relieves pain
> and from them the pharmacist compounds his mixture.
> There is no limit to the works of the Lord,
> who spreads health over the whole world.[128]

There could be no better illustration of the humane enlightenment of the school tradition.

A minor genre which is common to our two books (otherwise occurring only in the book of Job and a single psalm)[129] is the numerical saying—obviously easy to learn by heart and therefore good for teaching:

> There are three sights which warm my heart
> and are beautiful in the eyes of the Lord and of men:
> concord among brothers, amity among neighbours,
> and a man and his wife who are inseparable.[130]

The delightful numerical saying about the four smallest creatures in the book of Proverbs has particularly interesting features:

> Four things there are which are smallest on earth
> yet wise beyond the wisest:
> ants, a folk with no strength,
> yet they prepare their store of food in the summer;
> rock-badgers, a feeble folk,
> yet they make their home among the rocks;
> locusts, which have no king,
> yet they all sally forth in formation;
> the lizard, which can be grasped in the hand,
> yet is found in the palaces of kings.[131]

This listing of natural phenomena has some affinity with those lists of names—the *onomastica*—which were popular as a teaching device in the Egyptian schools. It seems clear enough that such texts provided a model for Ben Sira's great hymn on the wonders of Creation. He lists *on high*: the sky, sun, moon, stars, rainbow, lightning, hailstones, thunder, winds, snow, frost, ice, heat, clouds; and *below*: the sea,

---

[128] Ecclus. 38: 1–8.   [129] Job 5: 19–22; Ps. 62: 11, 12.
[130] Ecclus. 25: 1; cf. 23: 16–18; 25: 2, 7–11; 26: 5–8, 28; 50: 25, 26; Prov. 6: 16–19; 30: 15, 16, 18, 19, 21–3, 29–31.   [131] Prov. 30: 24–8.

islands, sea-monsters, and other strange and wonderful creatures:

> We have seen but a small part of his works,
> and there remain many mysteries greater still.[132]

Benedicite, omnia opera.

The most exhaustive (and no doubt for the pupils who had to copy it out, the most exhausting) of the Egyptian *onomastica* was the *Onomasticon of Amenope*, written about 1085 BC: 'Beginning of the teaching for clearing the mind, for instruction of the ignorant and for learning all things that exist: what Ptah created, what Thoth copied down, heaven with its affairs, earth and what is in it, what the mountains belch forth, what is watered by the flood, all things upon which Re has shone, all that is grown on the back of the earth, excogitated by the scribe of the sacred books in the House of Life, Amenope.'[133] Similar *onomastica* were used in the schools of Mesopotamia, but there the order of the phenomena was different and it is invariably the Egyptian order which is followed by the schoolmen of Israel.[134]

A final and fascinating similarity in literary genres between the book of Proverbs and Ecclesiasticus is their adoption of the 'aretalogy', that is, the hymnic form in the first person used by a god or a goddess in self-praise. In both books, it is taken over, with residual traces of myth, for the presentation of Wisdom as a divine female figure intimately related to the Creator of the universe and as sole ruler of heaven and earth. In Ecclesiasticus, the first-person mode of address is explicitly emphasized:

> Hear the praise of wisdom from her own mouth,
> as she speaks with pride among her people,
> before the assembly of the Most High
> and in the presence of the heavenly host:

---

[132] Ecclus. 42: 15–43: 33.
[133] Alan H. Gardiner, *Ancient Egyptian Onomastica*, vol. i (1947), p. 2*.
[134] See Pss. 104, 148; R. J. Williams, 'Egypt and Israel', in J. R. Harris (ed.), *The Legacy of Egypt* (1971), 283; R. J. Williams, 'A People Come Out of Egypt', *VT*, Supp. xxviii (1975), 248–9.

'I am the word spoken by the Most High;
it was I who covered the earth like a mist.
My dwelling-place was in high heaven;
my throne was in a pillar of cloud.
Alone I made a circuit of the sky
and traversed the depths of the abyss.
The waves of the sea, the whole earth,
every people and nation were under my sway.'[135]

The corresponding section in the book of Proverbs falls into three separable (and probably in origin independent) units. In the first,[136] Wisdom speaks with prophetic fervour:

Hear how wisdom calls
and understanding lifts her voice.
She takes her stand at the crossroads,
by the wayside, at the top of the hill;
beside the gate, at the entrance to the city,
at the approach by the portals she cries aloud:
'It is to you I call,
to all mankind I appeal:
understand, you simpletons, what it is to be shrewd;
you stupid people, understand what it is to have sense.'

In the second unit,[137] Wisdom represents herself as the source of intelligence, power, and, therefore, success in all human affairs:

From me come advice and ability;
understanding and power are mine.
Through me kings hold sway
and governors enact just laws.

But, in the third unit,[138] Wisdom suddenly claims for herself absolute primacy and, therefore, superiority, in the whole order of Creation:

The Lord created me the first of his works
long ago, before all else that he made . . .
When he set the heavens in place I was there,
when he girdled the ocean with the horizon,
when he fixed the canopy of clouds overhead
and confined the springs of the deep,

[135] Ecclus. 24: 1–6.   [136] Prov. 8: 1–11.   [137] Prov. 8: 12–21.
[138] Prov. 8: 22–31; cf. Job 15: 7, 8.

when he prescribed limits for the sea
so that the waters do not transgress his command,
when he made earth's foundations firm.
Then I was at his side each day,
his darling and delight,
playing in his presence continually,
playing over his whole world,
while my delight was in mankind.[139]

Since metaphysics and myth are but different forms of the same adventure in free-ranging imagination, it is not surprising that these aretalogies (and, particularly, the one in Proverbs) were brought into service by New Testament authors[140] and later Christian theologians engaged in trying to define the relationship between the Creator and Christ. This doctrinal development should not mislead us into supposing that speculation about Wisdom as a heavenly being was part of the school tradition; that would be to pump back into the aretalogies precisely those mythological concepts the writers had been at pains to pump out. To portray wisdom as going back to the very creation of the world was primarily a way of asserting its fundamental significance and the authority of its teachers. It is just possible that the schoolmen were also claiming that, in learning wisdom, men were responding to the Creator's design and therefore, so to speak, discovering the order of the universe.

At the end of our exploration, we may well find ourselves coming to the conclusion that what the book of Proverbs and Ecclesiasticus have to offer is really no more than a string of platitudes—platitudes decked out, maybe, in resonant and colourful language, but platitudes nevertheless. If this is our judgement, we shall have succeeded in identifying the purpose and method of those who taught by 'apt proverbs' and, incidentally, said something about ourselves. These sayings about how to behave and what to do were addressed to people's reason and good sense, which in a civilized society is a *common* sense; they were intended to win assent without further explanation or argument; they were designed to be

[139] The older the wisdom, the more authoritative; cf. Job 15: 7–9; Isa. 19: 11.
[140] Col. 1: 15–17; 2: 3; 1 Cor. 1: 24, 30; cf. Heb. 1: 3; John 1: 1–14; Rev. 4: 11; 22: 13.

memorable and repeated (platitudinously) over and over
again. By reciting or copying out these proverbs, the
schoolboys of Israel were being initiated into the moral
consensus of their community—and that was a major part of
their education in wisdom. Puzzlement about how this
worked out in practice is somewhat reduced (but not entirely
eliminated) when we realize that similar teaching methods
were being followed in the Greek world from the fourth
century BC and that throughout the Hellenistic and early
Roman periods, collections of memorable sayings were much
in demand.[141]

[141] See Excursus, pp. 41–4; cf. A. E. Harvey, *Strenuous Commands* (1990),
49–51.

V

PROPHETS AND TEACHERS

1. *Prophets*

The learned men of Israel's school tradition cared a great deal about books but very little about authors. That is why they preserved the oracles of the great independent prophets, but had no scruple about splicing them with a miscellany of material from other sources. As a result, so far from having direct access to what the prophets actually taught, we are confronted by four untidy anthologies labelled 'Isaiah', 'Jeremiah', 'Ezekiel', and 'the Book of the Twelve' (so-called) 'minor prophets'. These were compiled by editors in Jerusalem at various stages during the centuries following the return from the Babylonian Exile. It is highly probable that these men had very little idea of what the prophets had been saying to their own times (certainly far less than we have now) and that they went to the trouble of preserving and editing their oracles because they were regarded as old and sacred.[1] The only further clue to their purpose is to be found in the threefold pattern they imposed on their diverse material. In each collection, we have, first, a block of oracles on the judgement of Israel,[2] followed by a block of oracles on the judgement of the nations,[3] and, finally, a block of oracles on the salvation of Israel.[4] It would be a mistake to conclude that these editors were trying to stir up their contemporaries to expect the imminent Coming of the Kingdom and the End of the World (academics, on the whole, don't engage in that

---

[1] Cf. Job 8: 8–10; 15: 17, 18; John Barton, *Oracles of God* (1986), 93, 115, 140.
[2] Isa. 1–12; Jer. 1: 1–25: 14; Ezek. 1–24.
[3] Isa. 13–23; Jer. 25: 15–38, followed immediately, as in the Septuagint, by 46–51; Ezek. 25–32.   [4] Isa. 24–35; Jer. 26–35; Ezek. 33–48.

kind of thing); rather, in a low key, they seem to be restating
the familiar conviction of the school tradition that God who
created the world is in control of it and that his rule is orderly
and reliable. This belief is memorably expressed in the book
of Judith: 'All that happened then, and all that happened
before and after, was your work. What is now and what is yet
to be, you have planned.'[5]

The same affirmation of God's orderly plan for his world is
made in the celebrated parable of the farmer now included in
the book of Isaiah:[6]

> Will the ploughman spend his whole time ploughing,
>   breaking up his ground and harrowing it?
> Does he not, once he has levelled it,
>   broadcast the dill and scatter the cummin?

Just as the farmer knows what to do in due order and in the
end achieves his purpose, so does God, despite all appearances
to the contrary. The style as well as the thought of the parable
is characteristic of the schoolmen. The opening instruction:

> Listen and hear what I say,
> attend and hear my words

is unmistakably a teacher speaking; the rhetorical questions
depend on an intelligent recognition of what is natural and
normal;[7] and the last verse crackles with school language:

> Even this knowledge comes from the Lord of Hosts,
> whose counsel is wonderful
> and whose wisdom is great.[8]

The 'counsel' of God is a key term in Isaiah's own oracles
and it encapsulates the prophet's fundamental conviction
that God's sovereign purpose in history will prevail over all
the plans of men:

> The Lord of Hosts has sworn this oath:
> 'As I purposed, so most surely it will be;
> as I planned, so it will take place.'[9]

---

[5] Judith 9: 5.   [6] Isa. 28: 23–9.
[7] Isa. 28: 24–6; cf. Jer. 2: 32; 8: 4; 13: 23; 18: 14; Prov. 6: 27–9; Job 8: 11.
[8] Isa. 28: 29.
[9] Isa. 14: 24; cf. 14: 27; Prov. 19: 21.

Man's part in this purpose is simply one of passive acceptance—an unquestioning trust in what has been divinely ordained:

> In calm detachment lies your safety,
> your strength in quiet trust.[10]

Judah's offence is to withhold this trust and become involved in the intrigues of power politics;[11] 'those who are wise in their own sight and prudent in their own esteem'[12] are guilty of the cardinal sin of pride.[13] Isaiah has eliminated the schoolmen's characteristic notion of man's co-operation with Providence and reduced his message to an uncompromising choice to be made here and now: *either* absolute faith in God's sovereign ordering of events, *or* devastation and destruction.

Although Isaiah was much more dogmatic than most schoolmen and rejected their characteristic pragmatism, there are many indications that he shared their educational background.[14] To glance, first, at his literary style—and it would be reasonable to assume that he wrote down his own oracles—he too uses, like many of the schoolmen, sharp rhetorical questions with their appeal to common sense:

> Will the axe set itself up against the hewer,
> or the saw claim mastery over the sawyer,
> as if a stick were to brandish him who raises it?[15]

and he draws comparisons from the natural world to expose the unnaturalness of Judah's behaviour;

> I reared children and brought them up,
> but they have rebelled against me.
> An ox knows its owner
> and a donkey its master's stall;
> but Israel lacks all knowledge,
> my people has no discernment.[16]

[10] Isa. 30: 15; cf. 7: 4, 9; 28: 16; see p. 48.
[11] Isa. 7: 3–9; 8: 5–8; 18: 4–6; 20: 1–6; 22: 8b–14; 28: 14–22; 30: 1–5; 31: 1–3.   [12] Isa. 5: 21; cf. Prov. 3: 7; 26: 12.
[13] Isa. 2: 12–17; 3: 16, 17; 9: 8–10; 22: 15–19; cf. 10: 12–14.
[14] See R. T. Anderson, 'Was Isaiah a Scribe?', *JBL* 79 (1960), 57–8; J. W. Whedbee, *Isaiah and Wisdom* (1971).
[15] Isa. 10: 15; cf. 29: 16; see p. 171 n.
[16] Isa. 1: 2, 3; cf. Jer. 8: 7; Prov. 6: 6; 30: 24–8; Job 12: 7–9.

It is scarcely fortuitous that the prophet's rebuke is remarkably similar to one recorded in a standard Egyptian school text, which points to the teachability of the cow and the horse, in order to put to shame the unteachable pupil: 'And the cow will be fetched this year and will plough on the return of the year: it begins to hearken to the herdsman; it can all but speak. Horses brought from the field have forgotten their dams; they are yoked and go up and down on every manner of errand for His Majesty. They become like those that bore them, and they stand in the stable, whilst they do absolutely everything for fear of a beating. Even if I beat you with any kind of stick, you do not hearken.'[17]

The school tradition is even more obviously in the background of Isaiah's rejection of the sacrificial cult, a momentous break with the past, which he made in common with the other independent prophet.[18] The danger inherent in cultic worship was recognized in Egyptian schools as early as *The Instruction for Merikare* (c.2100 BC): 'more acceptable is the character of the straightforward man than the ox of the wrongdoer';[19] and the difference between rites and righteousness is further sharpened by the teachers of Israel:

> To do what is right and just
> is more acceptable to the Lord than sacrifice.[20]

> Does the Lord desire whole-offerings and sacrifices
> as he desires obedience?
> To obey is better than sacrifice,
> and to listen to him better than the fat of rams.[21]

---

[17] Caminos, 377; see also the advice given to a young scribe in *Papyrus Anasti*: 'Persevere in your daily tasks, and then you will achieve mastery over them. Do not pass a day lazy, or else you will be beaten; a lad's ear is actually on his back, and he listens when he is beaten. Pay attention and listen to what I have said, that it may be of use to you. Apes can be taught to dance and horses tamed; a kite can be put in a nest and a falcon caught by the wings. Persevere in seeking advice and do not tire. Write and do not dislike it', R. J. Williams, 'Scribal Training in Ancient Egypt', *JAOS* 92/2 (1972), 218.

[18] Isa. 1: 10–17; cf. Amos 4: 4, 5; 5: 21–4; Hos. 2: 11; 5: 6; 6: 6; 8: 13; Mic. 3: 12; 6: 6–8; Jer. 6: 19–21; 7: 21–3; 11: 15; Isa. 43: 22–4; Pss. 40: 6–8; 50: 7–15, 23; 51: 15–17.

[19] *LAE* 191; *ANET* 417b.

[20] Prov. 21: 3; cf. 21: 27; 15: 8; Ecclus. 34: 19, 20.

[21] 1 Sam. 15: 22.

But the rational, root-and-branch exposure of the whole sacrificial system as a complete nonsense is first encountered in Amos:

> I spurn with loathing your pilgrim-feasts:
> I take no pleasure in your sacred ceremonies.
> When you bring me your whole-offerings and your grain-
> offerings
> I shall not accept them,
> nor pay heed to your shared-offerings of stall-fed beasts.
> Spare me the sound of your songs;
> I shall not listen to the strumming of your lutes.
> Instead let justice flow on like a river
> and righteousness like a never-failing torrent.[22]

With language so charged with mockery and indignation, the shilly-shallying of commentators is explicable only in terms of their theological and ecclesiastical fixations.

Isaiah's vituperative language similarly expresses contempt as well as anger:

> Listen to the word of the Lord, you rulers of Sodom;
> give ear to the teaching of our God, you people of Gomorrah:
> Your countless sacrifices, what are they to me?
> says the Lord.
> I am sated with whole-offerings of rams
> and the fat of well-fed cattle;
> I have no desire for the blood of bulls,
> of sheep, and of he-goats,
> when you come into my presence.
> Who has asked you for all this?
> No more shall you tread my courts.
> To bring me offerings is futile;
> the reek of sacrifice is abhorrent to me.
> New moons and sabbaths and sacred assemblies—
> such idolatrous ceremonies I cannot endure.
> I loathe your new moons and your festivals;
> they have become a burden to me,
> and I can tolerate them no longer.
> When you hold out your hands in prayer,
> I shall turn away my eyes.
> Though you offer countless prayers,

[22] Amos 5: 21–4.

I shall not listen;
there is blood on your hands.
Wash and be clean;
put away your evil deeds
far from my sight;
cease to do evil, learn to do good.
Pursue justice, guide the oppressed;
uphold the rights of the fatherless,
and plead the widow's cause.[23]

Some of the offences for which Isaiah condemns Judah—
the oppression of the widow and orphan, murder, theft,
bribery and corruption in the courts—are to be found
specified in the Law, but many are not—self-aggrandize-
ment,[24] excessive wealth,[25] drunkenness,[26] pride,[27] cynical
scepticism[28]—and it is virtually certain that for these at least
(and probably for all of them), he was drawing on the core
curriculum of his school in Jerusalem.[29]

The authority for this teaching differed from the divine
demands of the Law and relied on an understanding that
moral obligation sprang from men's encounter with the way
things actually are in human life—the order of nature—and
that this order was obvious to all sensible people. Thus, there
was established a consensus about good and evil, which only
the anarchist would deny:

Woe betide those who call evil good and good evil,
who make darkness light and light darkness,
who make bitter sweet and sweet bitter.[30]

Isaiah is particularly sensitive to the threat of a complete
collapse of the social order, which would carry with it a
collapse of the moral order:

The Lord, the Lord of Hosts,
is about to strip Jerusalem and Judah
of every prop and stay . . .

---

[23] Isa. 1: 10–17.   [24] Isa. 9: 9–10; 22: 15–19.
[25] Isa. 3: 16–4: 1; 32: 9–14; cf. Prov. 20: 21; 21: 6.
[26] Isa. 5: 11–17, 22; 28: 1–13.
[27] Isa. 5: 21.   [28] Isa. 5: 19, 20; 22: 12–14; 29: 15, 16.
[29] See J. Barton, 'Ethics in Isaiah of Jerusalem', *JTS* 32/1 (1981), 1–18; 'Natural
Law and Poetic Justice in the Old Testament', *JTS* 30/1 (1979), 1–14.
[30] Isa. 5: 20.

> I shall appoint youths to positions of authority,
> and they will govern as the whim takes them.
> The people will deal oppressively with one another,
> everyone oppressing his neighbour;
> the young will be arrogant towards their elders,
> mere nobodies towards men of rank.[31]

One is reminded of the celebrated speech by Ulysses in Shakespeare's *Troilus and Cressida*:

> O! when degree is shak'd,
> Which is the ladder to all high designs,
> The enterprise is sick. How could communities,
> Degrees in schools, and brotherhoods in cities,
> Peaceful commerce from dividable shores . . .
> But by degree, stand in authentic place?
> Take but degree away, untune that string,
> And, hark! what discord follows.[32]

Comparably alarming accounts of the breakdown of order used to be circulated in the schools of Babylon and Egypt, and Job, later, was to lament that society had been turned upside-down.[33] In this respect, too, Isaiah was reflecting the school tradition, which was as conservative in its social mores as it was radical in its theological thinking.

Twenty years earlier, Amos had drawn on the same school tradition of order and natural law and declared that Israel's moral degeneration was simply nonsensical:

> Can horses gallop over rocks?
> Can the sea be ploughed with oxen?
> Yet you have turned into venom the process of law,
> justice itself you have turned into poison.[34]

Amos, of course, identified the morality of the schools with the personal will of Israel's God, but because it was based on a perception of how *human beings as such* were intended to

---

[31] Isa. 3: 1–5.   [32] I. iii. 101–10.

[33] See *The Prophecy of Neferti*, LAE 237–9; ANET 445b; *The Admonitions of an Egyptian Sage*, LAE 214, 218: 'Indeed, the builders [of pyramids have become] cultivators, and those who were in the sacred bark are now yoked [to it] . . . Indeed, public offices are opened and their inventories are taken away; the serf has become an owner of serfs. Indeed, [scribes] are killed and their writings are taken away. Woe is me because of the misery of this time.' See pp. 139–42.

[34] Amos 6: 12; cf. Jer. 18: 13–16.

behave, other nations could properly be judged by it. In the extended and carefully composed indictment of the neighbouring nations for their war crimes, which now introduces his collected oracles,[35] Amos takes it for granted that everybody would agree that such inhuman behaviour was obviously unnatural and, therefore, wrong:

> These are the words of the Lord:
> For crime after crime of the Ammonites
> I shall grant them no reprieve,
> because in their greed for land
> they ripped open the pregnant women in Gilead.
>
> For crime after crime of Moab
> I shall grant them no reprieve,
> because they burnt to lime
> the bones of the king of Edom.[36]

The difference between the moral teaching of Amos and that of (say) the schoolmen of the book of Proverbs is not in content, but in urgency. In Amos, there is so intense an involvement in the realities of the situation that moral platitudes catch fire:

> Listen to this,
> you cows of Bashan who live on the hill of Samaria,
> you who oppress the poor and crush the destitute,
> who say to your lords, 'Bring us drink':
> The Lord God has sworn by his holiness
> that your time is coming.[37]

Amos's moral fervour is in marked contrast to his low-key account of how he came to be God's spokesman:
'I was no prophet ... nor was I a prophet's son; I was a herdsman and fig-grower. But the Lord took me as I followed the flock and it was the Lord who said to me, "Go and prophesy to my people Israel." '[38] The four modest episodes entitled 'This was what the Lord God showed me'[39] belong to the class-room rather than the seventh heaven of the visionary: ' "What do you see, Amos?" "A plumb-line (sir!)",

---

[35] Amos 1: 6–2: 16.
[37] Amos 4: 1, 2 (*NEB*).
[39] Amos 7: 1–9; 8: 1–3.

[36] Amos 1: 13; 2: 1.
[38] Amos 7: 14, 15.

I answered . . . "What is that you are looking at, Amos?" he said. I answered, "A basket of ripe summer fruit." '[40] The same school background is to be found in his use of rhetorical questions, which were characteristically employed by teachers.[41]

Like Isaiah, Amos was probably educated at a school in Jerusalem (his home village was only twelve miles south of the city), and there he encountered an articulate moral tradition, which only needed to be taken seriously to expose the rottenness at the heart of Israel's life. Amos did just that, supported only by the conviction that God had called him to speak out.[42]

It was only a comparable, inescapable conviction that God had called him which compelled Jeremiah to stick to his agonizing task of telling his people that they had taken leave of their senses:

> You have duped me, Lord,
> and I have been your dupe;
> you have outwitted me and prevailed.
> All the day long I have been made a laughing-stock;
> everyone ridicules me.
> Whenever I speak I must needs cry out,
> calling, 'Violence!' and 'Assault!'
> I am reproached and derided all the time
> for uttering the word of the Lord.
> Whenever I said, 'I shall not call it to mind
> or speak in his name again,'
> then his word became imprisoned within me
> like a fire burning in my heart.
> I was weary with holding it under,
> and could endure no more.[43]

---

[40] Amos 7: 8; 8: 1, 2.

[41] Amos 3: 1–8; 6: 12; cf. Prov. 6: 27, 28; 30: 4; Job 8: 11.

[42] Hosea, who taught in the northern kingdom a little later than Amos, is peculiarly difficult to place in relation to the school tradition. His oracles were clearly edited in Jerusalem (1: 7; 4: 15; 6: 11; 11: 12; 12: 2) and presented as a book of moral instruction: 'Let the wise consider these things and let the prudent acknowledge them' (14: 9). However, his own ethical teaching, which is very limited in its range, seems to be based on Mosaic, rather than natural, law (4: 2, 6; 8: 1, 12).

[43] Jer. 20: 7–9. The external opposition and inner anguish which Jeremiah suffered are powerfully expressed in six personal laments: 11: 18–12: 6; 15: 10–21; 17: 14–18; 18: 18–23; 20: 7–11, 14–18.

Jeremiah shared the anger of Amos and Isaiah at his people's debauchery (especially when it was encouraged by idolatrous religion)[44] and, like them, was incensed by arrogant injustice. His courageous indictment of Shallum, the son and successor of King Josiah, could not be more explicit:

> Woe betide him who builds his palace on unfairness
> and completes his roof-chambers with injustice,
> compelling his countrymen to work without payment,
> giving them no wage for their labour!
> Woe to him who says,
> 'I shall build myself a spacious palace
> with airy roof-chambers and windows set in it;
> it will be panelled with cedar
> and painted with vermilion.'
> Though your cedar is so splendid,
> does that prove you a king?
> Think of your father; he ate and drank,
> dealt justly and fairly; all went well with him.
> He upheld the cause of the lowly and poor;
> then all was well.
> Did not this show he knew me? says the Lord.[45]

Here we have the fundamental affirmation of both the great prophets and the school tradition that it is in right human relations that God is known and served. However, Jeremiah goes a step beyond his predecessors in the depth and devastating simplicity of his diagnosis of Judah's condition. Everything about the life of his people is false—a perversion of the truth:

> Lying, not truth, holds sway in the land.
> They proceed from one wrong to another
> and care nothing for me.[46]
>
> prophets and priests are frauds,
> every one of them;
> they dress my people's wound,
> but on the surface only,
> with their saying, 'All is well.'
> All well? Nothing is well![47]

[44] Jer. 3: 2–5; 5: 7–9.   [45] Jer. 22: 13–16.   [46] Jer. 9: 3; cf. 9: 5, 6.
[47] Jer. 8: 10, 11; cf. 5: 30, 31; 7: 1–15; 23: 9–14.

Conquest and exile should be welcomed, for only such radical surgery could provide a cure.[48]

It is astonishing that such a message, which put the prophet's own life at risk,[49] was allowed to survive. Scholars are generally agreed that schoolmen associated with the production and promotion of Deuteronomy, to judge by their outlook and idiom, were those who came to the rescue.[50] It is very remarkable not only that the most anti-establishment collection of teaching in the whole of the Old Testament should have been preserved, edited, expanded, and transmitted by men close to the centre of power in Jerusalem, but also that they should have recorded so deliberately in biographical narratives that it was they who secured the survival of both the prophet and his oracles.[51] In making this claim (whatever its historical reliability), the schoolmen of Jerusalem were disclosing, if not the radicalism of their tradition, at least their willingness to be associated with what has been described as 'a frontal attack on the entire religious enterprise and world-view of his contemporaries'.[52] The preservation of the teaching of Jeremiah makes the writing of the book of Job somewhat less surprising.

The last of the independent prophets, whose anonymity compels us to call Second Isaiah,[53] bears witness to the school tradition, not only by his preoccupation with the work of the Creator,[54] but by his mature skill as a poet. He is a great imitator of conventional literary forms. His oracles of salvation are modelled on the traditional assurances given in the Jerusalem cult;[55] his trial scenes are taken from law-court procedures;[56] his snatches of hymns echo the Psalms;[57] and his disputations appear to reflect the kind of rhetoric and

[48] Jer. 24: 1–10; 29: 1–32; 38: 14–23.
[49] Jer. 11: 21–3; 26: 1–24; 37: 11–21; 38: 1–13.
[50] See such prose sections as: Jer. 7: 1–8: 3; 9: 12–16; 11: 1–14; 14: 11–16; 16: 1–18; 17: 19–27; 19: 1–20: 6; 22: 8–9. See E. W. Nicholson, *Preaching to the Exiles* (1970).
[51] Jer. 26: 24; 36: 1–32; 39: 11–14; 40: 1–6; 45: 1–5.
[52] W. A. Brueggemann, 'Jeremiah's Use of Rhetorical Questions', *JBL* 92 (1973), 374.   [53] Isa. 40–55.
[54] Isa. 40: 12–31; 45: 18, 19; 55: 8–11.
[55] Isa. 41: 8–13, 14–16; 43: 1–4, 5–7; 44: 1–5.
[56] Isa. 41: 1–5, 21–9; 43: 8–13; 45: 20–5.
[57] Isa. 42: 5, 10–13; 44: 23; 49: 13; cf. Pss. 104: 1–4; 117.

argumentation taught in the schools.[58] A good example of the latter is provided by the prophet's defence of his claim that God had chosen the pagan imperialist, King Cyrus, as the agent of his deliverance of Israel from Exile:

> Will the pot contend with the potter,
> or the earthenware with the hand that shapes it?
> Will the clay ask the potter what he is making
> or his handiwork say to him, 'You have no skill?'
> Will the child say to his father,
> 'What are you begetting?'
> or to his mother, 'What are you bringing to birth?'
> Thus says the Lord, Israel's Holy One, his Maker:
> Would you dare question me concerning my children,
> or instruct me in my handiwork?
> I alone made the earth
> and created mankind upon it.
> With my own hands I stretched out the heavens
> and directed all their host.
> With righteous purpose I have roused this man.[59]

The question about the pot and the potter also occurs in both Isaiah and Jeremiah[60] and, as we learn from the book of Job, the conclusion that the Creator cannot be questioned was part of the orthodoxy of the schools.[61] Again, it is the intellectual world of Job (and particularly the class-room rhetoric of the Lord's speech 'out of the tempest'),[62] which we encounter in the first of the prophet's disputations:

> Who has measured the waters of the sea in the hollow of his
>   hand,
> or with its span gauged the heavens?
> Who has held all the soil of the earth in a bushel,
> or weighed the mountains on a balance,
> the hills on a pair of scales?
> Who has directed the spirit of the Lord?
> What counsellor stood at his side to instruct him?
> With whom did he confer to gain discernment?
> Who taught him this path of justice,
> or taught him knowledge,
> or showed him the way of wisdom?[63]

[58] Isa. 40: 12–17, 18–26, 27–31; 55: 8–11.
[60] Isa. 29: 16; Jer. 18: 1–6.
[62] See pp. 143–5.
[59] Isa. 45: 9–13.
[61] See p. 149.
[63] Isa. 40: 12–14.

It may be mere coincidence that the figure of weighing and measuring the mountains occurs in a popular Egyptian school text satirizing a pupil's claim to incomparable knowledge,[64] but the language chosen by the prophet— 'instruct', 'discernment', 'knowledge', 'the way of wisdom'— clearly reveals the influence of his schooling.

So also does his rational and contemptuous dismissal of Babylon's makers of idols:

> Those who make idols are all less than nothing;
> their cherished images profit nobody;
> their worshippers are blind;
> their ignorance shows up their foolishness.[65]

The elaboration in prose which follows this oracle may, perhaps, be the work of a sympathetic schoolman who was editing the prophet's teaching, but it splendidly expresses the intellectual outlook of his circle: 'Such people neither know nor understand, their eyes made too blind to see, their minds too narrow to discern. Such a one will not use his reason; he has neither the wit nor the sense to say, "Half of it I have burnt, and even used its embers to bake bread; I have roasted meat on them and eaten it; but the rest of it I turn into this abominable object; really I am worshipping a block of wood." He feeds on ashes indeed! His deluded mind has led him astray, and he cannot recover his senses so far as to say, "This thing I am holding is a sham." '[66] It was in the same rational spirit and with the same grasp of reality that the earlier prophets had rejected the sham of the cult.

2. Teachers

The schoolmen who rallied to the cause of Jeremiah, whom for want of a better name we call 'the Deuteronomists', produced directly or indirectly no less than a quarter of the literature of the Old Testament. In addition to the book of Deuteronomy and the prose narratives in the book of Jeremiah, they were responsible for the history books of Joshua, Judges, Samuel, and Kings. These learned and humane men clearly dominated the educational establishment

---

[64] See p. 61.   [65] Isa. 44: 9.   [66] Isa. 44: 18–20.

of Jerusalem at the critical period of the collapse of the monarchy and subsequent Exile, when it became urgent to collect and consolidate Israel's historical and legal traditions and at the same time reinterpret them.[67]

The Deuteronomists were born teachers and an earnest desire to win the hearts and minds of their readers animates all their writing. One of their key terms, *torah*, usually translated 'law', really means *teaching*, as we may see when it is used to describe the preaching of the prophets,[68] or the instruction encapsulated in proverbs.[69] The Deuteronomists' use of *torah* makes it clear that they were far from thinking of their own book of law merely as a code to be obeyed; it was, rather, a book of God-given instructions to be taught, studied, and taken to heart. In the words of the charge given to Joshua: 'This book of the *torah* must never be off your lips; you must keep it in mind day and night so that you may diligently observe everything that is written in it. Then you will prosper and be successful in everything you do.' In his turn, Joshua charges the tribes in the same characteristically Deuteronomic language: 'But be very careful to keep the commands and the *torah* which Moses the servant of the Lord gave you: to love the Lord your God; to conform to all his ways; to observe his commandments; to hold fast to him; to serve him with your whole heart and soul.'[70]

The school setting of the Deuteronomists is clearly reflected in their style. References to learning and discipline abound,[71] their awareness of people's questions and problems points to their skill as teachers,[72] and (to mention a curious detail) there is much use of the term 'abomination', which, it seems, had long been established as a fierce expression of disapproval in the schools of Egypt and Babylon.[73] The high-

---

[67] See Moshe Weinfeld, *Deuteronomy and the Deuteronomic School* (1972).

[68] Isa. 1: 10; 5: 24; 8: 16, 20; 30: 9; Jer. 6: 19.

[69] Prov. 1: 8; 3: 1; 6: 20–3; 7: 2.

[70] Josh. 1: 8; 22: 5; cf. 23: 6; 1 Kgs. 2: 3; 2 Kgs. 10: 31; 17: 13; see Barnabas Lindars, 'Torah in Deuteronomy', in P. R. Ackroyd and B. Lindars (eds.), *Words and Meanings* (1968), 117–36.

[71] Deut. 5: 31; 6: 1; 17: 18, 19; cf. Prov. 2: 1; 3: 1; 4: 1–4, 10–13.

[72] Deut. 6: 20; 7: 17; 10: 12; 13: 1, 6; 17: 14; 18: 21.

[73] Deut. 7: 25; 12: 31; 17: 1; 18: 12; 20: 18; 22: 5; 23: 18; 25: 16; 27: 15; Prov. 3: 32; 11: 1, 20; 12: 22; 15: 8, 9, 26; 16: 5; 17: 15; 20: 10, 23; 21: 27; see *The*

flown language they use to describe their teaching is directly
paralleled in the hyperbole of the book of Proverbs. In the
latter, we find the schoolmaster in full spate:

> My son, keep my words;
> store up my commands in your mind.
> Keep my commands if you would live,
> and treasure my teaching as the apple of your eye.
> Wear them like a ring on your finger;
> inscribe them on the tablet of your memory.[74]

With this, we may compare an admonition from Deuteronomy, the opening words of which were adopted for the
Shema, later the watchword of Jewish monotheism: 'Hear,
Israel: the Lord is our God, the Lord our one God; and you
must love the Lord your God with all your heart and with all
your soul and with all your strength. These commandments
which I give you this day are to be remembered and taken to
heart; repeat them to your children, and speak of them both
indoors and out of doors, when you lie down and when you
get up. Bind them as a sign on your hand and wear them as a
pendant on your forehead; write them on the doorposts of
your houses and on your gates.'[75] This teaching was
presented as the way and source of 'life'—a central concept
for both the schoolmen of Deuteronomy and the schoolmen
of Proverbs,[76] and they refer to it as the nation's distinctive
'wisdom': 'I have taught you statutes and laws ... Observe
them carefully, for thereby you will display your wisdom and
understanding to other peoples. When they hear about all
these statutes, they will say, "What a wise and understanding
people this great nation is!" '[77]

One of the less attractive features of the school tradition
was the importance it attached to gaining a reputation in the
eyes of the world, and, unfortunately, this seems to have
coloured the view of at least some of the Deuteronomists of
Israel as the Chosen People. Promises of the nation's success,

---

Instruction of Amen-em-opet, ANET 423a, 423b; *LAE* 252, 254, 257. For
Babylonian usage, see Lambert, 117.

[74] Prov. 7: 1–3.
[75] Deut. 6: 4–9; cf. 11: 18–20; Prov. 1: 9; 3: 3; 6: 20–2.
[76] Deut. 30: 15–20; cf. 4: 1, 40; 30: 6; Prov. 2: 19; 5: 6; 6: 23; 10: 11, 17; 15:
24. [77] Deut. 4: 5, 6; cf. Prov. 1: 1–6; 3: 13–18.

summed up crisply and crudely in the assurance, 'you will always be at the top and never at the bottom',[78] punctuate the Deuteronomic writings and immediately recall the go-getting confidence characteristic of the schoolmen of the Ancient Near East. In the same vein, the familiar promise that 'the humble will possess the land and enjoy untold prosperity'[79] was politicized and nationalized to become an assertion that Palestine was 'the land which the Lord your God is giving you for all time'.[80] Few claims have entailed more fateful consequences.

It seems at first sight that the Deuteronomists' nationalism is also reflected in what appears to be their fanatical enthusiasm for Holy War: 'When the Lord your God brings you into the land which you are about to enter to occupy it, when he drives out many nations before you—Hittites, Girgashites, Amorites, Canaanites, Perizzites, Hivites, and Jebusites, seven nations more numerous and powerful than you—and when the Lord your God delivers them into your power for you to defeat, you must exterminate them ... You must not intermarry with them ... But this is what you must do to them: pull down their altars, break their sacred pillars, hack down their sacred poles, and burn their idols, for you are a people holy to the Lord your God, and he has chosen you out of all peoples on earth to be his special possession.'[81] Since it is virtually inconceivable that humane and sensible men like the Deuteronomists ever contemplated such mindless military exploits, one must conclude that the declaration is merely rhetorical—an appeal for religious loyalty during the social upheaval of the Exile.[82] Despite this chauvinistic huffing and puffing, the most characteristic feature of the Deuteronomists' version of the laws governing the waging of Holy War is that they are thoroughly desacralized and rationalized. Concern for sanctification is replaced by a concern for decent sanitation;[83] the ritual

[78] Deut. 28: 13; cf. 7: 17–24; 9: 1–3; 11: 22–5; 26: 19; 28: 10.
[79] Ps. 37: 11, 22, 29, 34; Prov. 2: 21; 10: 30.
[80] Deut. 4: 40; cf. 1: 8; 8: 1; 11: 9; 12: 10; 16: 20; 19: 10, 14; 21: 23; 24: 4; 26: 1.　　　　[81] Deut. 7: 1–6; cf. 20: 17.
[82] See Ezra 9: 1–10: 44; note especially 9: 1.
[83] Deut. 23: 9–14; cf. 1 Sam. 21: 3–6; Num. 31: 19, 24.

sounding of trumpets gives way to the sermonizing of priests;[84] spoil is devoted to pleasure instead of religious offerings;[85] and even the scorched-earth policy is modified by a common-sense discrimination between different kinds of tree.[86]

The reduction of sacral features in their exposition of Holy War is only one example of the way in which the Deuteronomists distance themselves from the cult and the old Canaanite kind of religion. The shutting-down of the rural sanctuaries and the centralizing of worship in Jerusalem, associated with the reform of King Josiah,[87] inevitably provoked a crisis in the practice of eating meat. The Deuteronomists are not in the least disturbed: 'When the Lord your God enlarges your territory . . . and you say to yourselves, "I should like to eat meat," because you have a craving for it, then you may freely eat it . . . you may slaughter a beast from the herds or flocks . . . and freely eat it in your settlements . . . both clean and unclean alike may eat it.'[88] The same permissive spirit has transformed the practice of tithing. Instead of being simply 'holy to the Lord', tithes could now be used for throwing a party in the precincts of the Temple: 'When . . . the journey (is) too great for you to carry your tithe, then you may convert it into money. Tie up the money and take it with you to the place which the Lord your God will choose. There you may spend it as you choose on cattle or sheep, wine or strong drink, or anything else you please, and there feast with rejoicing, both you and your family, in the presence of the Lord your God.'[89]

In view of the Deuteronomists' rational outlook, it is not surprising that they demythologize the Temple itself and radically reinterpret its significance. It is no longer the quasi-physical dwelling-place of God,[90] but the house in which only his Name dwells and the people offer their prayers.[91]

[84] Deut. 20: 1–4; cf. Num. 10: 9; 31: 6.
[85] Deut. 20: 14; cf. Josh. 6: 17–19, 24; Num. 31: 48–54.
[86] Deut. 20: 19, 20.
[87] 2 Kgs. 22: 1–23: 25; Deut. 12: 1–19.   [88] Deut. 12: 20–2.
[89] Deut. 14: 22–6; cf. Lev. 27: 30–3.
[90] Pss. 46: 4; 132: 13, 14; Exod. 29: 44–6.
[91] Deut. 12: 11; 14: 23; 16: 2; 1 Kgs. 9: 3; 11: 36; 2 Kgs. 21: 4.

The Ark is no longer God's footstool; it is now simply a safe-deposit for the tables of the law.[92] This revolutionary outlook is memorably expounded in the prayer which the Deuteronomists ascribe to Solomon at the dedication of the Temple: 'But can God indeed dwell on earth? Heaven itself, the highest heaven, cannot contain you; how much less this house that I have built! Yet attend, Lord my God, to the prayer and the supplication of your servant . . . that your eyes may ever be on this house night and day, this place of which you said, "My Name will be there." Hear your servant when he prays towards this place . . . Hear in heaven your dwelling and, when you hear, forgive.'[93] For these schoolmen, forgiveness is God's gift, after confession and prayer, without recourse to sin-offerings and guilt-offerings, or to the mediation of the priesthood. They will have no truck with go-betweens—not even angels.[94]

This remarkable shift in theological perspective is consolidated in the Deuteronomists' fundamental reinterpretation of the relationship between God and Israel. It is now declared to be a fellowship constituted by a bilateral covenant, which rests on mutual choice and Israel's continuing response.[95] The ancient sacral notion that Israel was inherently and inalienably God's special possession, as reflected, for example, in the triumphalist superstition that Zion was inviolable,[96] had been vehemently rejected by the independent prophets. These astounding laymen[97] declared that Israel's privileged position as the People of God exposed it even more directly to the demands of righteousness:

> You alone I have cared for
> among all the nations of the world;
> that is why I shall punish you
> for all your wrongdoing.[98]

> Listen to this, leaders of Jacob,
> you rulers of Israel,

---

[92] Deut. 10: 1–5; cf. Exod. 25: 10–22; 1 Sam. 4: 4; 2 Sam. 6: 2; 2 Kgs. 19: 15; Ps. 80: 1.   [93] 1 Kgs. 8: 27–30.
[94] Exod. 14: 19; 32: 34; cf. Deut. 26: 6–8; Exod. 23: 20–3; cf. Deut. 7: 1, 2.
[95] Ernest W. Nicholson, *God and His People* (1986), 191–217.
[96] Pss. 46; 48; Isa. 14: 32; 31: 4, 5.
[97] John Barton, *Oracles of God* (1986), 272–3.   [98] Amos 3: 2.

who abhor what is right
and pervert what is straight,
building Zion with bloodshed,
Jerusalem with iniquity.
Her leaders sell verdicts for a bribe,
her priests give rulings for payment,
her prophets practise divination for money,
yet claim the Lord's authority.
'Is not the Lord in our midst?' they say.
'No disaster can befall us.'
Therefore, because of you
Zion will become a ploughed field,
Jerusalem a heap of ruins,
and the temple mount rough moorland.[99]

The Deuteronomists gave this prophetic break-through formal theological shape by reinterpreting the special status of Israel in their concept of a *conditional* covenant, springing from God's love and inviting the People's love in response: 'What then, Israel, does the Lord your God ask of you? Only this: to fear the Lord your God, to conform to all his ways, to love him, and to serve him with all your heart and soul . . . To the Lord your God belong heaven itself, the highest heaven, the earth and everything in it; yet the Lord was attached to your forefathers by his love for them, and he chose their descendants after them. Out of all nations you were his chosen people, as you are this day. So now you must circumcise your hearts and not be stubborn any more, for the Lord your God is God of gods and Lord of lords, the great, mighty, and terrible God. He is no respecter of persons; he is not to be bribed; he secures justice for the fatherless and the widow, and he shows love towards the alien who lives among you, giving him food and clothing. You too must show love towards the alien, for you once lived as aliens in Egypt.'[100]

The Chosen People is emphatically represented as the *choosing* people—'Today I offer you the choice of life and good, or death and evil'—[101] and such is the greatness of God's mercy and his endowment of men with moral respons-

---

[99] Mic. 3: 9–12; cf. Isa. 1: 2–9, 10–17, 18–20, 21–6; 22: 8b–14; 28: 14–22.
[100] Deut. 10: 12–19; cf. 7: 7–10; 8: 7–19; 23: 7; see E. W. Heaton, 'Sojourners in Egypt', ET 58/3 (1946), 80–3. For 'love' as the bond of the covenant, see Deut. 5: 10; 7: 9; 11: 1, 13, 22; 13: 3; 19: 9; 30: 16, 20.   [101] Deut. 30: 15–20.

ibility, that a false choice, so far from being irreversible, may be redeemed by a change of heart, assisted (paradoxically) by divine grace: 'The Lord your God will circumcise your hearts . . . so that you will love him with all your heart and soul and you will live . . . Then you will obey the Lord once more and keep all his commandments.'[102]

Many scholars take the view that the Deuteronomists were directly indebted to the independent prophets for their break with the sacral Zionist theology and their insistence on moral response as the condition of the covenant.[103] It is difficult, however, to explain how this influence was mediated over so long a period as two centuries without a stable institution such as we are presupposing for the continuity of the school tradition. This suggests the alternative (or, additional) possibility that both the prophets and the Deuteronomists were indebted to the teaching current in the schools, which, as all the evidence indicates, was characteristically moral, rational, and independent of the sacral mentality and which, no doubt, was further fortified when the schoolmen became guardians of the oracles of the prophets. A hint of the ethos of this common educational background is to be found in a detached fragment of the book of Micah. It begins didactically, with a series of satirical questions:

> What shall I bring when I come before the Lord,
> when I bow before God on high?
> Am I to come before him with whole-offerings,
> with yearling calves?
> Will the Lord be pleased with thousands of rams
> or ten thousand rivers of oil?
> Shall I offer my eldest son for my wrongdoing,
> my child for the sin I have committed?
>
> The Lord has told you mortals what is good,
> and what it is that the Lord requires of you:
> only to act justly, to love loyalty,
> and to walk humbly with your God.[104]

The Deuteronomists believed that their moral teaching (like God himself)[105] was within everybody's reach and they took

---

[102] Deut. 30: 6–8; cf. Jer. 31: 31–4; Deut. 4: 25–31; 1 Kgs. 8: 33, 34, 46–53.
[103] Nicholson, *God and His People*, 201–17.
[104] Mic. 6: 6–8.   [105] Deut. 4: 7.

a delight in explaining it, so that its acceptance was based on personal understanding: 'This commandment that I lay on you today is not too difficult for you or beyond your reach. It is not in the heavens, that you should say, "Who will go up to the heavens for us to fetch it and tell it to us, so that we can keep it?" Nor is it beyond the sea, that you should say, "Who will cross the sea for us to fetch it and tell it to us, so that we can keep it?" It is a thing very near to you, on your lips and in your heart ready to be kept.'[106]

This sympathetic, human outlook can be pinned down unambiguously in the reinterpretation of particular laws. For example, the early law on unintentional homicide is terse and to the point: 'Whoever strikes another man and kills him must be put to death. But if he did not act with intent, but it came about by act of God, the slayer may flee to a place which I shall appoint for you.'[107] The Deuteronomists, concerned that people should *really* understand, provide an illustration: 'This is the kind of homicide who may take sanctuary there and save his life . . . for instance, the man who goes into a wood with another to fell trees, and as he swings the axe to cut a tree the head glances off the tree, hits the other man, and kills him. The homicide may take sanctuary in any one of these cities, and his life is to be safe.'[108] Again, the new version of the law for the emancipation of slaves becomes a plea for generosity addressed to the conscience of the individual: 'Should a fellow-Hebrew, be it a man or a woman, sell himself to you as a slave, he is to serve you for six years. In the seventh year you must set him free, and when you set him free, do not let him go empty-handed. Give to him lavishly from your flock, from your threshing-floor and your winepress. Be generous to him, as the Lord your God has blessed you.'[109]

The earnestness of the Deuteronomists' sympathy for the weak reverberates through their writings: 'When . . . one of your fellow-countrymen becomes poor, do not be hard-hearted or close-fisted towards him in his need. Be open-handed towards him and lend him on pledge as much as he

---

[106] Deut. 30: 11–14. [107] Exod. 21: 12, 13.
[108] Deut. 19: 4, 5. [109] Deut. 15: 12–14, 18.

needs.'[110] In a revealing phrase, Babylon is described as 'a nation of grim aspect with no regard for the old, no pity for the young'.[111] Festivals in Jerusalem are to be occasions for rejoicing, not only for the family, but also for all who depend on it: 'Rejoice before the Lord your God, with your sons and daughters, your male and female slaves, the Levites who live in your settlements, and the aliens, fatherless, and widows among you.'[112] The Deuteronomists attached more importance to compassion than to cult, and joy and generosity are the twin pillars of their reasonable faith.

[110] Deut. 15: 7, 8; cf. 10: 18; 14: 29; 24: 17–21; Jer. 7: 6; 22: 3; Prov. 22: 9; 28: 27.   [111] Deut. 28: 50.

[112] Deut. 16: 11; cf. 12: 7, 12; 26: 11.

VI

STORY-WRITERS

As every schoolboy used to know, the Old Testament is full of good stories, a fact so obvious as to make it curious that English Bible-readers were not stimulated to invent the novel until the end of the seventeenth century.[1] The nearest approximation to a modern novel in the Old Testament is, of course, the Story of Joseph in Genesis,[2] which has all the ingredients to guarantee its popularity—a hero who is 'handsome in both face and figure',[3] as well as being shrewd, sentimental, ruthless, unscrupulous, and, above all, highly successful, presented in a plot which crackles with danger, false accusations, and strong emotion. Joseph survives his elder brothers' conspiracy to get rid of him, prospers in prison after his master's wife had falsely accused him of rape, wangles the dispatch to Egypt of his beloved Benjamin, persuades his aged father to abandon his home and make the journey to Egypt, not to mention his thinking up an ingenious scheme which enabled the Pharaoh to absorb the whole of the country's resources into state-ownership.

In general outline, the Joseph Story closely resembles the favourite text-book in Egyptian schools, *The Story of Sinuhe*.[4] This, too, was a tale of an exile's success in a foreign country, recounting the adventures of an Egyptian courtier in Palestine, where he married the ruler's eldest daughter, was made 'chief of a tribe of the finest in his land', and settled in

---

[1] See Ian Watt, *The Rise of the Novel* (1963), 87.
[2] Gen. 37–50; the following passages are extraneous to the story: 38; 46: 8–27; 48; 49.
[3] Gen. 39: 6. Physical beauty is a constant theme of the school literature: see Gen. 12: 11; 24: 16; 26: 7; 29: 17; 1 Sam. 17: 42; 2 Sam. 11: 2; 13: 1; 14: 25, 27; 1 Kgs. 1: 4, 6; Dan. 1: 4.   [4] *ANET* 18–22; *LAE* 57–74; see pp. 57–9.

an area where wine was more common than water.[5] In his
old age, Sinuhe achieved his heart's desire to return to Egypt,
where he received both promotion at court and the gratifying
promise of a lavish burial.

If *The Story of Sinuhe* does no more than provide a general
indication that the author of the Joseph Story had encountered
Egyptian short stories in the Jerusalem school tradition, *The
Tale of the Two Brothers*, another exile's success story,
comes near to clinching the case for a direct Egyptian
connection.[6] The hero, Bata, described as 'a perfect man:
there was none like him in the entire land, for a god's virility
was in him', worked on his elder brother's farm. When he
returned home one day unexpectedly and there was nobody
else about, his sister-in-law tried to seduce him and, having
failed, faked evidence to suggest that Bata had beaten her up
and tried to rape her. To escape his brother's vengeance, Bata
went into exile, where (through a maze of myth and magic)
he ultimately became the King of Egypt.

It is highly probable that this naïve Egyptian tale (or some
version of it) is the source of the episode of Joseph and
Potiphar's voluptuous wife.[7] Bata had rejected his sister-in-
law's proposition on the grounds that it would be an offence
against the family: 'He argued with her, saying; "Now look,
you are (associated) with me after the manner of a mother,
and your husband is (associated) with me after the manner of
a father." '[8] Although Joseph declares that what the woman
is proposing is 'a sin against God', it is interesting to note that
(like Bata) he makes out a reasoned case against the betrayal
of a trust: ' "Think of my master," he said; "he leaves the
management of his whole house to me; he has trusted me
with all he has. I am as important in this house as he is, and
he has withheld nothing from me except you, because you are
his wife." '[9] Here then is an edifying tale, admirably fitted for
copying in the class-room.

The Story of Joseph as a whole is a propaganda exercise for
the school tradition which produced it. An Egyptian prayer
to Thot, the god of writing, put the matter succinctly: 'Better

[5] *LAE* 63.
[6] *ANET* 23–5; *LAE* 92–107.
[7] Gen. 39: 7–23.
[8] *LAE* 95–6; *ANET* 24a.
[9] Gen. 39: 8, 9.

is your profession than all professions. It makes (men) great.'[10] The hero is introduced at the age of 17 as reporting unfavourably on his brothers' management of the family's flock.[11] At the age of 30, now recognized as a man of 'vision and wisdom', he makes proposals for coping with the famine in Egypt and is appointed the Pharaoh's right-hand man with plenary powers. He immediately makes 'a tour of inspection through the land', displaying, no doubt, that 'zeal, firmness, and efficiency', which is so often claimed in late-Egyptian scribal correspondence.[12] In the end, Joseph demonstrates the value of his diplomatic training by winning the gratitude of the starving population, whose land and possessions he had contrived to confiscate; ' "You have saved our lives," the people said. "If it please your lordship, we shall be Pharaoh's slaves." '[13]

The hero's decisive action, which shows unambiguously that he is in charge of events, is, nevertheless, directed by the discreet but determinative hand of Providence—that 'divinity that shapes our ends, rough-hew them how we will'. On two occasions, the writer makes this dual control explicit: 'I am your brother Joseph, whom you sold into Egypt. Now do not be distressed or blame yourselves for selling me into slavery here; it was to save lives that God sent me ahead of you . . . It is clear that it was not you who sent me here, but God . . . You meant to do me harm; but God meant to bring good out of it.'[14] This problematic concept of a co-operative but unequal relationship between autonomous human action and divine providence is a commonplace in the school literature of Egypt, as, for example, in *The Instruction of Amen-em-opet*:

> The words which men say pass on one side,
>   the things which God does pass on another side.
>
> The tongue of a man is the steering oar of a boat,
>   And the Lord of All is its pilot.[15]

The idea finds expression in the book of Proverbs, from which Thomas à Kempis drew his classical formulation

[10] *LAE* 345.   [11] Gen. 37: 2.
[12] Gen. 41: 46; Caminos. 4, 5, 7, 15, 221, 293, 296.   [13] Gen. 47: 25.
[14] Gen. 45: 5, 8; 50: 20.   [15] *LAE* 258; *ANET* 423b, 424a.

Homo proponit sed Deus disponit.[16] However, despite their recognition of God's ultimate sovereignty, the story-writers always presuppose that the characters of their narratives are free to act and that it is they and no *deus ex machina* who determine the shape of the plots.

The Joseph Story also reflects its Egyptian ancestry in its sophisticated use of dialogue, as in the following anxious family argument about young Benjamin:

When the grain they had brought from Egypt was all used up, their father said to them, 'Go again and buy some more grain for us to eat.' Judah replied, 'But the man warned us that we must not go into his presence unless our brother was with us. If you let our brother go with us, we will go down and buy you food. But if you will not let him, we cannot go, for the man declared, "You shall not come into my presence unless your brother is with you." ' Israel said, 'Why have you treated me so badly by telling the man that you had another brother?' They answered, 'The man questioned us closely about ourselves and our family: "Is your father still alive?" he asked, "Have you a brother?" and we answered his questions. How were we to know he would tell us to bring our brother down?' Judah said to Israel his father, 'Send the boy with me; then we can start at once . . . I shall go surety for him, and you may hold me responsible . . . If we had not wasted all this time, we could have made the journey twice by now.'[17]

Before we leave this miniature masterpiece, it is worth noticing a number of otherwise insignificant features which reflect the influence of Egypt on the author's school tradition. Joseph dies at the age of 110—the ideal life-span for Egyptians;[18] the use of the schoolmen's term 'abomination';[19] the appearance of the Egyptian cliché, 'like the sand of the sea';[20] and, finally, the stiff-upper-lip taboo on any display of emotion, which was firmly established in educated society, is a recurrent feature of the story: 'Joseph, suddenly overcome by his feelings for his brother, was almost in tears, and he

---

[16] Prov. 16: 9; 19: 21; 20: 24; Thomas à Kempis, *De Imitatione Christi*, 1: 19; *The Instruction of Ptahhotep, LAE* 165.

[17] Gen. 43: 2–10; cf. Gen. 44: 18–34.

[18] Gen. 50: 22, 26; *The Instruction of Ptahhotep, ANET* 414b; *LAE* 175; Caminos, 143.   [19] Gen. 43: 32; 46: 34; see p. 106.

[20] Gen. 41: 49; cf. Gen: 32: 12; 2 Sam. 17: 11; 1 Kgs. 4: 20, 29; see *BAR* iv, paras. 190, 216, 217.

went into the inner room and wept. Then, having bathed his face, he came out and, with his feelings now under control, he ordered the meal to be served.'[21]

It has long been recognized that the Story of Joseph was the model for one of the stories in the first half of the book of Daniel. Like Joseph, Daniel is presented as the ideal representative of Israel, whose superior abilities are acknowledged at a foreign court. The heathen monarch is troubled by a dream, which defeats his own professional interpreters. In conscious reliance on divine inspiration, the hero is able to explain the dream, for which he is promoted to high office.[22]

The Daniel story is set in the period of the Babylonian Exile, when, for obvious reasons, the motif of the successful Jew in the Gentile world became pertinent. It is reflected in legends about the prophet Jeremiah[23] and King Jehoiachin,[24] and perhaps, even, in the Genesis stories about Abraham and his wife, Sarah.[25] Works of fiction from the second century BC, such as Tobit, Judith, and Esther, are also set in the period of Israel's dispersion among the nations. Thus, Tobit is an exile living in Assyria in the first half of the seventh century BC; Judith is an exile living in Babylon in the sixth century BC; and Esther is an exile living at the Persian court in the fifth century BC. The exilic setting was more, however, than a mere literary convention; popular fiction was actually circulating at this period among the Jews dispersed abroad, as the discovery at the beginning of this century of *The Story of Ahikar* has strikingly demonstrated.[26] The text (in Aramaic) was found at Elephantine, an island on the Nile, where a Jewish military colony had been established, probably in the sixth century BC. The work combines an account of the harrowing adventures of Ahikar, a trusted official of Sennacherib, the King of Assyria, and a collection of his wise sayings. Its phenomenal popularity is reflected in the fact that it was known in the school tradition of Jerusalem and has left

---

[21] Gen. 43: 30, 31; cf. Gen. 42: 24; 45: 1; Prov. 12: 16.
[22] Gen. 41; Dan. 2; cf. E. W. Heaton, *The Book of Daniel* (1956).
[23] Jer. 40: 1–6.
[24] 2 Kgs. 25: 27–30; see E. W. Heaton, 'Sojourners in Egypt', *ET* 58/3 (1946), 80–3.   [25] Gen. 12: 10–20; 20: 1–18.
[26] R. H. Charles, *Apocrypha and Pseudepigrapha of the Old Testament*, vol. ii (1913), 715–84; *ANET* 427–30; *DOTT* 270–5.

traces in the book of Proverbs,[27] some of the Psalms,[28] and
Ecclesiasticus;[29] in Tobit, both Ahikar and his nephew are
actually named.[30] In view of the development of loyalist
fiction in response to Israel's exposure to the Gentile world
after the fall of Jerusalem, it is not surprising that many
scholars now date the composition of the Story of Joseph
during this exilic period.[31]

There is a good deal in common between the Story of
Joseph and the infinitely more sensitive Story of Ruth. Once
again, the setting is famine, exile, and homecoming, with a
central character portrayed against a family background. The
book of Ruth, written perhaps about 400 BC, is a little gem.
The narrative is constantly enlivened by convincing dialogue,
which advances the plot and gives light and shade to its
characters, as we see in this opening scene: 'Naomi said to
her daughters-in-law, "Go back, both of you, home to your
own mothers. May the Lord keep faith with you, as you have
kept faith with the dead and with me; and may he grant each
of you the security of a home with a new husband." And she
kissed them goodbye. They wept aloud and said, "No, we
shall return with you to your people." But Naomi insisted,
"Go back, my daughters. Why should you come with me?
Am I likely to bear any more sons to be husbands for you? Go
back, my daughters, go; for I am too old to marry again. But
if I could say that I had hope of a child, even if I were to be
married tonight and were to bear sons, would you, then, wait
until they grew up? Would you on their account remain
unmarried? No, my daughters! For your sakes I feel bitter
that the Lord has inflicted such misfortune on me." At this
they wept still more. Then Orpah kissed her mother-in-law
and took her leave, but Ruth clung to her.'[32] The author had
a sharp eye for telling detail: 'When Boaz had eaten and
drunk, he felt at peace with the world and went and lay down

---

[27] *Ahikar*, VII, cf. Prov. 24: 17; *Ahikar*, XII, cf. Prov. 23: 13, 14.
[28] *Ahikar*, XXXI, cf. Ps. 141: 5; *Ahikar*, XXXVII, cf. Ps. 137: 9.
[29] *Ahikar*, XXX, cf. Ecclus. 9: 8; *Ahikar* XXVI, cf. Ecclus. 4: 26.
[30] Tobit 1: 21, 22; 2: 10; 11: 18; 14: 10.
[31] Donald B. Redford, *A Study of the Biblical Story of Joseph*, *VT*, Supp. xx
(1970); R. N. Whybray, *The Making of the Pentateuch* (1987), 240–2; E. W.
Heaton, 'The Joseph Saga', *ET* 59/5 (1948), 134–6.
[32] Ruth 1: 8–14; cf. 2: 2–16; 3: 1–6.

to sleep at the far end of the heap of grain. Ruth came quietly, turned back the covering at his feet and lay down. About midnight the man woke with a start; he turned over, and there, lying at his feet, was a woman!'[33]

If the Story of Joseph celebrates and commends the pursuit of success, the Story of Ruth celebrates and commends the virtue of fidelity: 'Where you go, I shall go, and where you stay, I shall stay. Your people will be my people, and your God my God.'[34] As so often in this literary tradition, the outcome is declared to be in the hands of a benevolent Providence. As Boaz says to Ruth: 'The Lord reward you for what you have done; may you be richly repaid by the Lord the God of Israel, under whose wings you have come for refuge.'[35]

Tales of marriage and sexual adventure were obviously appreciated by Israel's schoolmen, as, indeed, the teaching of the core curriculum would lead us to expect.[36] In addition to the episode of Potiphar's wife, Genesis includes the wooing of Rebecca for Isaac,[37] Jacob's quest for Rachel,[38] and Tamar's seduction of Judah.[39] All the stories are now fitted into the narrative as links in the patriarchal succession, but they have a liveliness of their own. Tamar, who 'took off her widow's clothes, covered her face with a veil, and then sat where the road forks', is as pert as the prostitute depicted as lying in wait in the book of Proverbs.[40] On the other hand, Jacob's falling in love with Rachel, who was 'beautiful in both face and figure', is presented with great delicacy: the seven years he worked for her 'seemed like a few days because he loved her'.[41] The story of Rebecca is dominated by the notion of the secret working of divine Providence, which is guiding the diplomatic quest of Abraham's servant: 'The man was watching quietly to see whether or not the Lord had made his journey successful.'[42] Such passive faith, together with a high regard for family life ('So she became his wife, and he loved her and was consoled for the death of his mother'[43]), recalls the ethos we found in *The Instruction of Ani*: 'Take to thyself

---

[33] Ruth 3: 7, 8. [34] Ruth 1: 16, 17. [35] Ruth 2: 12.
[36] See pp. 68–9. [37] Gen. 24: 1–67.
[38] Gen. 29: 1–35. [39] Gen. 38: 12–30.
[40] Gen. 38: 14; cf. Prov. 7: 6–23. [41] Gen. 29: 17, 20.
[42] Gen. 24: 21; cf. 24: 12, 27, 40, 42, 48, 56. [43] Gen. 24: 67.

a wife while thou art still a youth that she may produce a son
for thee . . . Be silent, and thou wilt be happy . . . Pray thou
with a loving heart, all the words of which are hidden, and he
will do what thou needest . . . When thou art a young man
and takest to thyself a wife and art settled in thy house, set
thy eye on how thy mother gave birth to thee and all her
bringing thee up as well.'[44]

This realistic narrative tradition about personal relationships is unambiguously represented in the story of Adam and
Eve.[45] Whereas the priestly writer's sonorous account of the
creation of the universe in the first chapter of Genesis, with
its background in Canaanite and Babylonian mythology,
presents an event of cosmic significance,[46] this earlier piece
describes in matter-of-fact language the origin of life on earth
and records the guaranteed continuity of mankind through
the union of men and women in marriage.

Many features of the story have an Egyptian background.
The symbolism of the potter's wheel and the *ankh* emblem of
life, familiar from Egyptian reliefs, are reflected in the
imagery of Adam's creation: 'The Lord God formed a human
being from the dust of the ground and breathed into his
nostrils the breath of life, so that he became a living
creature.'[47] Even the Garden of Eden, where 'the Lord God
made trees grow up from the ground, every kind of tree
pleasing to the eye and good for food' and in which Adam
and Eve took a stroll in the cool of the day, is reminiscent of
the gardens beautifully depicted in the Theban tomb paintings.[48] When it is said that Adam 'gave names to all cattle, to
the birds of the air, and to every wild animal', the writer, no
doubt, had in mind the *onomastica* much used in Egyptian
schools. These lists represented the ancients' characteristic

[44] *ANET* 420–1; Erman, *AE* 234–42.

[45] Gen. 2: 4–3: 19; the river of Eden in 2: 10–14 is a later addition.

[46] Gen. 1: 1–2: 3; see W. G. Lambert, 'A New Look at the Babylonian
Background of Genesis', *JTS* 16/2 (1965), 287–300.

[47] Gen. 2: 7; see J. B. Pritchard, *The Ancient Near East in Pictures Relating to the
Old Testament*, 2nd edn. (1969), fig. 569.

[48] Gen. 2: 9; 3: 8; see N. de Garis Davies, *Two Ramesside Tombs at Thebes*
(1927), pl. XVIII; W. Stevenson Smith, *The Art and Architecture of Ancient Egypt*
(1958), 130, 225.

approach to knowledge: to name a thing was to get it taped, as bird-watchers will appreciate.[49]

The writer retains his detached, laconic style even in describing so momentous an event as the creation of the first woman and the surgery it involves is reported with an almost clinical objectivity: 'The Lord God then put the man into a deep sleep and, while he slept, he took one of the man's ribs and closed up the flesh over the place. The rib he had taken out of the man the Lord God built up into a woman.'[50] The serpent, too, is thoroughly demythologized and as skilled in argument as the brightest of the schoolmen. The word chosen to describe it—'cunning'—is almost monopolized by the book of Proverbs, where it is used to commend the really clever man.[51]

The serpent's success in persuading our first parents to sample the forbidden fruit, we are told, opened their eyes and endowed them with the knowledge of good and evil.[52] Hitherto, they had enjoyed the blissful unawareness of the animal creation; now they had graduated to the God-like status of human beings with freedom and responsibility: 'Then the eyes of both of them were opened and they knew that they were naked; so they stitched fig-leaves together and made themselves loincloths'.[53] It is characteristic of the culture of Ancient Israel that sexuality typified the importance of moral choice[54] and that it should be associated in the school tradition with the burdensome concept of shame.[55]

The Story of Adam and Eve now stands as the frontispiece to the history of Israel and sets it in a universal context. It used to be possible to make a confident connection between the writer of this account of Creation and the first contributor to the historical narrative which follows, whom generations of students have known as 'the Yahwist'. However, the kind of critical analysis which once isolated discrete documents in the Pentateuch, and so came to ascribe this source to an early writer, now retains only a diminishing number of supporters

[49] Gen. 2: 19, 20; see Alan H. Gardiner, *Ancient Egyptian Onomastica* (1947); Barry J. Kemp, *Ancient Egypt* (1989), 29–30.   [50] Gen. 2: 21, 22.
[51] Gen. 3: 1; cf. Prov. 12: 16, 23; 13: 16; 14: 8, 15, 18; 22: 3; 27: 12.
[52] Gen. 2: 9; 3: 5.   [53] Gen. 3: 7.   [54] Cf. Lev. 18: 6–30.
[55] Gen. 9: 20–4; cf. Isa. 20: 4; Nahum 3: 5; Rev. 3: 18; Deut. 23: 10; 25: 11, 12.

and it is being increasingly suggested that the literary deposit as we now have it from Genesis to the end of 2 Kings reflects scholarly activity (of a somewhat desultory sort) no earlier than the sixth century BC.[56] However, despite this turbulence in academic opinion, it is sometimes possible to be confident in identifying a piece of narrative which must have come from the class-room of a school during the period of the monarchy. One such fragment occurs in the book of Numbers at the point when Israel is poised to enter the Promised Land and Moses sends an advance party to explore the terrain and report back: 'Make your way up by the Negeb, up into the hill-country, and see what the land is like, and whether the people who live there are strong or weak, few or many. See whether the country in which they live is easy or difficult, and whether their towns are open or fortified. Is the land fertile or barren, and is it wooded or not? Go boldly in and bring some of its fruit.'[57] The writer was clearly familiar with the training of officials, such as the Egyptian teacher Hori caricatured in his *Satirical Letter*.[58]

It is impossible to say whether the Jerusalem school tradition provided its students with any models or guidance for the composition of historical narrative. Schoolboys in Egypt were copying historical inscriptions as early as the sixteenth century BC,[59] and two centuries later experiments in narrative were being made both visually in temple reliefs with connected battle scenes[60] and also in literary compositions.[61] The long poem on the Battle of Qadesh, written about 1280 BC, seems to anticipate to a remarkable degree key features of the account of Israel's Exodus from Egypt.[62] It was written no doubt, for the greater glory of the Pharaoh, but it is presented as a celebration of the mighty acts of his god Amun. There came a point in the battle when Ramses

[56] R. N. Whybray, *The Making of the Pentateuch* (1987); Thomas L. Thompson, *Early History of the Israelite People* (1992), 356, 391, 398.
[57] Num. 13: 17–20.   [58] See pp. 60–1.
[59] ANET 232–3; Erman, AE 52–4; John Van Seters, *In Search of History* (1983), 127–87.
[60] K. A. Kitchen, in M. Liverani (ed.), *La Siria nel Tardo Bronzo* (1969), 92; Stevenson Smith, *Art and Architecture*, 222–4.
[61] ANET 233–4; BAR, vol. ii. paras. 1–25, 80–2.
[62] Erman, AE 260–70; ANET 255–6.

found himself surrounded by Hittite forces and deserted by his own troops:

And his majesty said: 'What is it then, my father Amun? Hath a father indeed forgotten his son? Have I done ought without thee? . . . And I never swerved from the counsels of thy mouth . . . What are these Asiatics to thee, Amun? Wretches that know not God . . . Amun hearkeneth unto me and . . . he calleth out behind me: 'Forward, forward! I am with thee, I thy father. Mine hand is with thee, and I am of more avail than an hundred thousand men, I, the lord of victory . . .'

I have found my courage again . . . I find that the two thousand five hundred chariots, in whose midst I was, lie hewn in pieces before my steeds. Not one of them hath found his hand to fight. Their hearts are become faint in their bodies for fear . . . I shouted out to my army: 'Steady, steady your hearts, my soldiers. Ye behold my victory, I being alone. But Amun is my protector, and his hand is with me . . . Now when my foot-soldiers and chariotry saw that . . . Amun, my father, was joined with me and made every land straw before me, they approached one by one . . . and they found that all peoples, among whom I had forced my way, were lying slaughtered in heaps.[63]

In a similar vein, the Exodus is depicted as a story of the Divine Warrior waging Holy War. As in the Egyptian poem, we have the complaint that God has forgotten his chosen, God's promise of victory, his provocation of panic in the enemy ranks, and his final act of total annihilation:

Pharaoh was almost upon them when the Israelites looked up and saw the Egyptians close behind, and in terror they clamoured to the Lord for help. They said to Moses, 'Were there no graves in Egypt, that you have brought us here to perish in the wilderness?' . . . But Moses answered, 'Have no fear; stand firm and see the deliverance that the Lord will bring you this day; for as sure as you see the Egyptians now, you will never see them again. The Lord will fight for you; so say no more.' . . . In the morning watch the Lord looked down on the Egyptian army . . . and he threw them into a panic . . . That day the Lord saved Israel from the power of Egypt. When the Israelites saw the Egyptians lying dead on the sea-shore, and saw the great power which the Lord had put forth against Egypt, the people were in awe of the Lord and put their faith in him and in Moses his servant.[64]

[63] Erman, AE 263–7.   [64] Exod. 14: 10–14, 24, 30, 31.

Whether or not this colourful Holy War language was taken over by the school tradition of Jerusalem specifically from Egyptian models, it can no longer be regarded as expressing a distinctively Israelite theology, since it is now seen to reflect a kind of religious rhetoric about gods acting for their people which was common throughout the Ancient Near East.[65] The most ludicrous use of it in the Old Testament is probably that of the Chronicler, when he describes how Judah's enemies (by the Lord's contrivance) were provoked into destroying each other by nothing more forbidding than the Temple Choir.[66]

The narrative skills of the Jerusalem school tradition are displayed at their best in the Story of David, an exciting novella of some fourteen chapters, originally independent of its context in the second book of Samuel.[67] If, as many scholars have thought, the composition was written in support of Solomon's succession to the throne, after the manner of Egyptian works of royal propaganda,[68] it is strange that the author should have chosen to tell a story in which all the principal characters are thugs. He has given us a tale of debauchery and treachery: of David's adultery with Bathsheba and his elimination of her decent husband;[69] Amnon's brutal rape and rejection of Tamar;[70] Absalom's avenging disposal of Amnon;[71] Absalom's public orgy on the roof with David's corps of concubines;[72] Joab's acts of treachery and butchery, with Absalom, Amasa, and Sheba as his victims;[73] and, finally, Solomon's summary and callous dispatching of Adonijah, Joab, and Shimei.[74] This is hardly an exemplary story of civilized values. It is, therefore, not altogether surprising that some scholars now favour the view that the story was written as a counterblast to the renewed

---

[65] B. Albrektson, *History and the Gods* (1967); cf. J. R. Porter, 'Old Testament Historiography,' in G. W. Anderson (ed.), *Tradition and Interpretation* (1979), 125–50.   [66] 2 Chron. 20: 1–23.

[67] 2 Sam. 9: 1–20: 26 with 1 Kgs. 1: 1–2: 46, excluding the annalistic material in 2 Sam. 10: 1–11: 1 and 12: 26–31.

[68] 1 Kgs. 2: 46; cf. *The Instruction of Amenemhet*, ANET 418–19; Erman, *AE* 72–4; *LAE* 193–7; *The Prophecy of Neferti*, ANET 444–6; Erman, *AE* 110–15; *LAE* 234–40; *The Story of Sinuhe*.

[69] 2 Sam. 11: 1–27.   [70] 2 Sam. 13: 1–22.

[71] 2 Sam. 13: 23–9.   [72] 2 Sam. 16: 20–2.

[73] 2 Sam. 18: 9–17; 20: 8–22.   [74] 1 Kgs. 2: 13–46.

enthusiasm for the restoration of the Davidic dynasty after the Exile and that it was added to the Deuteronomists' history at this late period.[75] Against this, one might argue that it is too sophisticated to have been devised simply as a political pamphlet or a religious tract.

The sophistication of the narrative as a literary composition suggests that whatever else the writer had in mind, he was motivated by a desire to entertain his readers.[76] The dramatis personae number no less than twenty-nine and, instead of being pickled in descriptive prose, they come alive by being presented in revealing conversations and a developing plot. The action covers some twenty years and, as Erich Auerbach pointed out, the author shows an awareness of time which is not to be found in most writers of antiquity: 'Achilles and Odysseus are splendidly described in many well-ordered words, epithets cling to them, their emotions are constantly displayed in their words and deeds—but they have no development, and their life-histories are clearly set forth once and for all ... But what a road, what a fate, lie ... between David the harp player, persecuted by his lord's jealousy, and the old king, surrounded by violent intrigues, whom Abishag the Shunammite warmed in his bed, and he knew her not.'[77]

The writer's fascination with people is particularly seen in the care he devotes to his minor characters—David's smart nephew, Jonadab,[78] the outraged Tamar in her long, sleeved robe,[79] the wise and formidable woman of Tekoah,[80] the eager young Ahimaaz, with his distinctive way of running,[81] Saul's grandson, Mephibosheth, who was crippled in both feet,[82] the endearing octogenarian, Barzillai, who had lost both his hearing and his sense of taste,[83] the fanatical Shimei who pelted David with stones,[84] and the wise woman of Abel, who saved her city by procuring Sheba's head.[85]

It is obvious that the writer had a strong visual imagination and took a delight in everyday detail. 'In all Israel,' we are

[75] See Van Seters, *In Search of History*, 289–91.
[76] See David M. Gunn, *The Story of David* (1978).
[77] Erich Auerbach (trans. Willard R. Trask), *Mimesis* (1953), 17–18.
[78] 2 Sam. 13: 3, 32, 33.
[79] 2 Sam. 13: 18, 19.
[80] 2 Sam. 14: 1–20.
[81] 2 Sam. 18: 19–30.
[82] 2 Sam. 9: 5–13; 19: 24–30.
[83] 2 Sam. 19: 31–40.
[84] 2 Sam. 16: 5–14; 19: 18–23.
[85] 2 Sam. 20: 14–22.

told, 'no man was so much admired for his beauty as
Absalom; from the crown of his head to the sole of his foot he
was without a flaw. When he cut his hair (as had to be done
every year, for he found it heavy), it weighed two hundred
shekels by the royal standard.'[86] The vignette of his election
campaign every morning at the city-gate is splendidly vivid:
'Whenever a man approached to prostrate himself, Absalom
would stretch out his hand, take hold of him, and kiss him.
By behaving like this to every Israelite who sought justice
from the king, Absalom stole the affections of the people.'[87]
After his death, when it was known that David was grieving
for his son, the troops, it is said, 'stole into the city like men
ashamed to show their faces after fleeing from a battle.'[88]

The writer most obviously reflects his pleasure in words
and images—indeed, almost to the point of caricature—in the
speeches he ascribes to Ahithophel and Hushai, the rival
counsellors consulted by Absalom.[89] The art of public
speaking had been cultivated for centuries as part of the
school training of officials[90] and one popular Egyptian
composition, *The Tale of the Eloquent Peasant*, well illustrates the high-flown, metaphor-studded rhetoric, which,
apparently, the schoolmen came to admire: 'O High Steward
my lord! . . . foster truth, foster all good and destroy evil,
even as satiety comes and ends hunger; (as) clothing (comes)
and ends nakedness; even as the sky becomes serene after a
high wind and warms all who are cold; like a fire which
cooks what is raw and like water which quenches thirst
. . .'[91] And so on.

The writer of the Story of David reveals his familiarity with
a comparable tradition when he has Ahithophel and Hushai
draw rhetorical clichés straight from the text-book: 'I shall
bring all the people over to you *as a bride is brought to her
husband* . . . You know that your father and the men with
him are hardened warriors and *savage as a bear in the wilds
robbed of her cubs* . . . The courage of the most resolute and
lion-hearted will melt away . . . Here is my advice. Wait until

---

[86] 2 Sam. 14: 25–7; cf. 17: 17–22; perhaps the writer overworks the word
'beautiful', see p. 115 n.   [87] 2 Sam. 15: 1–6.
[88] 2 Sam. 19: 3.   [89] 2 Sam. 16: 20–17: 14.
[90] See Excursus, pp. 41–4.   [91] *LAE* 43–4; Erman, *AE* 126.

the whole of Israel, from Dan to Beersheba, is gathered about you, *countless as grains of sand on the seashore*, and then march to battle with them in person. When we come on him somewhere . . . and descend on him *like dew falling on the ground*, not a man of his family or of his followers will be left alive. If he retreats into a town, all Israel will bring ropes to that town, and we shall drag it into a ravine until not a stone can be found on the site.'[92] We are told that 'when Ahithophel saw that his advice had not been taken he saddled his donkey, went straight home to his own town, gave his last instructions to his household, and then hanged himself'. In this kind of society, you could not live with shame.[93]

The animation of the story is not, however, only a matter of language; it is also generated by the writer's skill in structuring his material. The unity of the narrative through many changes of scene is secured by the presentation of David, who is always either at the centre of the picture, or in close touch with what is happening. Events occurring simultaneously are systematically related as foreground and background and this is achieved for the most part by the unremitting activity of messengers, about whose vocational training, the writer, no doubt, was well informed.[94] Changes of scene, conspiracy, rumour, and news are exploited throughout to produce a satisfying sense of complexity and depth. Above all, they enable the writer to demonstrate his skilful handling of dramatic irony.

As an example of dramatic irony, it is worth looking more closely at the incomparable story of Bathsheba and Uriah.[95] At first, it moves slowly through the episode of Uriah's conscientious refusal to go home to sleep; it gathers pace as David conspires with Joab; and it mounts to an intolerable tension as the king is kept waiting for the news of Uriah's fate. Then, with consummate artistry, the writer gives David's response in flat platitudes—the lingua franca of the hypocrite: 'David told the messenger to say this to Joab: "Do

---

[92] 2 Sam. 17: 1–14; for the stock Egyptian description 'as sand of the shore', see p. 118 n.   [93] 2 Sam. 17: 23.

[94] 2 Sam. 11: 18, 19; 15: 10, 13, 36; 17: 17–22; 19: 11. The duties of an Egyptian messenger are described in *BAR*, vol. ii, para. 682.

[95] 2 Sam. 11: 1–27.

not let the matter distress you—there is no knowing where
the sword will strike. Press home your attack on the city, take
it and raze it to the ground"; and to tell him to take
heart.'[96]

Conspiracy is exploited to good effect in another notable
episode. Because the reader knows that the lascivious Amnon
is only pretending to be ill, Tamar's devoted attention,
described almost in slow motion, is all the more moving: 'She
took some dough, kneaded it, and made the cakes in front of
him; having baked them, she took the pan and turned them
out before him . . . Tamar took the cakes she had made and
brought them to Amnon her brother in the recess.' After the
rape, she suffers the ultimate humiliation of rejection: 'The
servant turned her out and bolted the door. She had on a long
robe with sleeves, the usual dress of unmarried princesses.
Tamar threw ashes over her head, tore the robe that she was
wearing, put her hand on her head, and went away, sobbing
as she went.'[97]

However, the writer's supreme achievement in dramatic
irony is his account of the death of Absalom and the cliff-
hanging suspense he creates in describing David as he receives
reports of the approach of men who appear to be messengers:
'David was sitting between the inner and outer gates and the
watchman had gone up to the roof of the gatehouse by the
wall of the town. Looking out and seeing a man running
alone, the watchman called to the king and told him. "If he is
alone," said the king, "then he is bringing news." The man
continued to approach, and then the watchman saw another
man running. He called down into the gate, "Look, there is
another man running alone." The king said, "He too brings
news." The watchman said, "I see by the way he runs that the
first runner is Ahimaaz son of Zadok." The king said, "He is
a good man and shall earn the reward for good news." ' Hard
on the news, comes the denouement: 'The king was deeply
moved and went up to the roof-chamber over the gate and
wept, crying out as he went, "O, my son! Absalom my son,
my son Absalom! Would that I had died instead of you! O
Absalom, my son, my son." '[98] There can be no doubt that

---

[96] 2 Sam. 11: 25.   [97] 2 Sam. 13: 1–19.   [98] 2 Sam. 18: 19–33.

the Story of David is the work of an educated and gifted man writing in a mature literary tradition.

It is impossible to determine why the stories we have been reviewing were written in the first place and how they were used before they were taken over by editors to fill out and illustrate their own compositions. The various possibilities are not, of course, mutually exclusive. Whether it be propaganda for some dynasty or institution, or moral teaching about human relations, the story was more likely to achieve its purpose if, at the same time, it entertained its readers. Since dons are not necessarily dull, there is no need to exclude story-writing simply for its own sake from the pursuits of the learned. As Solomon is virtually a *nom de plume* for Israel's schoolmen,[99] the description they left of his wisdom may be taken to mirror some of their own interests: 'God gave Solomon deep wisdom and insight, and understanding as wide as the sand on the seashore, so that Solomon's wisdom surpassed that of all the men of the east and of all Egypt . . . his fame spread among all the surrounding nations. He propounded three thousand proverbs, and his songs numbered a thousand and five. He discoursed of trees, from the cedar of Lebanon down to the marjoram that grows out of the wall, of beasts and birds, of reptiles and fish.'[100]

We have no means of deciding and there is no need to decide which items in this eulogy should be ascribed to the quick-witted entertainment of the court and which to the more earnest business of the schools. The same educated and civilized people were involved in both. The vignette celebrating the visit of the Queen of Sheba to Jerusalem affirms its international reputation for both wisdom and prosperity: 'When she came to Solomon, she talked to him about everything she had on her mind. Solomon answered all her questions; not one of them was too hard for the king to answer. When the queen of Sheba observed all the wisdom of Solomon, the palace he had built, the food on his table, the courtiers sitting around him, and his attendants standing

---

[99] Prov. 1: 1; 10: 1; 25: 1; Eccles. 1: 1, 12, 13, 16; S. of S. 1: 1.
[100] 1 Kgs. 4: 29–33; on *onomastica*, see pp. 88–9.

behind in their livery ... she was overcome with amazement.'[101] Of the topics covered by these royal tycoons we are not informed. However, the lavish setting of the encounter suggests that, as well as discussing the economics of the spice trade, they engaged in courtly badinage, of which, no doubt, both the Islamic and Ethiopian legends made much too much.[102]

Banquets were almost certainly the setting for recitals of such love poems as now make up the collection entitled 'Solomon's Song of Songs'. It is fairly clear that its editor wished to exploit the Solomonic tradition: the king's songs numbered 'a thousand and five' and such ostentation was just the thing for flattering his macho hero.[103] The collection's vivid cameos standing out in relief against a green background of trees and flowers—like the figures on a Wedgwood china jug—do not cohere to make a plot and the dialogues are often difficult to distinguish from soliloquies, but the total impact of the poems conveys the essence of a love-story. And love-stories are told to give pleasure. The way in which the poems present the couple's intimate thoughts and feelings, their delight in physical beauty and their joyful celebration of sexual relations, as well as the mastery of language which conveys all this, suggest that they emanate from the kind of schoolmen who wrote short stories for entertainment. We have good evidence of their popularity from the threat of a disapproving rabbi at the end of the first century AD: 'Whoever sings the Song of Songs with tremulous voice in a banquet hall and [so] treats it as a sort of ditty has no share in the world to come.'[104]

For our present purpose, it is fortunately not necessary to unravel the layers of allegorical interpretation in which over the centuries both Judaism and Christianity cocooned the Song, at once to supply a fig-leaf for the lovers' unashamed nakedness and to provide stimulating teaching about the intimate relationship between God and his People. Theodore,

---

[101] I Kgs. 10: 1–10.
[102] See E. Ullendorff, 'The Queen of Sheba', *BJRL* 45 (1962–3), 486–504.
[103] I Kgs. 4: 32; S. of S. 1: 4, 12; 6: 8, 9; 8: 11, 12.
[104] Roland E. Murphy, *The Song of Songs* (1990), 13 n. 53.

bishop of Mopsuestia in the fifth century, to his great credit, rejected this inflated (if not fatuous) interpretation and in writing to a friend said that the Song was simply love poetry written by Solomon and of no great significance for Christians. Astonishingly, this letter was used as part of the evidence when he was posthumously condemned at the Second Council of Constantinople in AD 553.[105]

Happily, historical criticism and that openness to fact of which it is the fruit have liberated the poems to be what they always were—lyrics embodying the yearning of a man and woman to consummate their mutual love:

> My beloved spoke, saying to me:
> 'Rise up, my darling;
> my fair one, come away.
> For see, the winter is past!
> The rains are over and gone;
> the flowers appear in the countryside;
> the season of birdsong is come,
> and the turtle-dove's cooing is heard in our land;
> the green figs ripen on the fig trees
> and the vine blossoms give forth their fragrance.
> Rise up, my darling;
> my fair one, come away.'[106]

The lovers' encounters are set in an idyllic pastoral landscape heavily scented with erotic suggestiveness:

> I am my beloved's, his longing is all for me.
> Come, my beloved, let us go out into the fields
> to lie among the henna bushes;
> let us go early to the vineyards
> and see if the vine has budded or its blossom opened,
> or if the pomegranates are in flower.
> There I shall give you my love,
> when the mandrakes yield their perfume,
> and all choice fruits are ready at our door,
> fruits new and old
> which I have in store for you, my love.[107]

---

[105] Ibid. 22.   [106] S. of S. 2: 10–13.
[107] S. of S. 7: 10–13; mandrakes were a recognized aphrodisiac; cf. Gen. 30: 14–17; for Egypt, see *LAE* 299.

The poems are given a tranquil domestic dimension by the recurrent image of the garden:

> My beloved has gone down to his garden,
> to the beds where balsam grows,
> to delight in the gardens, and to pick the lilies.
> I am my beloved's, and my beloved is mine . . .[108]

and in one of the central poems of the collection, the garden comes to symbolize the woman herself—exquisite and alluring:

> You have stolen my heart, my sister,
> you have stolen it, my bride . . .
> Your two cheeks are an orchard of pomegranates,
> an orchard full of choice fruits:
> spikenard and saffron, aromatic cane and cinnamon
> with every frankincense tree,
> myrrh and aloes
> with all the most exquisite spices.
> My sister, my bride, is a garden close-locked,
> a garden close-locked, a fountain sealed.[109]

The garden's exotic variety (including specimens foreign to Palestine, like aromatic cane, cinnamon, frankincense, myrrh, and aloes) suggests not only the imaginative exuberance of the poet, but the possibility of his indebtedness to more than a merely native tradition. The picture he presents is strongly reminiscent of the civilized domesticity of well-stocked Egyptian gardens as they are depicted in Theban tomb paintings. It is improbable that this similarity is fortuitous, since, as we have seen, the schoolmen of Jerusalem seem to have been familiar with the love songs written by their opposite numbers in Egypt.

One of the most notable common features of the Egyptian love songs and the Song of Songs is their use of the literary genre to which the Arabic term *wasf* has been given, meaning a description of a lover's physical beauty.[110] Papyrus Harris 500 provides a brief Egyptian example of its characteristically extravagant metaphorical language:

---

[108] S. of S. 6: 2, 3; cf. 6: 11, 12.
[109] S. of S. 4: 9, 13, 14, 12; cf. *LAE* 308–9.
[110] S. of S. 4: 1–7; 5: 10–16; 6: 4–7; 7: 1–7; cf. *LAE* 315–16.

Distracting is the foliage of my pasture;
[the mouth] of my girl is a lotus bud,
her breasts are mandrake apples,
her arms are [vines],
[her eyes] are fixed like berries,
her brow a snare of willow
and I the wild goose![111]

With this we may compare the even more bizarre similes used of the beautiful woman of the Song of Songs:

How beautiful you are, my dearest, how beautiful!
Your eyes are doves behind your veil,
your hair like a flock of goats streaming down Mount Gilead.
Your teeth are like a flock of ewes newly shorn,
freshly come up from the dipping;
all of them have twins, and none has lost a lamb.
Your lips are like a scarlet thread,
and your mouth is lovely;
your parted lips behind your veil
are like a pomegranate cut open.
Your neck is like David's tower,
which is built with encircling courses;
a thousand bucklers hang upon it,
and all are warriors' shields.
Your two breasts are like two fawns,
twin fawns of a gazelle
grazing among the lilies.[112]

The comparison of the woman's heavily bejewelled neck to the (unknown) tower of David prepares us for the one and only detailed description of the physique of her lover, which progresses for its language from exotic (and erotic) nature to monumental masonry:

My beloved is fair and desirable,
a paragon among ten thousand.
His head is gold, finest gold,
His locks are like palm-fronds,
black as the raven.
His eyes are like doves beside pools of water,
in their setting bathed as it were in milk.

[111] *LAE* 299.
[112] S. of S. 4: 1–5; 'beautiful' occurs in the Song eleven times.

His cheeks are like beds of spices, terraces full of perfumes;
his lips are lilies, they drop liquid myrrh.
His arms are golden rods set with topaz,
his belly a plaque of ivory adorned with sapphires.
His legs are pillars of marble set on bases of finest gold;
his aspect is like Lebanon, noble as cedars.
His mouth is sweetness itself, wholly desirable.
Such is my beloved . . .[113]

Since the Egyptian poets appear not to have exploited their native art and statuary for laudatory language, the suggestion that it was they who taught this stylistic feature to the poets of Palestine is highly improbable.[114] There is no doubt, however, that such language was much admired, as we may conclude from an uncharacteristically appreciative comment from Ben Sira:

As beautiful as the sunrise in the Lord's heavens
is a good wife in a well-ordered home.
As bright as the light on the sacred lampstand
is a beautiful face with a stately figure.
Like a golden pillar on a silver base
is a shapely leg with a firm foot.[115]

We knew that our respected tutor went to banquets and told his pupils not to interrupt the music and now we learn that he paid attention to the words of the songs.[116]

---

[113] S. of S. 5: 10–16.

[114] Murphy, *Song of Songs*, 43 n. 195; 71 n. 303.   [115] Ecclus. 26: 16–18.

[116] Ecclus. 32: 4–6. Ben Sira even uses the flowery language of the *wasf* to describe the high-priest Simon: 50: 5–10.

VII

HONEST DOUBTERS

In his *History of Religions* published eighty years ago, G. F. Moore acutely remarked: 'It is a common observation that it is not the people whose life seems to us most intolerable that are most discontented with life; despair is a child of the imagination and pessimism has always been a disease of the well-to-do, or at least the comfortably off.'[1] Job and Ecclesiastes (or their creators) give some support to this bold generalization. Both were comfortably off and both were well endowed with imagination. They were the products of a school tradition which nurtured confidence, based on the understanding that the universe was well managed and that life could be well managed too. All you had to do was to learn the ropes.

The presuppositions of this comfortable outlook—'God's in his heaven—All's right with the world'—had been questioned from time to time over the centuries,[2] but Job and Ecclesiastes are the only major works in the Old Testament deliberately undertaken to articulate the doubt and debate then current in the schools. They are generally thought to come from the fifth or fourth and third centuries BC respectively, but we have no evidence to support the speculation that it was at this period that the age-old conflict between the theories of the theologians and the facts of life became more than usually acute.

---

[1] G. F. Moore, *History of Religions* (1913), i. 286, quoted by Robert Gordis in 'The Social Background of Wisdom Literature', *HUCA* 18 (1943/4), 104.
[2] James L. Crenshaw, 'The Birth of Scepticism in Ancient Israel', in *The Divine Helmsman: Lou H. Silberman Festschrift* (1980), 1–19; 'Popular Questioning of the Justice of God in Ancient Israel', *ZAW* 82 (1970), 380–95; see pp. 164–70.

1. *Job*

Few would dissent from the judgement that the book of Job is a most powerful piece of writing. The impact it makes is derived from the principal author's marvellous use of language and mature skill as a poet. His passion determines the reader's response and his understanding of what the work is about. By this criterion, there can be no doubt that its subject is the justice of God: 'Can it be that a hater of justice is in control?'[3] As if simply to raise the question were not sufficiently daring, it is presented here through a sustained exposition of God's *injustice*.

In view of the familiar and moving icon of Job covered with boils and sitting among the ashes, it is important to recognize that the debate ranges far beyond his personal fortunes. He declares, for example, that God is indifferent to the suffering of the poor at the hands of oppressors:

> The wicked move boundary stones,
> and pasture flocks they have stolen . . .
> They drive off the donkey belonging to the fatherless,
> and lead away the widow's ox with a rope.
> They snatch the fatherless infant from the breast
> and take the poor person's child in pledge.
> They jostle the poor out of the way;
> the destitute in the land are forced into hiding together . . .
> Far from the city, they groan as if dying,
> and like those mortally wounded they cry out;
> *but God remains deaf to their prayer.*[4]

God also remains indifferent to the arrogance and prosperity of the wicked:

> Why do the wicked live on,
> hale in old age, and great and powerful?
> They see their children settled around them,
> their descendants flourishing,
> their households secure and safe;
> *the rod of God's justice does not reach them.*
> Their bull breeds without fail;

---

[3] Job 34: 17.
[4] Job 24: 2, 3, 9, 4, 12; cf. *The Admonitions of an Egyptian Sage*: 'Where is he (the supreme god) today? Is he asleep? Behold, his power is not seen', *LAE* 226.

their cow calves and does not cast her calf.
Like flocks they produce babes in droves,
and their little ones skip and dance;
they rejoice with tambourine and lyre
and make merry to the sound of the flute.
They live out their days in prosperity,
and they go down to Sheol in peace.
They say to God, 'Leave us alone;
we do not want to know your ways!
What is the Almighty that we should worship him,
or what should we gain by entreating his favour?'[5]

But Job accuses God of more than mere indifference; he is
directly responsible for natural disasters and social disorder:

When a sudden flood brings death,
he mocks the plight of the innocent.
When a country is delivered into the power of the wicked,
he blindfolds the eyes of its judges.[6]

It is, however, in relation to his own misfortunes that Job,
'speaking out in the bitterness of my soul',[7] allows his
indictment of God to escalate to blasphemous heights:

Do you find any advantage in oppression,
in spurning the work of your own hands
while smiling on the policy of the wicked? . . .
Your hands shaped and fashioned me;
and will you at once turn and destroy me? . . .
You granted me life and continuing favour,
and your providence watched over my spirit.
Yet this was the secret purpose of your heart,
and I know what was your intent:
that, if I sinned, you would be watching me
and would not absolve me of my guilt . . .[8]

When we enquire more closely into the cause of Job's
suffering, it becomes clear that it arose from alienation from
his community and psychological dislocation, rather than
physical disease.[9] He was the victim of a social revolution, in

---

[5] Job 21: 7–15.   [6] Job 9: 23, 24; cf. 12: 10–25.
[7] Job 10: 1.   [8] Job 10: 3, 8, 12, 13, 14; cf. 7: 13, 14, 20; 14: 17.
[9] In the prose Prologue, Job is represented as suffering from some form of skin
disease (2: 7, 8), but in the poem only four passages suggest this possibility and they
more probably refer to estrangement (19: 17) and hardship (30: 17, 18, 30; 7: 5).

which power was seized by tyrants and everything turned upside-down. As we learn from his final speech, Job had a good deal to lose:

> If only I could go back to the old days,
> to the time when God was watching over me,
> when his lamp shone above my head,
> and by its light I walked through the darkness!
> If I could be as in the days of my prime,
> when God protected my home,
> while the Almighty was still there at my side,
> and my servants stood round me,
> while my path flowed with milk,
> and the rocks poured forth streams of oil for me!
> When I went out of my gate up to the town
> to take my seat in the public square,
> young men saw me and kept back out of sight,
> old men rose to their feet,
> men in authority broke off their talk
> and put their hands to their lips;
> the voices of the nobles died away,
> and every man held his tongue.
> They listened to me expectantly
> and waited in silence for my counsel.
> After I had spoken, no one spoke again . . .
> When I smiled on them, they took heart;
> when my face lit up, they lost their gloomy looks.
> I presided over them, planning their course,
> like a king encamped with his troops . . .
>   I was a father to the needy,
> and I took up the stranger's cause.
> I broke the fangs of the miscreant
> and wrested the prey from his teeth.[10]

But the miscreants got their own back. They were, it would appear, the *nouveaux riches*—wealthy, with 'stacks of clothes', bloated and ruthless.[11] Job became their victim:

> But now I am laughed to scorn
> by men of a younger generation,
> men whose fathers I would have disdained
> to put with the dogs guarding my flock . . .

---

[10] Job 29: 2–10, 21, 22, 24, 25, 16, 17; cf. 4: 3, 4; 31: 1–23, 31, 32.
[11] Job 15: 27–33; 20: 15, 19–21; 21: 27–34; 27: 16.

Now I have become the target of their taunts;
my name is a byword among them.
They abhor me, they shun me,
they dare to spit in my face.
They run wild and savage me;
at sight of me they throw off all restraint . . .
Terror after terror overwhelms me;
my noble designs are swept away as by the wind,
and my hope of deliverance vanishes like a cloud . . .
God himself has flung me down in the mud.[12]

The reversal of Job's fortunes by social revolution echoes a theme which is recurrent in the pessimistic literature emanating from learned circles in Egypt and Babylon. *The Admonitions of an Egyptian Sage*, written about 2000 BC, laments at great length the fact that society has been turned upside-down:

Indeed, poor men have become owners of wealth, and he who could not make sandals for himself is now a possessor of riches . . . Indeed, noblemen are in distress, while the poor man is full of joy. Every town says: 'Let us suppress the powerful among us' . . . The men of rank can no longer be distinguished from him who is nobody . . . the serf has become an owner of serfs.[13]

Two Babylonian texts, written about 1200 BC, further illustrate the theme. In this respect, at least, it is plain to see why *The Poem of the Righteous Sufferer* has been called 'the Babylonian Job':

My strength is gone; my appearance has become gloomy;
My dignity has flown away, my protection made off . . .
The courtiers plot hostile action against me . . .
'I will make him vacate his post' . . . 'I will seize his position' . . .
'I will take over his estate' . . .
I, who strode along as a noble, have learned to slip by unnoticed.
Though a dignitary, I have become a slave . . .
When my acquaintance sees me, he passes by on the other side.
My family treats me as an alien.[14]

The acrostic poem known as *A Dialogue about Human Misery*, or, *The Babylonian Theodicy*, is equally explicit

[12] Job 30: 1, 9–11, 15, 19.
[13] *LAE* 212, 215, 218; *ANET* 441–4; Erman, *AE*, pp. xxix–xxx, 92–108.
[14] Lambert, 33, 35; *ANET* 434–7.

about the social revolution and laments the emergence of the *nouveaux riches*:

> The rogue has been promoted, but I have been brought low . . .
> I have to bow beneath the base fellow that meets me;
> The dregs of humanity, like the rich and opulent, treat me with contempt.
> The vegetarian [devours] a noble's banquet,
> While the son of the notable and the rich [subsists] on carob . . .
> People extol the word of a strong man who is trained in murder,
> but bring down the powerless, who has done no wrong . . .
> And as for me, the penurious, a nouveau riche is persecuting me.[15]

These Egyptian and Babylonian precedents suggest the possibility that the author of Job is writing within a convention well established in the circles of the schoolmen of the Ancient Near East, rather than presenting the actual experience of a particular individual or group in his own community. A choice between these alternatives will depend on what we judge to be the author's purpose and that, in turn, will depend on how much of the book we ascribe to his pen.

From its inception to its highly complicated and diverse final edition, the book of Job was a product of the schoolmen. Nearly a third of the work, by common critical consent, comes from writers other than the principal poet. Most obviously, the superb poem on the inaccessibility of wisdom in chapter 28 is independent of its present context and evidently belongs to the editorial process.[16] The same could be said of the set-pieces on the ostrich,[17] the crocodile,[18] and the whale,[19] which overload the concluding speech made by the Lord 'out of the tempest'.

The reader soon becomes aware of other set-pieces, even though they have been placed in more or less appropriate contexts. Job's final assertion of his innocence, for example,

[15] Lambert, 77, 87, 81, 87; *ANET* 438–40.   [16] See pp. 174–5.
[17] Job 39: 13–18.   [18] Job 40: 15–24.   [19] Job 41: 1–34.

takes the form of a comprehensive 'negative confession' comparable to those we find in the Egyptian *Book of the Dead*.[20] It is, indeed, conceivable that this splendid statement of moral values was originally the conclusion of the book:

> If my accuser had written out his indictment . . .
> I should plead the whole record of my life
> and present that in court as my defence.
> Job's speeches are finished.[21]

However the original book ended, a confident and clever young don, named Elihu, found it deplorable and, not being a man of few words, contrived to add six extra chapters by way of correction.[22] The speeches of Elihu are usually dismissed as falling far below the soaring literary and spiritual heights of the main poem, but it is only fair to recognize that he does at least see the point and stick to it.[23] His purpose is to defend the 'justice of my Maker' against what he calls Job's 'endless ranting against God'.[24] He takes it for granted that Job is a sinner; what he must do is to humble himself in God's presence and 'wait for his word'.[25]

Elihu's counsel is followed to the letter in the present ending of the poem, when Job recants and submits in response to the Lord's speech 'out of the tempest':

> I know that you can do all things
> and that no purpose is beyond you . . .
> . . . I have spoken of things
> which I have not understood,
> things too wonderful for me to know . . .
> I knew of you then only by report,
> But now I see you with my own eyes.
> Therefore I yield,
> repenting in dust and ashes.[26]

If this was how the poem ended when Elihu encountered it, it is difficult to see why he thought it stood in need of his own contribution by way of correction. It is more probable that

---

[20] Job 31: 5–40: *ANET* 34–6. [21] Job 31: 35, 37, 40.
[22] Job 32–7; see pp. 159–63. [23] Job 33: 8–12; 34: 5–9; 35: 2–4.
[24] Job 36: 3; 34: 37; cf. 34: 7; 35: 16. [25] Job 34: 7–9, 37; 35: 14.
[26] Job 42: 2, 3, 5, 6.

the Lord's speech and Job's submission were added by an editor who followed Elihu (if not, indeed, by Elihu himself). The conventional character of the speech favours this view.[27] So far from being a personal communication to this particular sufferer who longed for God to be approachable, the Lord's detailed survey of his own wonderful works as the omnipotent Creator is little more than a hectoring diatribe based on a regular *onomasticon* of the natural order. It uses a whole series of questions intended to point the contrast between human ignorance and divine omniscience:

> Who is this who darkens counsel with words devoid of
>   knowledge?
> Brace yourself and stand up like a man;
> I shall put questions to you, and you must answer.
> Where were you when I laid the earth's foundations?
> Tell me, if you know and understand.
> Who fixed its dimensions? Surely you know! ...
> In all your life have you ever called up the dawn
> or assigned the morning its place? ...
> Have you comprehended the vast expanse of the world?
> Tell me all this, if you know ...
> Did you proclaim the rules that govern the heavens
> or determine the laws of nature on earth?[28]

By a curious quirk of archaeological good fortune, as we noticed earlier, a model for this kind of inquisition has survived in the form of a burlesque of a viva voce examination in the scribal schools of Egypt. It purports to show how a teacher called Hori deflated his more conceited pupils:

> Come, set (me) on the way southward to the region of Acre.
> Where does the Achshaph road come? At what town?

---

[27] The use of the name 'Yahweh' in 38: 1 distinguishes the speech from the poem, in which God is called El, Shaddai, or Eloah. What appears to be a fragment of a poem similar to Yahweh's speech occurs in the enigmatic 'Sayings of Agur', which have found their way into the book of Proverbs (30: 1–4). Its rhetorical questions about creation, including the sarcastic comment, 'Surely you know!', are intended, like Yahweh's speech, to make the point that no one can know God (cf. Job 38: 4, 5).

[28] Job 38: 2–5, 12, 18, 33; cf. Ecclus. 43: 1–26; Ps. 148: 1–13; S. of III Ch. 35–60; see G. von Rad, 'Job XXXVIII and Ancient Egyptian Wisdom', in *The Problem of the Hexateuch and Other Essays* (1965), 281–91.

Pray, teach me about the mountain of User.
  What is its head like?
Where does the mountain of Shechem come?[29]

And so on. Is it not ironical that the Lord's speech in Job, for which profound spiritual claims have been made, should correspond so closely in form and tone to the Egyptian caricature? Presumably, its author was familiar with conventional school teaching material and drew on it as a way of showing how Job was reduced to size and to abject submission—despite his declaration:

> Till I cease to be, I shall not abandon my claim of innocence,
> I maintain and shall never give up the rightness of my cause;
> so long as I live, I shall not change.[30]

Job had asked, 'Would he exert his great power to browbeat me?' and had answered, 'No; God himself would never set his face against me.'[31] The editor responsible for the crass insensitivity of the Lord's speech and Job's final humiliation thought differently.

Although the poet's insight into human suffering is focused in the person of Job and presented as the *cri de cœur* of an individual, his work is neither a drama nor a dialogue involving personal confrontation. The successive 'speeches' of the poem differ to a limited degree in content, but they show no real development of thought and no response to what other 'speakers' have to say. Their use of conventional material also favours the conclusion that Job and the three Comforters are simply intended to represent different points of view in a theological debate which was evidently exercising the minds of educated people.

Job, of course, speaks for the honest doubters. To the orthodox Comforters his views are 'the long-winded ramblings of an old man', glib and irreverent talk, 'hot-air arguments'—outrageous and depraved.[32] However, like most theological opinions (including radical ones), Job's assertions were far from novel. Given the unquestioned belief that God is

[29] *ANET* 477; see von Rad, 'Job XXXVIII', 287–91; see pp. 60–1.
[30] Job 27: 5, 6.   [31] Job 23: 6.
[32] Job 8: 2; 11: 2, 3; 15: 2; 20: 3; 22: 5.

directly responsible for everything that exists and happens in the world, it was inevitable that throughout history questions should have been raised about his justice and it is not surprising that there were precedents in the school tradition of the Ancient Near East for both the subject and the literary form of the book.[33]

Written in Babylon about 1200 BC, *The Poem of the Righteous Sufferer* presents the total despair of a man of some standing in his community. Despite his punctilious piety, he has been forsaken by Marduk, his god, and reduced to a social outcast and physical wreck. The poet goes beyond the current teaching that 'undeserved' suffering was punishment for sins known to the gods but unknown to men, and roundly declares that the gods are not merely inscrutable, but act on principles which are the very reverse of human moral values:

> I instructed my land to keep the god's rites,
> And provoked my people to value the goddess's name.
> I made praise for the king like a god's,
> And taught the populace reverence for the palace.
> I wish I knew that these things are pleasing to one's god!
> What is proper to oneself is an offence to one's god,
> What in one's own heart seems despicable is proper to one's god.
> Who knows the will of the gods in heaven?[34]

The same radical questioning occurs in the other Babylonian work we mentioned earlier, known as *A Dialogue about Human Misery*, or *The Babylonian Theodicy*. It takes the form of an academic discussion between two friends, in which the sufferer rejects outright the dogma that men always get what they deserve:

> Those who neglect the god go the way of prosperity,
> While those who pray to the goddess are impoverished and
>   dispossessed.[35]

---

[33] R. J. Williams, 'Theodicy in the Ancient Near East', *CJTh*, ii/1 (1956), 14–26; John Gray, 'The Book of Job in the Context of Near Eastern Literature', *ZAW* 82 (1970), 251–69.
[34] Lambert, 41; compare the Sumerian/Akkadian proverb; 'The will of a god cannot be understood, the way of a god cannot be known. Anything of a god [is difficult] to find out', Lambert, 266.   [35] Lambert, 75.

The friend declares that such thoughts are perverse:

You have forsaken right and blaspheme against your god's
   designs.[36]

The sufferer must recognize that men cannot fathom the
god's purpose:

The divine mind, like the centre of the heavens, is remote;
Knowledge of it is difficult . . .[37]

However, some consolation may be found in the knowledge
that men are wicked *by divine appointment*, since the gods
themselves

> Gave perverse speech to the human race.
> With lies, and not truth, they endowed them for ever.[38]

With this astonishing abandonment of belief in the gods'
moral governance of the world, the sufferer abandons his
complaint.

Some fifteen hundred years before the book of Job, an
Egyptian schoolman had produced a poetic work, now
known as *The Man who was Tired of Life*, which takes the
form of a dialogue between a sufferer and his soul (or other
'self') on the desirability of suicide.[39] The man was utterly
miserable at seeing and suffering the collapse of a moral
order in society:

> To whom can I speak today?
> Hearts are rapacious
> And everyone takes his neighbour's goods . . .
> Men are contented with evil
> And goodness is neglected everywhere . . .
> There are no just persons
> And the land is left over to the doers of wrong.[40]

---

[36] Lambert, 77.   [37] Lambert, 87; cf. Job 11: 7–11; 37: 23.
[38] Lambert, 89. A Sumerian poem on a righteous sufferer from about 2000 BC
similarly affirms that the gods planned and instituted evil: 'Never has a sinless child
been born to its mother'; see S. N. Kramer, ' "Man and his God": A Sumerian
Variation on the "Job" motif', in M. Noth and D. Winton Thomas (eds.), *Wisdom
in Israel and in the Ancient Near East*, VT, Supp. iii (1955), 179.
[39] *LAE* 201–9; Erman, *AE*, pp. xxix, 86–92; an alternative title for the work is
'The Dispute of a Man with his BA ('soul')'.   [40] *LAE* 206, 207.

Although the composition is a speculative work and not a direct account of an individual's experience, it is presented, like the poem of Job, in hauntingly personal terms:

> Behold, my name is detested,
> Behold, more than the smell of vultures
> On a summer's day when the sky is hot.
> To whom can I speak today?
> Faces are averted,
> And every man looks askance at his brethren ...
> To whom can I speak today?
> I am heavy-laden with trouble
> Through lack of an intimate friend.[41]

In the circumstances, his only friend was Death:

> Death is in my sight today ...
> Like sitting under an awning on a windy day ...
> As when a man returns home from an expedition.[42]

Although Job is never said to have contemplated suicide, he passionately lamented the day of his birth:

> Perish the day when I was born,
> and the night which said, 'A boy is conceived!' ...
> Why was I not stillborn,
> why did I not perish when I came from the womb?
> For now I should be lying in the quiet grave ...
> why should the sufferer be born to see the light?
> Why is life given to those who find it so bitter? ...
> They are glad when they reach the grave.[43]

Even though it cannot be established that the Joban poet was familiar with any of the writings which have survived for comparison, and even though his achievement was vastly superior in both quality and scale, the existence of this intellectual tradition among the schoolmen of the Ancient Near East (represented most probably in other works now lost to us) strengthens the case for preferring an academic rather than a simplistic biographical interpretation of his work.

[41] *LAE* 205, 207. [42] *LAE* 208.
[43] Job 3: 3, 11, 13, 20, 22; cf. 10: 18, 19; cf. *The Admonitions of an Egyptian Sage*: 'Would that there were an end of men, without conception, without birth! Then would the land be quiet from noise and tumult be no more', *LAE* 217.

It is easy to resist a biographical interpretation of Job's Comforters. In their three rounds of speeches, they are the spokesmen for the current orthodoxy of the school tradition. It rested on three principal beliefs: (1) God, the Creator, is the source and controller of everything in nature and human life,[44] (2) Man, his creature, is fallible and cannot fathom God's ways;[45] (3) God gives every man what he deserves.[46] The traditional character of this teaching is confirmed by the structure of many of the Comforters' speeches, which betrays their reuse of stock material (to be found, no doubt, in the school library). After a brief introduction which acknowledges the new context in the form of a rebuke to Job, there regularly follows one or more conventional set-pieces. Thus, Zophar, having accused Job of glib and irreverent talk, produces a poem on the mystery of God:

> Is this spate of words to go unanswered?
> Must the glib of tongue always be right?
> Is your endless talk to reduce others to silence?
> When you speak irreverently, is no one to take you to
>   task? . . .
> Can you fathom the mystery of God,
> or attain to the limits of the Almighty?
> They are higher than the heavens.
>   What can you do?
> They are deeper than Sheol.
>   What can you know?
> In extent they are longer than the earth
> and broader than the ocean.[47]

Poems gloating over the fate of the wicked are constantly being recycled, as, for example, by Bildad:

> How soon will you bridle your tongue?
> Show some sense, and then we can talk.

But, of course, genuine dialogue was not the poet's style and he is content to copy out a blow-by-blow account of the fate awaiting the evildoer:

---

[44] Job 5: 8–16; cf. 12: 13–23.   [45] Job 4: 17; 11: 7–11; 25: 2–6.
[46] Job 4: 7, 8; 8: 20; 11: 14–20; 15: 17–35; 18: 5–21; 20: 4–29; 22: 4, 5, 29; 27: 7–23; cf. Prov. 10: 3; 15: 25.   [47] Job 11: 2, 3, 7–9.

> No, it is the evildoer whose light is extinguished,
> from whose fire no flame will rekindle . . .
> His vigorous stride is shortened,
> and he is tripped by his own policy . . .
> Terror of death suddenly besets him
> so that he cannot hold back his urine . . .
> Disease eats away his skin,
> death's firstborn devours his limbs . . .
> He leaves no issue or offspring among his people,
> no survivor where once he lived.
> In the west people are appalled at his end;
> in the east they shudder with horror.[48]

Another standard poem, celebrating the 'great and unsearch-able things, marvels beyond all reckoning' of the Creator, is allocated to Eliphaz:

> For my part, I would make my appeal to God;
> I would lay my plea before him . . .
> He gives rain to the earth
> and sends water over the fields;
> he raises the lowly on high,
> and the mourners are lifted to safety;
> he frustrates the plots of the crafty,
> and they achieve no success . . .
> he saves the destitute from their greed,
> and the needy from the clutches of the strong.
> So the poor have hope again,
> to the outrage of the unjust.[49]

This is followed immediately by a further set-piece on the good fortune which awaits those who recognize that suffering is a divine warning:

> Happy indeed are they whom God rebukes!
> Therefore do not reject the Almighty's discipline.
> For, though he wounds, he will bind up;
> the hands that harm will heal . . .
> In famine he will deliver you from death,
> in battle from the menace of the sword.
> You will be shielded from the scourge of slander,
> unafraid when violence comes . . .
> You will know that all is well with your household,

[48] Job 18: 2, 5–21.   [49] Job 5: 8–16; cf. 9: 4–10.

you will look around your home and find nothing amiss;
you will know that your descendants will be many
and your offspring like grass, thick on the earth.
You will come to the grave in sturdy old age
as sheaves come in due season to the threshing-floor.
We have enquired into all this, and so it is;
this we have heard, and know it to be true for you.[50]

The complexity and obscurity of the editorial process
which underlies the Joban literary cornucopia makes it
impossible to speak in simple terms of its meaning and
message. The best we can do is to try to make sense of its
different strata. As it now stands, framed in the prose
prologue and epilogue, frightening and comforting like a
bedtime story, the account of Job's fortunes in the book as a
whole asserts that commitment to God and goodness is not
necessarily cupboard-love; Satan lost his wager and the hero
lived happily ever after (or very nearly so).[51] However, when
we consider simply the poem in isolation, there can be no
doubt that it is brought to a calculated climax in the Lord's
speech 'from the tempest'[52] and Job's recantation in response
to it.[53] The fact that it provides no answer to any of the
questions raised in the earlier speeches of Job and the
Comforters gives interpreters ample scope to indulge their
own particular theological preferences. This climax, it is said,
is to affirm the need to acknowledge the mystery of the divine
and the limitations of human knowledge. It is to point the
contrast between the power of God and the weakness of men.
It is to rebuke the pride of men in setting themselves up as
God. It is to declare that the justice of God is not only
different from but greater than the justice of men (whatever
that could possibly mean). And so on.

But there is a further possibility and it is based on the view
that the poem had a meaning before editors added the Lord's
speech and Job's submission. This has the advantage of
giving due weight to the impact of the passionate language in
which Job expresses his outrage at the *sheer unintelligibility*
of life as he had experienced it. What made it worse was the

---

[50] Job 5: 17–27; cf. Ecclus. 2: 1–5. For further 'set-pieces', see Job 8: 1–7, 8–19;
15: 1–16, 17–35; 20: 1–3, 4–29.   [51] Job 1: 1–2: 13; 42: 7–17.
[52] Job 38: 1–41: 6; 40: 6–34.   [53] Job 42: 2, 3, 5, 6.

fact that God was not available, so that things could be
sorted out:

> God is not as I am, not someone I can challenge,
> and say, 'Let us confront one another in court.'
> If only there were one to arbitrate between us
> and impose his authority on us both.[54]

> If only I knew how to reach him,
> how to enter his court,
> I should state my case before him
> and set out my arguments in full;
> then I should learn what answer he would give
> and understand what he had to say to me.[55]

> I call out to you, God, but you do not answer,
> I stand up to plead, but you keep aloof.[56]

The sustained protest of Job's speeches challenged the two
principal (and plainly contradictory) dogmas which had
become fossilized in the school tradition. The first held (as
the hymn puts it) that God moves in a mysterious way his
wonders to perform, while the second asserted that, on the
contrary, his way in the world is not in the least mysterious
and may be traced with confidence in the prosperity of the
righteous and the suffering of the wicked. The first—the
belief in God's absolute and unqualified transcendence,
which Job finds so particularly galling—is summed up in the
words of Elihu: 'God is so great that we cannot know him.'[57]
The second—the belief that God invariably gives men what
they deserve—is simply proved false by Job's experience of
innocent and disproportionate suffering:

> If the appeal is to force, see how mighty he is;
> if to justice, who can compel him to give me a hearing?
> Though I am in the right, he condemns me out of my own
>   mouth;
> though I am blameless, he makes me out to be crooked . . .
> But it is all one; therefore I declare,
> 'He destroys blameless and wicked alike.'[58]

[54] Job 9: 32, 33; cf. 16: 21. Note the presupposition that God and men share the
same concept of justice. [55] Job 23: 3–5.
[56] Job 30: 20; cf. 9: 15, 16. [57] Job 36: 26.
[58] Job 9: 19, 20, 22.

The moral courage and intellectual integrity of the poet in opposing the views of his fellow schoolmen eclipse the arguments of the Comforters and the attempts of later editors to make Job respectably orthodox:

> Nevertheless I would speak with the Almighty;
> I am ready to argue with God,
> while you go on smearing truth with your falsehoods,
> one and all stitching a patchwork of lies.[59]

The book of Job does not explain God's action in the world, but it encourages the believer to be intellectually honest and jettison any theological claims, no matter how venerable their ancestry, which are found to be simply untrue.

2. *Ecclesiastes*

The second of our honest doubters, Ecclesiastes, is the prisoner of a memorable slogan. 'Vanity of vanities, vanity of vanities,' says the Speaker, 'all is vanity' (or even more dismissively in the Revised English Bible, 'Futility, utter futility, everything is futile'); such is the doleful note on which the book now begins and ends.[60] However, the actual application of the description in the body of the work is much more discriminating and has a stronger claim to represent the teacher's thought. The things specified as being futile include the pursuit of such luxury and fame as Solomon indulged in,[61] the common fate awaiting wise and foolish, man and beast,[62] a lifetime of anxious work of which the fruits will be enjoyed only by others,[63] the rivalry between 'high achievers',[64] the inability of the workaholic and the lover of money ever to be satisfied,[65] and the unjust fortunes of the righteous and the wicked.[66] The analysis is gloomy, but it is not berserk.

Any soundly based interpretation of this work must give due weight to the fact that Ecclesiastes was a teacher: 'So the

---

[59] Job 13: 3, 4.
[61] Eccles. 2: 1–11.
[63] Eccles. 2: 20–3.
[65] Eccles. 4: 7, 8; 5: 10, 11.

[60] Eccles. 1: 2; 12: 8.
[62] Eccles. 2: 12–17; 3: 19, 20; 9: 3.
[64] Eccles. 4: 4.
[66] Eccles. 7: 15; 8: 14.

Speaker, in his wisdom, continued to instruct the people. He turned over many maxims in his mind and sought how best to set them out. He chose his words to give pleasure, but what he wrote was straight truth. The sayings of the wise are sharp as goads, like nails driven home . . .'[67] The author of this epilogue, which has been thought to reflect the style of the colophons with which scribes in the Ancient Near East rounded off their documents,[68] may well have been responsible for collecting the master's maxims to produce the present formless compilation.

Like the poet of the book of Job, Ecclesiastes is a literary stylist, exploiting a variety of genres favoured by the schoolmen, and elaborating his basic observations with rhetorical flourishes to such an extent that they seem far removed from the immediacy of personal concern. A man who *really* finds 'all things wearisome' and has come to 'hate life'[69] is unlikely to wax so eloquent about the sun and the wind and the streams which inconsequentially run into the sea.[70] In adopting Solomon as his pseudonym, he is following an established convention of Israel's school tradition[71] and reflecting the familiar form of the Egyptian royal instruction. The idea that there is a 'proper time' for everything, which Ben Sira was to find useful in parrying awkward questions,[72] is presented in a polished version of the kind of list they used in the class-room:

> For everything its season, and for every activity under heaven
>   its time:
> a time to be born and a time to die;
> a time to plant and a time to uproot;
> a time to kill and a time to heal;
> a time to break down and a time to build up;
> a time to weep and a time to laugh;
> a time for mourning and a time for dancing;
> a time to scatter stones and a time to gather them;
> a time to embrace and a time to abstain from embracing;
> a time to seek and a time to lose;

[67] Eccles. 12: 9–11.
[68] Michael Fishbane, *Biblical Interpretation in Ancient Israel* (1985), 29–32.
[69] Eccles. 1: 8; 2: 17.   [70] Eccles. 1: 5–8.
[71] Eccles. 1: 12–2: 26.   Ecclus. 39: 17, 21, 34.

a time to keep and a time to discard;
a time to tear and a time to mend;
a time for silence and a time for speech;
a time to love and a time to hate;
a time for war and a time for peace.[73]

Among his literary forms, even a miniature narrative ('There was once a small town with few inhabitants . . .') has found its way into the compilation as an example of 'wisdom'.[74] In his only direct reference to religious practice, which is notably lacking in enthusiasm, Ecclesiastes adopts the admonition form, much used by teachers in addressing their pupils: 'Go circumspectly when you visit the house of God . . . Do not be impulsive in speech . . . God is in heaven and you are on earth, so let your words be few.'[75]

There was, however, nothing conventional in Ecclesiastes' own quest as a schoolman. He set out to discover what he called 'the reason in things'—'a worthless task,' he comments dryly, 'that God has given to mortals to keep them occupied'.[76] As a detached and penetrating observer, he came to conclusions which his go-getting contemporaries must have found extremely unpalatable. It is evident that they were caught up in an acquisitive society, which was dominated by money and driven by aggressive individualism. Ecclesiastes' aim is to get his pupils to face reality and recognize that the rat-race is futile: 'I considered all toil and all achievement and saw that it springs from rivalry between one person and another'; 'No one who loves money can ever have enough, and no one who loves wealth enjoys any return from it.'[77]

Beyond these daily frustrations, there looms the final frustration of death, which renders all life's achievements transitory and insignificant: 'All came from the dust, and to the dust all return.'[78] Death is the great leveller; the same fate overtakes the wise man and the fool,[79] man and beast,[80] 'this is what is wrong in all that is done here under the sun: that one and the same fate befalls everyone.'[81] Death, for Ecclesiastes, is the enemy of justice, because, although he

[73] Eccles. 3: 1–8.   [74] Eccles. 9: 13–16.   [75] Eccles. 5: 1, 2.
[76] Eccles. 7: 25; 1: 13; cf. 4: 15; 8: 9.   [77] Eccles. 4: 4; 5: 10; 6: 7.
[78] Eccles. 3: 20; 8: 8.   [79] Eccles. 2: 12–16.
[80] Eccles. 3: 19–20.   [81] Eccles. 9: 3; cf. 7: 2.

recognizes the *fact* that 'the just person gets what is due to the unjust, and the unjust what is due to the just',[82] he retains, nevertheless, the traditional *doctrine* that men are appropriately rewarded and punished in this life.

It is probable, however, that his preoccupation with death has a more profound and immediate motivation. The fact of death is the most obvious denial that a man is the master of his life: 'time and chance govern all . . . no one knows when his hour will come.'[83] Life is not what a man is able to make of it (a sort of do-it-yourself job), as many of Ecclesiastes' ambitious contemporaries evidently supposed. It is, rather, a gift of God and a gift to be enjoyed: 'it is good and proper for a man to eat and drink and enjoy himself in return for his labours here under the sun, throughout the brief span of life which God has allotted him. Moreover, it is a gift of God that everyone to whom he has granted wealth and riches and the power to enjoy them should accept his lot and rejoice in his labour. He will not brood overmuch on the passing years, for God fills his time with joy of heart.'[84] Joy sounds through this work quite as clearly as the tolling of vanity.[85]

Some of Ecclesiastes' cheerful advice, however, must have provoked hollow laughter outside his own affluent stratum of society: 'So I commend enjoyment,' he writes, 'since there is nothing good for anyone to do here under the sun but to eat and drink and enjoy himself; this is all that will remain with him to reward his toil throughout the span of life which God grants him here under the sun.'[86] 'Academic', in its pejorative sense, fairly describes Ecclesiastes' detached attitude to the less fortunate members of society; he observed the poor and the oppressed, but was not moved to action: 'If in some province you witness the oppression of the poor and the denial of right and justice, do not be surprised at what goes on, for every official has a higher one set over him, and the highest keeps watch over them all.' The bureaucracy, evidently, inspired no confidence and was ineffective: 'I considered all the acts of oppression perpetrated under the

[82] Eccles. 8: 14.   [83] Eccles. 9: 11, 12.   [84] Eccles. 5: 18–20.
[85] Eccles. 2: 24, 25; 3: 12, 13; 9: 7–9; 11: 8, 9; cf. Robert K. Johnston, ' "Confessions of a Workaholic": A Reappraisal of Qoheleth', *CBQ* 38 (1976), 14–28.   [86] Eccles. 8: 15.

sun; I saw the tears of the oppressed, and there was no one to comfort them.'[87] And that was it; Ecclesiastes was no Amos.

Even from his comfortable ivory tower, Ecclesiastes recognizes with commendable honesty that intellectual mastery was no more possible than mastery by means of money. Perhaps it was this limitation which he found the most irksome of all. Their education, he tells his pupils, will not solve life's problems, remove its uncertainties, or reveal its *modus operandi*: 'I applied my mind to acquire wisdom and to observe the tasks undertaken on earth . . . and always I perceived that God had so ordered it that no human being should be able to discover what is happening here under the sun. However hard he may try, he will not find out; the wise may think they know, but they cannot find the truth of it.'[88] The teacher himself has to admit that wisdom—'the reason in things'—eluded him: 'whatever has happened lies out of reach, deep down, deeper than anyone can fathom.'[89]

The responsibility for the whole incomprehensible human situation lies entirely with God, whose rule is absolute and arbitrary. He is 'the maker of all things'[90] and everything has been determined by him in advance: 'Whatever exists has already been given a name; it is known what human beings are and they cannot contend with one who is stronger than they.'[91] This, under God, is man's fate and he is not free to change his condition: 'Consider God's handiwork; who can straighten out what he has made crooked? When things go well, be glad, but when they go ill, consider this: God has set the one alongside the other in such a way that no one can find out what is to happen afterwards.'[92]

Unlike the author of Job, who took it for granted that the Almighty shared his understanding of morality and could follow an argument, Ecclesiastes does not berate God. More radically, he reduces him to a bare concept—Transcendent Sovereignty—emptied of all the values which man could understand and share: 'the righteous and the wise and whatever they do are under God's control; *but whether they will earn love or hatred they have no way of knowing*.'[93] The

[87] Eccles. 5: 8; 4: 1.   [88] Eccles. 8: 16, 17; cf. 6: 12; 10: 14.
[89] Eccles. 7: 24, 25; cf. Ecclus. 16: 20, 21.   [90] Eccles. 11: 15.
[91] Eccles. 6: 10.   [92] Eccles. 7: 14.   [93] Eccles. 9: 1.

sovereignty of God is no longer the sovereignty of the Good. In total contrast to some of our most adventurous modern theologians, who abandon what they call the 'realist' concept of God and identify 'the divine' with man's own moral engagement, Ecclesiastes quite clearly retains a 'realist' concept of God and abandons the fundamental conviction of the school tradition that he is to be identified with goodness.[94] Theologically, we are left with little more than a formal category representing the inscrutable and the unpredictable. Pastorally, however, Ecclesiastes offers valuable counsel to any society eroded by self-interested individualism and dominated by overweening ambition to get on in the world. Recognize, he says, your human limitations; make the best of things; life is not a task to be mastered, but a gift to be enjoyed.

[94] See Iris Murdoch, *Metaphysics as a Guide to Morals* (1992), 452–3, 455–6; see pp. 177–9.

VIII

BELIEF AND BEHAVIOUR

1. *Elihu*

The schoolmen of the Old Testament were never tempted to engage in the academic pursuit of systematic theology, but, as we have seen, they did worry about the goodness of God. Although this problem arose from their everyday experience and not from theoretical speculation, they did their best to think it through and make a rational response. We have a particularly good example of their efforts in the discourse of Elihu in the book of Job.[1] These six chapters were a late addition to the Job material made by an angry young man—a teacher who (as a prefatory note tells the reader) 'became . . . angry because Job had made himself out to be more righteous than God, and angry with his three friends because they had found no answer to Job and so let God appear wrong'.[2]

The young Elihu's pert self-confidence in lecturing his elders and betters has not, on the whole, commended him to professors of the Old Testament. In consequence, they have been inclined to overlook the representative significance of his exposition, as illustrating an enlightened version of the current orthodoxy of the schools. Even if distinctly humourless, his approach is that of a thoughtful man:

> Let us then examine for ourselves what is right;
> let us together establish the true good.[3]

> I shall search far and wide to support my conclusions,
> as I ascribe justice to my Maker.
> There are, I claim, no flaws in my reasoning;
> before you stands one whose conclusions are sound.[4]

---

[1] Job 32–7.   [2] Job 32: 2, 3.   [3] Job 34: 4.   [4] Job 36: 3, 4.

Elihu's style is that of the better sort of tutor—sympathetic and encouraging:

> Answer me, if you can,
> marshal your arguments and confront me.
> In God's sight I am just what you are;
> I too am only a handful of clay.
> Fear of me need not abash you,
> nor any pressure from me overawe you.[5]

> If you have anything to say, answer me;
> speak, for I shall gladly find you proved right.[6]

The source of Elihu's confidence is hinted at in his reference to his 'Maker', that is to say, his belief in the abilities bestowed on human beings as created by God:

> But it is a spirit in a human being,
> the breath of the Almighty, that gives him understanding.[7]

> My heart assures me that I speak with knowledge,
> that my lips speak with sincerity.
> For the spirit of God made me,
> the breath of the Almighty gave me life.[8]

> God, my Maker . . .
> who grants us more knowledge than the beasts of the earth
> and makes us wiser than the birds of the air.[9]

In the theological tradition reflected here, the basic manifestation of God is the order of nature (including human nature), which he created and perpetually upholds:

> Who committed the earth to his keeping?
> Who but he established the whole world?
> If he were to turn his thoughts inwards
> and withdraw his life-giving spirit,
> all flesh would perish on the instant,
> all mortals would turn again to dust.[10]

Moreover, the natural order is a medium of God's present action in the world:

> At God's command wonderful things come to pass;
> great deeds beyond our knowledge are done by him.

[5] Job 33: 5–7.   [6] Job 33: 32.   [7] Job 32: 8.
[8] Job 33: 3, 4.   [9] Job 35: 10, 11.   [10] Job 34: 13–15.

For he says to the snow, 'Fall over the earth';
to the rainstorms he says, 'Be violent,'
and at his voice the rains pour down unchecked.
He shuts everyone fast indoors,
and all whom he has made are quiet;
beasts withdraw into their lairs
and take cover in their dens.[11]

Elihu is particularly fascinated by the movement of light and clouds:

the clouds spread his light,
as they travel round in their courses,
directed by his guiding hand to do his bidding
all over the habitable world;
whether for punishment or for love
he brings them forth.[12]

It is less clear how Elihu conceived of God as acting in a more particular way through public events or individual lives;

God is pre-eminent in majesty;
who wields such sovereign power as he?[13]

but all we are told is that he turns on wrongdoers in the night 'and they are crushed', or that 'he strikes them down as a public spectacle'.[14] What, however, is quite clear is that God's actions, so far from being arbitrary, are always directed to upholding the moral order:

Can it be that a hater of justice is in control?
Do you disparage a sovereign whose rule is so fair,
who says to a prince, 'You scoundrel,'
and calls the nobles blackguards to their faces;
who shows no special respect to those in office
and favours the rich no more than the poor?
All alike are God's creatures . . .[15]

Far be it from God to do evil,
from the Almighty to play false!
For he requites everyone according to his actions
and sees that each gets the reward his conduct deserves.[16]

[11] Job 37: 5–8; cf. 36: 27, 28, 31.   [12] Job 37: 11–13.
[13] Job 36: 22.   [14] Job 34: 25, 26.   [15] Job 34: 17–19.
[16] Job 34: 10, 11; cf. 36: 5, 6.

This is the standard, fateful formulation, which looks reasonable enough, until it is put to the test of experience. Then, it would appear, there are occasions when God is either impotent or immoral. Elihu seeks to avoid this fearful conclusion by suggesting that misfortune is not necessarily a punishment for wrongdoing; it may, rather, be a God-given warning:

> Those who suffer he rescues through suffering
> and teaches them by the discipline of affliction.[17]

If a sinner responds to the warning in penitence, God will forgive him 'again and yet again', so that 'he may enter his presence with joy' and 'enjoy the full light of life'.[18] This unexpectedly personal language suggests that the writer was familiar with the kind of spirituality we find reflected in many of the psalms,[19] but, paradoxically, when he actually speaks of singing God's praises, it is in a context which affirms his utter transcendence and denies that men may ever know him:

> Remember, then, to sing the praises of his work,
> as mortals have always sung them.
> All mankind gazes at him;
> the race of mortals look on from afar.
> Consider: God is so great that we cannot know him;
> the number of his years is past searching out.[20]

God is 'greater than any mortal';[21] he is not accountable for his actions;[22] and he is completely unaffected by what men do:

> Your wickedness touches only your fellow-creatures;
> any right you do affects none but other mortals.[23]

Clearly, these insights and affirmations would not easily fit together to make a coherent theology. How could the Creator who endowed men with intelligence and the freedom to use it exercise an absolute control over everything that is? How could God be so far removed from the world and yet act in the world in particular events? How could it be maintained

---

[17] Job 36: 15; cf. 33: 15–25.
[18] Job 33: 26–30.
[19] Pss. 16: 11; 17: 15; 73: 23–8.
[20] Job 36: 24–6.
[21] Job 33: 12.
[22] Job 34: 24; cf. 37: 20.
[23] Job 35: 8.

that God's goodness was invariably demonstrated in the lives of individuals? How could the utterly transcendent God admit the penitent sinner to the light of his presence? At the end of his discourse, Elihu admits that making sense of God is really quite beyond him:

> Teach us then what to say to him;
> for all is dark, and we cannot marshal our thoughts . . .
> At one moment the light is not seen,
> being overcast with cloud;
> then the wind passes by and clears it away,
> and a golden glow comes from the north.
> But the Almighty we cannot find;
> his power is beyond our ken,
> yet in his great righteousness he does not pervert justice.
> Therefore mortals pay him reverence,
> and all who are wise fear him.[24]

To adopt the writer's splendid phrase, 'a golden glow' highlights two principal themes of this exposition for further exploration: 'God and Goodness' and 'God and the Natural Order'. They are recurrent in the theological tradition of the schools and account for much of its distinctive character.

2. God and Goodness

The gut-feeling that good actions follow the grain of the universe is what, presumably, underlies the age-old conviction that virtue should be rewarded and wrongdoing punished. In theological terms, if God's understanding of what is good corresponds to that of men (and how could it be otherwise?), and if (contrary to Elihu) he is responsive to what men do, he will give them what they deserve. This teaching, based on the way things ought to be, was used for encouragement and warning and became orthodox in the school tradition:

> Depend upon it: an evildoer will not escape punishment,
> but the righteous and all their offspring will go free.[25]

Despite the fact that this dogma so obviously flies in the face of so much human experience, it was commonly held in

---

[24] Job 37: 19, 21–4.
[25] Prov. 11: 21; cf. 10: 30; 12: 21; 13: 21, 25; 14: 11; Ps. 37: 25.

the Ancient Near East and persisted in Israel for centuries,
provoking, as we have already seen in the case of Job and
Ecclesiastes, much anguish:

> Why do the wicked prosper
> and the treacherous all live at ease?[26]

> How long, Lord, will you be deaf to my plea? . . .
> Your eyes are too pure to look on evil;
> you cannot countenance wrongdoing.
> Why then do you countenance the treachery of the wicked?
> Why keep silent when they devour those who are more
>   righteous?[27]

> Where is the God of justice?[28]

Unfortunately, none of Israel's teachers was prepared to
question the assumption that God's way with the world
meant that he was directly responsible for everything that
happened and that he could, if he so wished, intervene to put
things right.

Nearly a thousand years before the principal author of the
book of Job roundly accused God of failing to live up to the
moral standards recognized in common by him and his
creatures, a Babylonian teacher advanced the view that the
suffering of the innocent indicated not so much a moral
failure on the god's part as a totally different and inscrutable
understanding of what 'moral' meant;

> What is proper to oneself is an offence to one's god,
> What in one's own heart seems despicable is proper to one's
>   god.[29]

With the outstanding exception of Ecclesiastes, Israel's
teachers were never prepared to adopt so radical an
explanation, since it would have meant abandoning their
most distinctive belief, namely, that God was to be understood
(over and above all other attributes) in terms of *goodness*—
that objective goodness of which human beings are aware in
and through their everyday experience.[30] In the school
tradition, theology was primarily *moral* theology.

---

[26] Jer. 12: 1.   [27] Hab. 1, 2, 13.
[28] Mal. 2: 17; cf. Zeph. 1: 12; Ezek. 8: 12; 9:9.
[29] Lambert, 41.   [30] See pp. 178–9; cf. Job 9: 32–5; 16: 21.

The kind of discussion which took place in the schools is reflected in a somewhat ponderous exposition (probably from the early years after the Exile), which found its way into the book of Ezekiel.[31] It is a teacher's response to the accusation that 'the Lord acts without principle',[32] because, as the current proverb put it:

> Parents eat sour grapes,
> and their children's teeth are set on edge.[33]

The standard doctrine that men receive their just deserts is firmly upheld, but now on a strictly individual basis: 'It is the person who sins that will die';[34] the righteous man will not be affected by the sins of others. The terms in which the righteous man is described again illustrate the emphatic moral understanding of godliness in the school tradition: 'he oppresses no one, he returns the debtor's pledge, he never commits robbery; he gives his food to the hungry and clothes to those who have none. He never lends either at discount or at interest, but shuns injustice and deals fairly between one person and another.'[35] This individualistic interpretation of the doctrine of retribution was adopted by the Chronicler, who cheerfully rewrote history to make it fit the theory. Each individual king was made to get exactly what he deserved. Thus, Manasseh's many years on the throne were more than a bad king ought to have had and so the Chronicler turned him into a reformed character.[36] On the other hand, Josiah died too young for a good king and so the Chronicler invented his involvement in an act of religious rebellion.[37]

A comparable and probably contemporary fragment from the school debate on the goodness of God is preserved in the Genesis story of the Lord's visit to inspect Sodom and Gomorrah. Even he is made to sound like a former pupil, now employed as an official in the Home Office: 'I shall go down and see whether their deeds warrant the outcry reaching me. I must know the truth.'[38] It is recounted how

[31] Ezek. 18: 1–32. [32] Ezek. 18: 25, 29; cf. 33: 17–20.
[33] Ezek. 18: 2; cf. Jer. 31: 29, 30; Lam. 5: 7.
[34] Ezek. 18: 4; cf. Deut. 24: 16. [35] Ezek. 18: 7, 8.
[36] 2 Chron. 33: 12, 13. [37] 2 Chron. 35: 21–24.
[38] Gen. 18: 21–33; on getting at 'the truth' by diligent investigation, see Deut. 13: 14; 17: 4.

Abraham boldly challenged the Lord face to face (in a way Job longed for but was denied) on the subject of indiscriminate punishment: 'Will you really sweep away innocent and wicked together?'[39] He pressed the point with pedantic persistence: for the sake of fifty, forty-five, forty, thirty, twenty, and even as few as ten innocent inhabitants, the Lord promises to spare the city. This adventurous modification of the strictly orthodox position reaffirms the belief that God and men share a common understanding of what is meant by good: 'Should not the judge of all the earth do what is just?'[40]

We should hardly have expected that the psalmists, preoccupied as they were with liturgy, would have been greatly involved in this school debate. There is little such recognition of moral problems in our own hymn books. It is, however, an extraordinary fact that as many as a third of the psalms are pieces about religious doubts and difficulties and, even though they all end on a note of confidence, it is a confidence which had been explicitly called into question.[41] Some of these compositions unmistakably reflect the idiom and outlook of the school tradition.[42]

Psalm 37, for example, is an acrostic set-piece, presenting a conventional instruction for the righteous on how to cope with the provocative and perplexing prosperity of the wicked. The advice is: keep cool; do not be angry or envious, but, rather, trust in the Lord; wait patiently and quietly since the wicked will soon be brought to judgement.[43] No shadow of doubt is allowed to dim the brazen dogma of just deserts, which finds here its most notorious expression:

---

[39] Gen. 18: 23.   [40] Gen. 18: 25.

[41] Pss. 10; 14; 53; see R. Davidson, 'Some Aspects of the Theological Significance of Doubt in the Old Testament', *Annual of the Swedish Theological Institute*, 7 (1970), 41–52.

[42] Pss. 1; 34; 37; 49; 73; 112. Ps. 1, in its use of the 'Blessed' formula (cf. Pss. 34: 8; 112: 1; 127:5; Prov. 3: 13; 8: 32; 28: 14) and of the parable of the fruitful tree (cf. Jer. 17: 7–8; *The Instruction of Amen-em-opet*, *ANET* 422; *LAE* 246), echoes a didactic tradition which can be traced back to the schools of Egypt (see Leo G. Perdue, *Wisdom and Cult* (1977), 328–9). Its present position as the introduction to the whole Psalter suggests that the psalms had become detached from their original cultic use and were now presented for study and reflection.

[43] Cf. Job 4: 7–9; 20: 4, 5.

> I have been young and now have grown old,
> but never have I seen the righteous forsaken
> or their children begging bread.[44]

Psalm 73 is also the work of a schoolman and its subject the prosperity of the wicked, whom he describes with devastating penetration:

> They are sleek and sound in body . . .
> Their eyes gleam through folds of fat,
> while vain fancies flit through their minds.
> Their talk is all mockery and malice;
> high-handedly they threaten oppression . . .
> They say, 'How does God know?
> Does the Most High know or care?'
>
> I set my mind to understand this
> but I found it too hard for me,
> until I went into God's sanctuary,
> where I saw clearly what their destiny would be.[45]

The psalmist first adopts the conventional answer about the imminent destruction of the wicked, but he goes beyond it. He recognizes that the problem was not so much the prosperity of the wicked in relation to the goodness of God, but the quality of his own faith:

> My mind was embittered,
> and I was pierced to the heart.
> I was too brutish to understand,
> in your sight, God, no better than a beast.
> Yet I am always with you;
> you hold my right hand . . .
> Whom have I in heaven but you?
> And having you, I desire nothing else on earth.[46]

Here was an educated man of simple piety, who found assurance at a level deeper than that offered by the current orthodoxy.

As we have seen, the goodness of God was questioned with unprecedented candour in the books of Job and Ecclesiastes; the work of Ben Sira illustrates how the problem was still

---

[44] Ps. 37: 25.   [45] Ps. 73: 4, 7, 8, 11, 16, 17.
[46] Ps. 73: 21–3, 25.

exercising the minds of schoolmen at the beginning of the second century BC.[47] This experienced tutor made his own confident orthodoxy explicit at the beginning of his collected teaching:

> Consider the past generations and see:
> was anyone who trusted the Lord ever disappointed?
> Was anyone who stood firm in the fear of him ever abandoned?
> Did he ever ignore anyone who called to him?[48]

> His mercy is great, but great also his condemnation;
> he judges each by what he has done.
> He does not let the wrongdoer escape with his plunder
> or try the patience of the godly too long.[49]

It is hardly surprising that this tidy view of God's good governance of the world continued to be challenged:

> Do not say, 'I have no master';
> the Lord, you may be sure, will call you to account.
> Do not say, 'I sinned, yet nothing happened to me';
> it is only that the Lord is very patient.[50]

> Who is to declare his acts of justice
> or who will wait for them,
> their fulfilment being so remote?[51]

Ben Sira's basic response to such scepticism, embellished with borrowings from Greek popular philosophy, was to reaffirm his belief that the world is as good as it could possibly be:

> I have been convinced of all this from the beginning;
> I have thought it over and left it in writing:
> all that the Lord has made is good,
> and he supplies every need as it arises.
> Let no one say, 'This is less good than that,'
> for all things prove good at their proper time.[52]

At the root of the problem of theodicy is the presupposition that God, as absolute sovereign, can and does intervene

---

[47] See J. L. Crenshaw, 'The Problem of Theodicy in Sirach: On Human Bondage', *JBL* 94 (1975), 47–64.   [48] Ecclus. 2: 10.
[49] Ecclus. 16: 12, 13.   [50] Ecclus. 5: 3, 4.
[51] Ecclus. 16: 22.   [52] Ecclus. 39: 32–4; see pp. 19–23.

directly and particularly in human affairs. There are slight indications that Ben Sira is feeling his way towards a different view. In his exposition of the Creation, we encounter the suggestion that it is through the natural order, and not by the unmediated manipulation of particular events, that God exercises his responsibility for the world:

> From the beginning good was created for the good,
> and evil for sinners.
> The basic necessities of human life
> are water, fire, iron, and salt,
> flour, honey, and milk,
> the juice of the grape, oil and clothing—
> all these are good for the godfearing,
> but turn to evil for sinners.[53]

The author of the Wisdom of Solomon took the hint and developed (albeit somewhat crudely) the idea that God ruled the world through his sovereignty in Creation: 'For creation, serving you its Maker, strains to punish the unrighteous and relaxes into benevolence towards those who put their trust in you.'[54] Entirely congruous with this small step towards a less directly interventionist conception of God's *modus operandi* is the great emphasis which Ben Sira gives to the Creator's endowment of men for responsible freedom:

> The Lord created human beings from the earth . . .
> He clothed them with power like his own
> and made them in his own image . . .
> He fashioned tongues, eyes, and ears for them,
> and gave them minds with which to think.
> He filled them with understanding and knowledge
> and showed them good and evil.[55]

> The Lord has imparted knowledge to mortals,
> that by their use of his marvels he may win praise;
> by means of them the doctor relieves pain
> and from them the pharmacist compounds his mixture.
> There is no limit to the works of the Lord,
> who spreads health over the whole world.[56]

[53] Ecclus. 39: 25–7; however, in the following verses (39: 28–31), natural phenomena are directly interventionist. [54] Wisd. 16: 24.
[55] Ecclus. 17: 1, 3, 6, 7. [56] Ecclus. 38: 6–8.

> When in the beginning God created the human race,
> he left them free to take their own decisions.[57]

It is ironical that a school teacher of the second century BC should have shown more perception than most 'biblical theologians' of the twentieth century AD.

3. *God and the Natural Order*

So large and elusive a subject is, perhaps, best approached through some small, concrete, nugget of experience. And so let us begin with the proverb. The characteristic function of a proverb is to pin down a regular relationship between an action and its moral consequence, so that even an unsystematic collection of proverbs can establish a general pattern of principles to guide the individual as he makes a decision in particular circumstances.[58] The authority of the proverbs is derived not from any extrinsic source (as in the case of the Law, regarded as embodying the revealed will of God), but from rational judgements made by men in response to their experience of the world and consolidated over the years as the common sense of the community. Since human nature remains fairly constant, it is not surprising that the basic moral teaching of the school tradition of Israel should have had a great deal in common with that of Egypt and that it should have been paralleled in the Greek world.[59] It embodied not only the common sense of successive societies; it represented common sense *tout court*. The schoolmen sometimes make this point explicit by the deft use of nonsensical questions to expose the obviously *nonsensical*

---

[57] Ecclus. 15: 14; cf. M. F. Wiles, *God's Action in the World* (1986), 90: 'The absence of divine intervention in relation to so many evils and disasters in the world is because such direct action is logically incompatible with the kind of world that God has chosen to create'; p. 93: 'The nature of such a creation is . . . incompatible with the assertion of further particular divinely initiated acts within the developing history of the world.'

[58] See A. E. Harvey, *Strenuous Commands* (1990), 155.

[59] Cf. ibid. 52: 'The entire structure of Greek popular ethics rested on the assumption that the good action is the *sensible* action; the appeal is always ultimately to the mind; if you think things out you will see that this is the right or appropriate thing to do. But it is precisely this appeal to prudence and rationality that is characteristic of Hebrew wisdom from the Book of Proverbs onwards.'

nature of wrongdoing. In the book of Proverbs, we have, for example:

> Can a man kindle a fire in his bosom
> without setting his clothes alight?
> If a man walks on live coals,
> will his feet not be scorched?
> So is he who commits adultery with his neighbour's wife.[60]

As we have seen,[61] the prophets, similarly, use questions inviting the answer, 'Of course not', to make clear the sheer *unnaturalness* of the people's behaviour, as when Jeremiah asks:

> Will a girl forget her finery
> or a bride her wedding ribbons?
> Yet times without number
> my people have forgotten me.[62]

In one of his oracles, Jeremiah seems to be disclosing a further aspect of what he understood by 'unnatural'; Judah's sins are not simply contrary to normal human behaviour, but contrary to the behaviour enshrined in and upheld by the natural order itself:

> But this people has a rebellious and defiant heart;
> they have rebelled and gone their own way.
> They did not say to themselves,
> 'Let us fear the Lord our God,
> who gives us the rains of the autumn
> and brings showers in their turn,
> and brings us unfailingly,
> fixed harvest seasons.'
> *But your wrong doing has upset nature's order,*
> *and your sins have kept away her bounty.*[63]

---

[60] Prov. 6: 27–9; cf. Job 6: 5, 6; 8: 11.

[61] See p. 95.

[62] Jer. 2: 32; cf. 13: 23; Amos 6: 12; see J. L. Crenshaw, 'Questions, dictons et épreuves impossibles', in *La Sagesse de l'Ancien Testament*, Bibliotheca Ephemeridum Theologicarum Lovaniensium, 51 (1979), 96–111. We find comparable rhetorical questions in *The Instruction of Amenemhet*: 'Have women ever marshaled the ranks? Are brawlers nourished within a house? Are the waters opened up or the earthen banks destroyed?' (i.e. Do men deliberately destroy the irrigation channels?), *LAE* 195.

[63] Jer. 5: 23–5. The primeval covenant with Noah described in Gen. 9: 8–17 is understood to embrace mankind and all living creatures and guarantee stability in

Isaiah, similarly, affirms that to do wrong is to offend against the God-given order of Creation:

> Woe betide those who seek to hide their plans
> too deep for the Lord to see!
> When their deeds are done in the dark
> they say, 'Who sees us? Who knows of us?'
> *How you turn things upside down,*
> as if the potter ranked no higher than the clay!
> Will the thing made say of its maker,
> 'He did not make me'?
> Will the pot say of the potter, 'He has no skill'?[64]

To say that morality has its source and authority in the natural order must mean that it is the product of man's reflection on his experience of the world. The resulting consensus about good and bad behaviour appeals, not to any kind of special revelation, but to moral principles fashioned by rational thought. This is seen very clearly in the so-called 'negative confession' included in the book of Job:

> If I ever rejected the plea of my slave or slave-girl
> when they brought a complaint against me,
> what shall I do if God appears?
> What shall I answer if he intervenes?
> Did not he who made me in the belly make them?
> Did not the same God create us in the womb?[65]

The same insight into the moral significance of the work of the Creator is encapsulated in a saying in Proverbs, which is also found in the school literature of Egypt:

> To oppress the poor is to insult the Creator;
> to be generous to the needy is to do him honour.[66]

The importance which is attached to God's creation of the world in the school tradition should not tempt us into over-

---

the order of creation. Later rabbis elaborated the so-called Noachian precepts, 'the way of all the earth', which applied to non-Jews and represented the Jewish equivalent for the Stoic 'Law of Nature'; see C. H. Dodd, 'Natural law in the Bible', *Theology* (May and June 1946); *New Testament Studies* (1953), 129–42.

[64] Isa. 29: 15, 16; see John Barton, 'Ethics in Isaiah of Jerusalem', *JTS* 32/1 (Apr. 1981), 8–13.   [65] Job 31: 13–15.
[66] Prov. 14: 31; cf. 17: 5; 22: 2; 29: 13; see pp. 50–1; 75.

much theorizing about a quasi-metaphysical relationship between order in the cosmos, order in the political sphere, order in human society, and order in the life of the individual.[67] It is clear that such a concept of the world as being ordered in a sacral unity, expounded in myth and maintained by ritual, was central to the religion of many of Israel's neighbours in the Ancient Near East.[68] But Israel's own understanding was quite different. God was always represented as transcendent over his Creation and not bound up with it, and its order, established by him, was maintained not by ritual but by righteousness. The contrast is well illustrated by Ben Sira's instruction on this theme, celebrating with admirable clarity God's establishment of an orderly universe, which enables man, made in his image, to exercise his capacity for responsible choice:

> When in the beginning the Lord created his works . . .
> he disposed them in an eternal order . . .
> The Lord created human beings from the earth . . .
> and gave them minds with which to think . . .
> Their eyes saw his glorious majesty,
> and their ears heard the glory of his voice.
> He said to them, 'Refrain from all wrongdoing,'
> and he taught each his duty towards his neighbour.[69]

An attentive, moral engagement with other people in ordinary life is the way in which human beings become aware of the wonders of Creation and the way in which they hear the Creator's voice.[70]

The suggestion is sometimes made that the schoolmen consciously invented what is now called 'creation theology', in order to meet a crisis of faith, when sceptics began to question God's just governance of the world. This view, however, seems over-dramatic and fails to recognize that the wonders of Creation had always been a topic in the teaching of the schools. Both in Egypt and in Israel, boys were familiar

---

[67] See Barton, 'Ethics in Isaiah of Jerusalem', 13–17.

[68] Ernest W. Nicholson, 'Israelite Religion in the Pre-Exilic Period', in James D. Martin and Philip R. Davies (eds.), *A Word in Season* (1986), 20–6; Ernest W. Nicholson, *God and His People* (1986), 193–209.

[69] Ecclus. 16: 24–17: 14; cf. 15: 14–16.

[70] Roland E. Murphy, 'Wisdom and Creation', *JBL* 104/1 (1985), 3–11.

with *onomastica*—those orderly lists of all the things which exist—from the time they began to read and write.[71]

It is true, nevertheless, that poems in the book of Job and Ecclesiasticus, exuberantly celebrating the Creator's 'great and unsearchable things, marvels beyond all reckoning',[72] are used to teach men to recognize their finitude and the limitations of their knowledge:

> Listen, Job, to this argument;
> Stop and consider God's wonderful works.
> Do you know how God assigns them their tasks,
> how he sends light flashing from his clouds?
> Do you know how the clouds hang poised overhead,
> as wonderful work of his consummate skill?
> Sweltering there in your stifling clothes,
> when the earth lies sultry under the south wind,
> can you as he does beat out the vault of the skies,
> hard as a mirror of cast metal?[73]

Prescinding the Lord's notorious speech 'from the tempest', which was crudely cobbled together to browbeat poor Job—

> Did you proclaim the rules that govern the heavens,
> or determine the laws of nature on the earth?[74]

we are able to respond spontaneously to the superb poem on the unfathomable wisdom of God in Job 28. The technological skills of men are indeed amazing, but they fall short of being able to control and explain everything:

> Man sets his hand to the granite rock
> and lays bare the roots of the mountains;
> he cuts galleries in the rocks,
> and gems of every kind meet his eye;

[71] *The Instruction for Merikare* (c.2100 BC) has an account of Creation, which includes the idea of man made in God's image: 'Provide for men, the cattle of God, for He made heaven and earth at their desire. He suppressed the greed of the waters, he gave the breath of life to their noses, for they are likenesses of Him which issued from his flesh. He shines in the sky for the benefit of their hearts; He has made herbs, cattle, and fish to nourish them', *LAE* 191; *ANET* 417b.
[72] Job 5: 9; 9: 10; cf. 5: 8–16; 11: 7–9; 38: 1–41: 34; Ecclus. 16: 24–17: 14; 39: 15–35; 42: 15–43: 33.
[73] Job 37: 14–18. [74] Job 38: 33; see pp. 144–5.

he dams up the sources of the streams
and brings the hidden riches of the earth to light.

But where can wisdom be found,
and where is the source of understanding? . . .
God alone understands the way to it,
he alone knows its source;
for he can see to the ends of the earth
and observe every place under heaven.[75]

Ecclesiastes, in a similar vein, asserts unequivocally the limits of human understanding: 'I applied my mind to acquire wisdom . . . and always I perceived that God has so ordered it that no human being should be able to discover what is happening here under the sun. However hard he may try, he will not find out; the wise men may think they know, but they cannot find the truth of it.'[76]

The pessimism of Ecclesiastes is, of course, exceptional, but even the intellectually confident school tradition, which he is criticizing, had always acknowledged that the ways and works of God transcended man's grasp. Our ignorance of what is going to happen tomorrow is a recurrent theme of the Egyptian school literature,[77] and centuries later Ben Sira is found warning his pupils to recognize that there are mysteries they cannot penetrate:

Do not pry into things too hard for you
or investigate what is beyond your reach.
Meditate on what the Lord has commanded;
what he has kept hidden need not concern you.[78]

The idea that we know enough for all practical purposes had already been formulated (characteristically) by the Deuteronomists: 'There are things hidden, and they belong to the Lord our God, but what is revealed belongs to us and our children for ever; it is for us to observe all that is prescribed in this law.'[79] For a less pragmatic and more elevated affirmation of the transcendence of God, we must return to Ben Sira:

[75] Job 28: 9–12, 23, 24.
[76] Eccles. 8: 16, 17; cf. 6: 12; 7: 23–5; 10: 14; Ecclus. 3: 17–24; 16: 20, 21.
[77] See p. 48; cf. Prov. 27: 1.
[78] Ecclus. 3: 21, 22; 17: 30.   [79] Deut. 29: 29.

He who lives for ever is the Creator of the whole universe;
the Lord alone will be proved supreme.
To whom is it given to unfold the story of his works?
Who can fathom his mighty acts?
No one can measure his majestic power, still less tell the full
    tale of his mercies.
They can neither be diminished nor increased,
and the wonders of the Lord cannot be fathomed.
When anyone finishes he is still only beginning,
and when he stops he will still be at a loss.[80]

It is in the context of the school tradition's powerful affirmation of the transcendence of God that we are most likely to make sense of its 'Man proposes, God disposes' dichotomy—revealing the tension between man's freedom to choose and act and God's overall and final control:

The human mind may be full of schemes,
    but it is the Lord's purpose that will prevail.[81]

Since belief in God necessarily involves an acknowledgement of our creaturely finitude and frailty, such language is at one level wholly intelligible. Its weakness, however, is that it fails to safeguard the conviction that our experience of freedom is God-given and authentic and, therefore, his chosen *modus operandi* for fulfilling his purpose.

The schoolmen had another, less theologically treacherous, way of affirming God's transcendence and that was in paeans of praise and thanksgiving:

However much we say, our words will always fall short;
the end of the matter is: God is all.
Where can we find the skill to sing his praises?
For he is greater than all his works . . .
Honour the Lord to the best of your ability,
yet still is he high above all praise.
Summon all your strength to extol him,
and be untiring, for you will always fall short.

Who has seen him, that he can describe him?
Can anyone praise him as he truly is?

---

[80] Ecclus. 18: 1–7.
[81] Prov. 19: 21; see pp. 52–3; 58–9; 117–18.

We have seen but a small part of his works,
and there remain many mysteries greater still.[82]

4. *Final Reflections*

'Religion', Iris Murdoch has written recently, 'is a mode of
belief in the unique sovereign place of goodness or virtue in
human life. One might put it flatly by saying that there is
something about moral value which goes *jusqu'au bout* . . . It
adheres essentially to the conception of being human and
cannot be detached.'[83] Such an understanding is not,
perhaps, true of all religions, but it was realized in Israel by
that remarkable triumph of conscience over cult which was
initiated by a few extraordinary laymen, of whom we know
the names of Amos, Micah, Isaiah, and Jeremiah, with the
evident backing of their old school teachers. Nobody will ever
know what triggered their emergence on the public scene, or
how far they themselves were innovators, but we may be
confident that they owed a great deal to the moral teaching
current in the school tradition and that it was the sympathetic
attitude of the schoolmen which ensured the preservation and
transmission of their oracles. This, of course, is not to ignore
the evidence that after the Exile the school tradition
smothered the burning radicalism of their message in layers
of editorial wrapping and lost touch with them as persons in
a particular historical context.

It is easy to understand the great prophets' rapport with
the school tradition and why, for example, the Deuteronomists took up the cause and work of Jeremiah. For all their
moral fervour, they were pre-eminently humane and rational
men. They dismissed the sacrificial cult as ludicrous. Unlike
the cultic prophets, with whom they are still often mistakenly
associated, they were not frenzied charismatics, exploiting
music to get themselves hyped-up;[84] they did not claim to be
miracle-workers;[85] or powerful professionals in prayer;[86]

---

[82] Ecclus. 43: 27–32; cf. 17: 8, 10; 39: 15, 16; Pss. 8; 33; 104; 147; 148.
[83] Iris Murdoch, *Metaphysics as a Guide to Morals* (1992), 426.
[84] 1 Sam. 10: 5, 6; 19: 19–24; 1 Kgs. 22: 1–12.
[85] 2 Kgs. 2: 12–25; 4: 1–44; 6: 1–23; 13: 14–21; Jer. 21: 1–10.
[86] 1 Kgs. 13: 6; 17: 20–2; 18: 36–9; cf. Jer. 37: 1–10; 42: 1–22.

nor were they diviners or clairvoyants.[87] They were realists,
who saw the life of their society in its true colours and
became involved in a courageous campaign to restore its
human values.

The impressively wide-ranging collection of moral teaching
current in the school tradition, presented characteristically in
the specific detail of proverbs, bears witness to the fact that it
is part of ordinary living to judge between right and wrong
and part of ordinary thinking to believe in objective value. As
Hugh Rice put it in a recent Oxford University Sermon:
'Most people believe that some things are right and others
wrong; most people believe that some things are good and
others bad . . . There is, however, an alternative picture . . .
This is the view that there are in reality *no* truths that this is
good and that is bad; there are no *facts* about good and bad,
no *facts* about right and wrong; the only facts in this vicinity
are facts about people's desires and aversions, likes and
dislikes, loves and hatreds. But this is not the ordinary view
of things. Whatever we say when we philosophize, our
ordinary ways of talking betray us.'[88] Iris Murdoch, who
believes passionately that good is experienced by ordinary
people in ordinary ways, makes the same point: 'The
ordinary person does not, unless he is corrupted by philosophy, believe that he creates values by his choices. He thinks
that some things really are better than others.'[89]

For the school tradition of Israel, the good which human
beings encounter as an objective and transcendent reality,
was not (as for Dame Iris) anything like a Platonic Idea,[90] but
the very being of God—God who is the creator and
continuing source of all that is. Man with his God-given
endowment as a creature naturally tries to make sense of his
environment and the schoolmen taught their pupils to find in

[87] 2 Sam. 12: 14; 2 Kgs. 5: 25–7; 6: 12.
[88] Hugh Rice, 'Ordinary Thinking and Belief in God' (1992).
[89] Iris Murdoch, *The Sovereignty of Good* (1970), 97; cf. Murdoch, *Metaphysics*, 508–9.
[90] Ibid. 508: 'No existing thing could be what we have meant by God. Any existing God would be less than God . . . God does not and cannot exist. But what led us to conceive of him does exist and is *constantly* experienced and pictured. That is, it is real as an Idea, and is *also* incarnate in knowledge and work and love.' Cf. ibid. 428.

the law and order of the universe a manifestation of the character of God as goodness.[91]

Unfortunately, the insight of this understanding of God's presence and influence in the world, inspiring and enabling the achievement of what is good, was never fully developed in the school tradition. It would have provided an alternative to the entrenched belief that God acts directly and particularly in human affairs to uphold righteousness and punish wrongdoing. We find this damaging conviction applied indiscriminately to individuals, as in the psalms and proverbial literature, and to nations, as in the prophetic books and the Deuteronomic history of Israel.

Belief in such divine intervention was so deep-rooted a part of religion in ancient sacral societies that it was wholly indifferent to evidence and survived the fact that it gave rise to so much agonized disappointment. 'If God is able to intervene, why doesn't he?' was the question to which no satisfactory answer was ever forthcoming. Indeed it could hardly be formulated, as long as correct cultic forms (whether in word or ritual action) were held to exercise irresistible power and achieve their ends *ex opere operato*. Although the school tradition was to a large degree independent of this sacral world, it did, nevertheless, encourage the expectation of divine intervention by its understanding of petitionary prayer. Words of Ben Sira illustrate how this practice was a form (albeit a weakened one) of the old way of manipulating the supernatural, or (in personal terms) of bringing pressure to bear on God:

> The prayer of the humble pierces the clouds;
> before it reaches its goal there is no comfort for him.
> He does not desist until the Most High intervenes,
> giving the just their rights and seeing justice done.[92]

Since it is hardly deniable that prayer, in the basic sense of asking God to intervene, does not work, it is surprising and significant that the practice still flourishes. This suggests that there is something in it which is so fundamentally related to

[91] 'As Aquinas was to insist, the work of creation is best seen as the natural overflow of God's goodness', Wiles, *God's Action in the World*, 27.
[92] Ecclus. 35: 17; cf. Prov. 15: 8.

our human condition as to be unaffected by its inefficacy.
The reason seems to be that, whatever the surface meaning of
the words we use, prayer is the means by which we
acknowledge our creatureliness. The purpose of this acknowledgement is to relate ourselves to our human situation and to
enable us to cope with it. Men and women face every kind of
suffering, and prayer, although powerless to change the
empirical circumstances, is a means of changing our response
to them and of reaffirming, in an act of trust, that, despite
everything, the world and our life within in it make sense.
Contrary to what Ecclesiastes thought, our finitude does not
condemn us to futility.

Many reflective people urgently need help to see beyond
the false claims for prayer and related ritual practices which
are still encountered in the life of the Church. This
accommodation to the cultic presuppositions of ancient
paganism (for that is the source of the problem) would have
been avoided if only the Lord's Prayer had been resolutely
upheld as the determinative model: 'Our Father . . . Thy will
be done . . . For Thine is the Kingdom.' This is the beginning
and end of all our prayers and this is the context in which we
may freely, without inhibition and without superstition,
express our gratitude, expose our griefs, and so acknowledge
our finitude.

The last of our final reflections also raises a question about
the practice of the Church. As we have seen, the school
tradition characteristically found its authority in the capacity
of human beings to discern moral norms by the light of
nature. Most Old Testament scholars have shown a lament-
able reluctance to recognize this understanding and some
have rejected it with passionate and dogmatic hostility. Thus,
for example, the widely read teacher W. Eichrodt: 'The
divine will keeps its secret; in its secret hiddenness it remains
impenetrable and does not yield itself to his creatures as the
ground of being which is accessible to the human spirit . . .
This excludes the possibility of deriving the law of one's
being from universal law, or of understanding it as a special
case within the general order . . . Every attempt to spy out
this Lord's plans, and to derive the reasonableness of the
world's laws and the perfection of the lawgiver from the

harmony of the whole world as grasped by the human mind, is bound to come to grief on the absolute lordship of the Creator.'[93]

The error of dismissing or marginalizing this 'natural law' tradition in the Old Testament is suggested by the recognition it is given in the New. The teaching of Jesus often presupposes that human relations, such as those of parent and child, disclose the Creator's pattern for life[94] and, remarkably, it is God's action in Creation which is invoked for what is generally thought of as the most distinctive of all Christian obligations: 'Love your enemies and pray for your persecutors; only so can you be children of your heavenly Father, who causes the sun to rise on good and bad alike, and sends the rain on the innocent and the wicked . . . There must be no limit to your goodness, as your heavenly Father's goodness knows no bounds.'[95]

It is, however, Paul who provides the most explicit exposition of Creation as the source of revelation for all mankind. In the first of two passages in the Epistle to the Romans, he is telling Gentiles how their knowledge of God makes them morally responsible: 'For all that can be known of God lies plain before their eyes; indeed God himself has disclosed it to them. Ever since the world began his invisible attributes . . . have been visible to the eye of reason, in the things he has made. Their conduct, therefore, is indefensible.'[96] In the second passage, Paul is goading his fellow-Jews by calling their attention to good pagans: 'When Gentiles who do not possess the law carry out its precepts by the light of nature, then, although they have no law, they are their own law; they show that what the law requires is inscribed on their hearts, and to this their conscience gives supporting witness.'[97]

If it is accepted that the law of God is, indeed, written on the heart of man by the very fact of his creation by God, the Church must think again about its role as a teacher of morality. There is still a hankering after a Christian ethic

[93] W. Eichrodt, *Man in the Old Testament* (1951), 29, quoted by John Barton, *Understanding Old Testament Ethics*, JSOT (1978), 51.
[94] Matt. 7: 11; Mark 10: 1–9; Luke 12: 57–9.
[95] Matt. 5: 44–8.   [96] Rom. 1: 19, 20.   [97] Rom. 2: 14, 15.

which is distinctive in substance as well as psychological stimulus and a disposition to represent as morally binding what are no more than ecclesiastical inventions and clerical preferences.

The school tradition we have been exploring leaves us in no doubt that, even though moral judgements are fashioned out of individual experience, there is a vital role for moral tradition and moral training. The establishment of a *communis sensus* based on what C. S. Lewis called 'the ultimate platitudes of Practical Reason' was never more needed.[98] If the Church acknowledges the authenticity of moral judgements made outside its membership, it has an obligation to use what influence it has, in co-operation with other institutions (whether religious or not), to achieve an educational system which includes explicit teaching about human behaviour—a *school tradition* in which, as in ancient Israel, you learn how to live, even as you learn how to read and write. 'It is not for us,' wrote my revered father-in-law, C. H. Dodd, as he ended his own Bampton Lectures in America forty years ago, 'to recommend *our* ethic, the Christian ethic as a specialized system characteristic of our community. It is for us to bear witness to what the Gospel declares about the eternal nature of God as revealed in Christ, out of which all moral obligation flows.'[99]

[98] See B. M. Mitchell, 'Is there a Distinctive Christian Ethic?', in William J. Abraham and Robert W. Prevost (eds.), *How to Play Theological Ping-Pong* (1990), 46–51.   [99] C. H. Dodd, *Gospel and Law* (1951), 82–3.

IX

RETROSPECT

It was no part of the purpose of this study to argue the case for the existence of schools in Ancient Israel. From the outset, their work has been taken for granted and the aim has been to demonstrate how it throws new light on much of the literature of the Old Testament and provides an explanation (otherwise missing) of its growth and transmission.

Our exploration of Israel's school tradition started out with tentative criteria and nothing approaching a definition. Instead of declaring at the outset what precisely we were looking for, we adopted the method of reviewing a fairly wide range of Old Testament literature in the hope and expectation that a distinctive stance and style would become evident. There is no escaping the possibility that a pre-conceived notion of the goal influenced the initial choice of texts. If this has exposed us to the risk of arguing in a circle, it has not inhibited the literary evidence from making its own impact; and that is what matters.

The selection of the literature to be reviewed has not, however, been entirely arbitrary. Obviously it began with those works long recognized as being in some degree 'intellectual' and conventionally (but not very usefully) ascribed to a hypothetical 'wisdom tradition'.[1] This selection was then extended to include writings which, though not explicitly 'intellectual', exhibit features reflecting an educated literary background.[2] These are the texts which, in recent years, have come to be represented as the product of an imagined 'Wisdom Movement', thus exacerbating the

---

[1] Proverbs, Job, Ecclesiastes, Ecclesiasticus.

[2] The Story of Adam and Eve, the Story of Joseph, the Story of David, the oracles of Amos, Isaiah, Jeremiah, the Deuteronomists.

methodological confusion on this subject in Old Testament scholarship. To these two groups of texts, others have been added on the (perhaps more subjective) grounds of their general similarity.[3]

From this pragmatic approach, a school tradition has emerged, which, while far from being monochrome and inflexible, notably stands apart from a number of ambitious writings of the post-exilic period, such as the books of Chronicles, Leviticus, and Numbers. The work of the Chronicler, for example, belongs to a different mental universe. Its outlook is dominated by the bustling activities of priests and Levites, whose lives are devoted to the daily cultus and administration of the Temple.[4] This was the very cultic establishment from which the great independent prophets, encouraged by their school teachers, had tried to extricate Israel before the Exile and which now, after the hiatus of the Exile, had been enthusiastically re-founded. All the hallowed superstitions about the Temple as a supernatural power-house were all once again being embraced: 'When Solomon had completed the house of the Lord . . . the Lord appeared to him by night and said: "I have heard your prayer and I have chosen this place to be my house of sacrifice. When I shut up the heavens and there is no rain, or command the locusts to consume the land, or send a pestilence on my people, and then my people . . . submit and pray to me and seek me and turn back from their evil ways, I shall hear from heaven and forgive their sins and restore their land." '[5]

Equally naïve are the Chronicler's statistics: 'King Solomon offered a sacrifice of twenty-two thousand oxen and a hundred and twenty thousand sheep';[6] the figures for Levites are equally fantastic: 'The Levites were enrolled from the age of thirty upwards, their males being thirty-eight thousand in all. Of these, twenty-four thousand were to be responsible for the maintenance and service of the house of the Lord, six thousand to act as officers and magistrates, and four thousand to be door-keepers, and four thousand to praise the Lord with the musical instruments which David had produced

---

[3] The Story of Ruth, the Story of Sodom and Gomorrah, Second Isaiah, Song of Songs.   [4] 2 Chron. 8: 12–14.
[5] 2 Chron. 7: 11–14.   [6] 2 Chron. 7: 5; cf. 1 Chron. 29: 21.

for the service of praise ... They were to be on duty continually before the Lord every morning and evening, giving thanks and praise to him.'[7] The author seems to have shared the Levites' passion for bureaucratic detail and his narrative bristles with lists, registers, and records. The only hint of an intellectually more demanding role is the claim that the Levites accompanied the priests as they went round the towns of Judah teaching the Law[8] and were capable of expounding its meaning: 'They read from the book of the law of God clearly, made its sense plain, and gave instruction in what was read.'[9]

The Law which the Levites taught, to judge by the books of Leviticus and Numbers, was compiled and elaborated in a milieu of considerable professional sophistication. The extra-ordinarily complicated regulations governing the different sacrificial rites and the tortuous ramifications of ritual cleanliness, while not exactly reflecting a liberal education, certainly presuppose a highly specialized form of diagnostic and legal training. For this purpose, there must have been in Ezra's time some kind of Seminary attended by priests and teachers of the Law and, to speculate on the basis of analogies (Ugarit, for example, with its High Priest's library and school), it was almost certainly part of the Temple establishment. The less academic training of the Levites as 'skilled musicians ... secretaries, clerks, or door-keepers'[10] was probably one of the Seminary's subsidiary responsibilities and it is plausible to assume that this is where most of the psalms were composed.

It is widely recognized that many of the psalms, as we now have them in the post-exilic edition of the Psalter, were directly taken over from the liturgical prayers of the pre-exilic Temple, or modelled on them. Most obviously, those which centred on the king, as, for example, when he celebrated his coronation,[11] or his wedding,[12] or offered sacrifice before and after battle,[13] originated in the period of the monarchy. This adds weight to the strong probability that the Temple Seminary was active in some form before the Exile.

[7] 1 Chron. 23: 3–5, 30.   [8] 2 Chron. 17: 7–9.   [9] Neh. 8: 8.
[10] 2 Chron. 34: 13.   [11] Pss. 2; 10.   [12] Ps. 45.
[13] Pss. 18; 20; 44; 72; 89; 132; 144.

There can be no doubt about the pre-exilic origin of the centre of learning and teaching which maintained the non-sacerdotal school tradition, although in recent years scholars have become more critical of the view that it was founded by Solomon himself.[14] It is, indeed, arguable that the idea of a far-reaching 'Solomonic Enlightenment' is based on late and unreliable sources,[15] but there is enough archaeological evidence of the king's enterprise to support the conclusion that he needed a great many administrators and started a school for their training.[16] By the eighth century, at least, this royal establishment had developed into a fully-fledged teaching institution after the Egyptian model. Its continuing vitality after the Exile is demonstrated by the impressive editorial work of the Deuteronomists, the compilation of the books of the prophets, the nurturing of radical critics of the prevailing orthodoxy like the Joban poet and Ecclesiastes, and the remarkably stable tradition of teaching which Ben Sira inherited.

There was a fundamental difference between this school tradition and the instruction of the Seminary. The school tradition was primarily moral and intellectual, whereas the instruction of the Seminary was professionally religious and institutional. The two had different concepts of authority. Whereas the school tradition encouraged men to use their minds and trained them to become conscientious members of the community, the instruction of the Seminary rested on unquestioning obedience to the Law of Moses and its purpose was to keep Israel separate from the world. The school tradition embraced the world, including the whole creation, whereas the instruction of the Seminary was rooted in the nation's past.

---

[14] David W. Jamieson-Drake, *Scribes and Schools in Monarchic Judah* (1991), 11–15, 147–56; A. Lemaire, *Sagesse et écoles*, VT xxxiv 3 (1984), 270–81; R. N. Whybray, 'Wisdom Literature in the Reigns of David and Solomon', in T. Ishida (ed.), *Studies in the Period of David and Solomon* (1982), 13–26.

[15] R. B. Y. Scott, 'Solomon and the Beginnings of Wisdom in Israel', in M. Noth and D. Winton Thomas (eds.), *Wisdom in Israel and in the Ancient Near East*, VT, Supp. iii (1955), 262–79.

[16] E. W. Heaton, *Solomon's New Men* (1974), 66–92. After an interval of twenty years, I should be more cautious in assessing Solomon's achievement, but I still take the view that there is too much smoke to deny the fire.

However, too sharp a distinction between the School and the Seminary would clearly be an over-simplification. First, it must be recognized that over the centuries, as the Law came to dominate and regulate the whole life of post-exilic Judaism, learned and ingenious rabbinic interpreters found ways of escaping the strait-jacket of unqualified obedience and regained a degree of intellectual freedom and individual choice. Second, it must be recognized that the school tradition was broad in its scope and, as we learnt from Ben Sira, provided the intellectual context for a variety of perspectives and concerns. The book of Deuteronomy, for example, reveals a significant relationship between the work of the priests and the school tradition. Before the Exile, the schoolmen of Jerusalem, although detached from the cultic life of the Temple, almost certainly co-operated with the priests in their role as magistrates in the courts, administering civil as well as religious law.[17] One may further speculate that the schoolmen were involved in the transmission of the case-law of these courts, alongside the 'Book of the Covenant',[18] which, eventually, the author of Deuteronomy inherited and expounded in his characteristically humane fashion. The Deuteronomists were also heirs to the tradition of Israel's special status as the Chosen People, but what they transmitted was a version of the covenant reinterpreted in so fundamental a way as to remove its guarantee of security and make it compatible with the moral priorities of the school tradition.

The schoolmen had always been, so to speak, the librarians of Israel—the collectors and guardians of texts. In the post-exilic period, they began to play a new and highly influential role in producing new (and enlarged) editions of the texts in their possession, which had now come to be regarded as 'Scripture'. Their aim was to provide books of moral instruction—a development already discernible in the Deuteronomists' presentation of the history of the kings of Israel and Judah as a story with a moral. Similarly, the oracles of the pre-exilic prophets were edited and amplified

---

[17] Deut. 17: 8–13; 21: 5; 2 Chron. 19: 8–11.
[18] Exod. 20: 24–23: 9.

to provide moral guidance for the present age.[19] Again, it is the Deuteronomists who most clearly illustrate this literary initiative in their edition of Jeremiah. Such re-processed prophetic teaching came to be thought of as a back-up for the all-authoritative Law of Moses and, indeed, 2 Maccabees explicitly represents Jeremiah as appealing to the people 'never to let the law be far away from their hearts'.[20] The literary circle in which this view was held is of some interest, since it produced the story of Judas Maccabaeus and was clearly self-consciously academic: 'These five books of Jason', we read, 'I shall attempt to summarize in a single work; for I was struck by the mass of statistics and the difficulty which the sheer bulk of the material occasions to those wishing to master the narratives of this history. I have tried to provide entertainment for those who peruse for pleasure, an aid for students who must commit the fact to memory, and in general a service to readers. The task which I have taken on myself in making this summary is no easy one; it means hard work and late nights.'[21] This is the language and outlook of Ben Sira's grandson in the preface to his translation of Ecclesiasticus and they are redolent of the school tradition at its most confident and mature.[22]

It is obvious that in one way or another the post-exilic community was responsible for the present form of the whole of the Old Testament and it is equally obvious that we lack the data which would enable us to apportion its books between the different sectors of Jerusalem's educational establishment. The law books, the work of the Chronicler, and most of the psalms we may confidently assign to the Temple Seminary, which was probably increasingly involved in providing instruction and instructors in the Law. Alongside, we have the sector of the educational establishment with which this study has been concerned and which accounts for the impressive continuity and stability of the school tradition from the pre-exilic period to the time of Ben Sira. Within this

---

[19] John Barton, *The Oracles of God* (1986), 156–8: 'There is probably no book in the Latter Prophets that lacks some evidence of this desire of the redactors to show the relevance of older prophets and history to contemporary ethical needs.'

[20] 2 Macc. 2: 3.

[21] 2 Macc. 2: 23–6.

[22] See p. 7.

tradition, it is impossible to propose any further break-down. We do not know whether it represents the teaching and literary activity of more than one type of school, or of different levels and special interests within a single comprehensive establishment. In a period covering two or three hundred years, many permutations and combinations are not only conceivable, but intrinsically probable.

There can, however, be little doubt that together the Temple Seminary and the school tradition have left their stamp on all the books of the Old Testament. In addition to works written in the post-exilic period, all the literature already in the school libraries and received as 'Scripture' was edited and given a more uniform and didactic interpretation. It is probable that this process of redaction involved the virtual elimination of the old Yahwistic theology, which postulated a God who acted and acts in history. He is now thought of as making himself known through man's everyday experience of life in the world he created, regulated by the Law and guided by the Prophets.

It would, however, be too theoretical to claim that the post-exilic schoolmen self-consciously substituted a new 'theology of creation' for the old 'theology of revelation in history'. What they appear to have done is to bring to the surface and articulate the theological convictions which the school tradition had always presupposed. Its moral teaching appealed to the responsibility and equality of men as creatures made in God's image and its intellectual and aesthetic awareness, together with a strong sense of the transcendent, focused attention on the wonder and order of the Creation.

The theology of the school tradition, with its moral and rational stamina, cannot be dismissed as an eccentric development on the margin of Old Testament thought, as the ideas of 'wisdom' books like Job and Ecclesiastes used to be.[23] It may now be seen as transmitting, undergirding, and reinterpreting a major part of Israel's heritage, and this offers a serious challenge to the conventional exposition of what

[23] John Barton, 'Natural Law and Poetic Justice in the Old Testament', *JTS* 30/1 (1979), 8–9.

passes for 'Old Testament theology'. It also offers a fundamental challenge to those versions of Christian theology
which perpetuate Israel's precarious triumphalism by representing the Church as the exclusive recipient and sole
guardian of the truth about God and his world.

CHRONOLOGICAL TABLES

1. *The Literature of Ancient Egypt*

A Table of Approximate Dates

OLD KINGDOM—2695–2160 BC
Dynasties III–VIII   *The Instruction of Ptahhotep*

FIRST INTERMEDIATE PERIOD 2160–1991 BC
Dynasties IX–XI   *Kemyt*
    The Instruction for Merikare
    The Tale of the Eloquent Peasant
    The Man who was Tired of Life
    The Admonitions of an Egyptian Sage

MIDDLE KINGDOM 1991–1785 BC
Dynasty XII   *The Instruction of Amenembet*
    The Prophecy of Neferti
    The Story of Sinuhe
    The Satire on the Trades
    Hymn to the Nile

SECOND INTERMEDIATE PERIOD 1785–1540 BC
Dynasties XIII–XVII

NEW KINGDOM 1540–1070 BC
Dynasties XVIII–XX   *The Instruction of Ani*
    The Instruction of Amen-em-opet
    The Story of Wenamun
    The Satirical Letter of Hori
    The Onomasticon of Amenope
    Love Songs

THIRD INTERMEDIATE PERIOD 1070–712 BC
Dynasties XXI–XXIV

LATE DYNASTIC PERIOD 712–332 BC
Dynasties XXV–XXXI   *The Instruction of*
Onchsheshonqy
Papyrus Insinger

2. *The Literature of the Old Testament*

A Selection with Approximate Dates

BC
1000 David *c.*1000–961
Solomon
*c.*961–922

SOUTHERN KINGDOM	NORTHERN KINGDOM	
	Jeroboam I 922–901	
900		*Proverbs*
800		
Azariah (Uzziah) 783–742		*Amos* *Hosea*
	Jeroboam II 786–746	*Isaiah* *Micah*
	Fall of	
Hezekiah 715–687	Northern Kingdom 721	
700		
Josiah 640–609		*Jeremiah*
600		
Fall of Jerusalem 587		
Exile 587–?		*Second Isaiah* *The Deuteronomists*
500		
Ezra ?397–		
400		*Ruth* *Job* *1 & 2 Chronicles*

Alexander conquers
   Palestine 333
Ptolemies rule Pales-
   tine 325–198

300   *Ecclesiastes*
                           Song of Songs

200 Seleucids rule Pales-
   tine 198–63   *Ecclesiasticus*
                           Tobit

Antiochus Epi-
   phanes 175–163
Desecration of the   *Daniel*
   Temple 167   *Judith*
                           Esther

INDEX OF BIBLICAL REFERENCES

Page numbers refer to the footnotes

OLD TESTAMENT

Genesis
1 : 1–2 : 3 122
1 : 26–31 8
2 : 4–3 : 19 122
2 : 7 122
2 : 9 122, 123
2 : 10–14 122
2 : 19, 20 123
2 : 21, 22 123
3 : 1 123
3 : 5 123
3 : 7 123
3 : 8 62, 122
9 : 8–17 171
9 : 20–4 123
12 : 10–20 119
12 : 11 115
18 : 21–33 165
18 : 23 166
18 : 25 166
20 : 1–18 119
24 : 1–67 121
24 : 12, 27, 40, 42, 48,
    56 121
24 : 16 115
24 : 21 121
24 : 67 121
26 : 7 115
29 : 1–35 121
29 : 17 115, 121
29 : 20 121
30 : 14–17 133
32 : 12 118
37–50 115
37 : 2 117
38 115
38 : 12–30 121
38 : 14 121
39 : 6 115

39 : 7–23 116
39 : 8, 9 116
41 119
41 : 8 2
41 : 46 117
41 : 49 118
42 : 24 119
43 : 2–10 118
43 : 30, 31 119
43 : 32 118
44 : 18–34 118
45 : 1 119
45 : 5, 8 117
45 : 8 58
46 : 8–27 115
46 : 34 118
47 : 25 117
48 115
49 115
50 : 20 58, 117
50 : 22, 26 118

Exodus
4 : 10 43
7 : 11 2
14 : 10–14, 24, 30,
    31 125
14 : 19 110
20 : 24–23 : 9 187
21 : 12, 13 113
23 : 20–3 110
25 : 10–22 110
28 : 3 65
29 : 44–6 109
31 : 3–11 65
32 : 34 110
35 : 31–3 65
35 : 35 65
36 : 8 65

Leviticus
18 : 6–30 123
27 : 30–3 109

Numbers
10 : 9 109
13 : 17–20 124
31 : 6 109
31 : 19, 24 108
31 : 48–54 109

Deuteronomy
1 : 8 108
4 : 1, 40 107
4 : 5, 6 107
4 : 7 112
4 : 25–31 112
4 : 40 108
5 : 10 111
5 : 31 106
6 : 1 106
6 : 4–9 107
6 : 20 106
7 : 1, 2 110
7 : 1–6 108
7 : 7–10 111
7 : 9 111
7 : 17–24 108
7 : 17 106
7 : 25 106
8 : 1 108
8 : 7–19 111
9 : 1–3 108
10 : 1–5 110
10 : 12–19 111
10 : 12 106
10 : 18 114
11 : 1, 13, 22 111
11 : 9 108
11 : 18–20 107

Deuteronomy (cont.):
11 : 22–5 108
12 : 1–19 109
12 : 7, 12 114
12 : 10 108
12 : 11 109
12 : 20–2 109
12 : 31 106
13 : 1, 6 106
13 : 3 111
13 : 14 165
14 : 22–6 109
14 : 23 109
14 : 29 114
15 : 7, 8 114
15 : 12–14, 18 113
16 : 2 109
16 : 11 114
16 : 20 108
17 : 1 106
17 : 4 165
17 : 8–13 187
17 : 14 106
17 : 18, 19 106
18 : 12 106
18 : 21 106
19 : 4, 5 113
19 : 9 111
19 : 10, 14 108
20 : 1–4 109
20 : 14 109
20 : 17 108
20 : 18 106
20 : 19, 20 109
21 : 5 187
21 : 23 108
22 : 5 106
23 : 7 111
23 : 9–14 108
23 : 10 123
23 : 18 106
24 : 4 108
24 : 16 165
24 : 17–21 114
25 : 11, 12 123
25 : 16 106
26 : 1 108
26 : 6–8 110
26 : 11 114
26 : 19 108
27 : 15 106
28 : 10 108
28 : 13 108

28 : 50 114
29 : 29 175
30 : 6–8 112
30 : 6 107
30 : 11–14 113
30 : 15–20 107, 111
30 : 15, 19 21
30 : 16, 20 111
⋯ ⋯ ⋯ ⋯

Joshua
1 : 8 106
6 : 17–19, 24 109
22 : 5 106
23 : 6 106
⋯ ⋯ ⋯

Judges
16 : 13, 14 2

Ruth
1 : 8–14 120
1 : 16, 17 121
2 : 2–16 120
2 : 12 121
3 : 1–6 120
3 : 7, 8 121

1 Samuel
4 : 4 110
10 : 5, 6 177
15 : 22 96
17 : 4–51 58
17 : 42 115
19 : 19–24 177
21 : 3–6 108

2 Samuel
1 : 17, 18 37
6 : 2 110
8 : 15–18 33
9 : 1–20 : 26 126
9 : 5–13 127
10 : 1–11 : 1 126
11 : 1–27 126, 129
11 : 2 60, 115
11 : 18, 19 129
11 : 25 130
12 : 14 178
12 : 26–31 126
13 : 1–22 126
13 : 1–19 130
13 : 1 115
13 : 3, 32, 33 127

13 : 18, 19 127
13 : 23–9 126
14 : 1–20 127
14 : 25–7 128
14 : 25, 27 115
15 : 1–6 128
15 : 10, 13, 36 129
16 : 5–14 127
16 : 20–2 126
16 : 20–17 : 14 128
17 : 1–14 129
17 : 11 118
17 : 17–22 128, 129
17 : 23 129
18 : 9–17 126
18 : 19–33 130
18 : 19–30 127
19 : 3 128
19 : 11 129
19 : 18–23 127
19 : 24–30 127
19 : 31–40 127
20 : 8–22 126
20 : 14–22 127
20 : 23–6 33

1 Kings
1 : 1–2 : 46 126
1 : 4, 6 115
2 : 3 106
2 : 13–46 126
2 : 46 126
3 : 1 35
4 : 1–6 33
4 : 20, 29 118
4 : 29–34 66
4 : 29–33 131
4 : 32 132
7 : 14 65
8 : 27–30 110
8 : 33, 34, 46–53 112
9 : 3 109
9 : 27 65
10 : 1–10 132
11 : 36 109
11 : 41 66
13 : 6 177
14 : 19 37
14 : 29 37
16 : 14 37
17 : 20–2 177
18 : 36–9 177
22 : 1–12 177

2 Kings
2 : 12–25 177
4 : 1–44 177
5 : 25–7 178
6 : 1–23 177
6 : 12 178
10 : 31 106
13 : 14–21 177
17 : 13 106
18 : 17–37 34
18 : 24 35
19 : 15 110
21 : 4 109
22 : 1–23 : 25 109
25 : 26 35
25 : 27–30 119

1 Chronicles
22 : 15 65
23 : 3–5, 30 185
29 : 21 184

2 Chronicles
7 : 5 184
7 : 11–14 184
8 : 12–14 184
17 : 7–9 41, 185
19 : 8–11 187
20 : 1–23 126
29 : 34 41
33 : 12, 13 165
34 : 12, 13 41
34 : 13 185
35 : 3 41
35 : 21–4 165
35 : 25 37

Ezra
7 : 6, 10 41
9 : 1–10 : 44 108

Nehemiah
8 : 7–12 41
8 : 8 185

Esther
1 : 13 2

Job
1 : 1–2 : 13 151
1 : 1, 8 83
2 : 7, 8 139

3 : 3, 11, 13, 20,
    22 148
4 : 3, 4 140
4 : 7–9 166
4 : 7, 8 149
4 : 17 149
5 : 8–16 149, 150, 174
5 : 9 174
5 : 17–27 151
5 : 19–22 88
6 : 5, 6 171
7 : 5 139
7 : 13, 14, 20 139
8 : 1–7, 8–19 151
8 : 2 145
8 : 8–10 93
8 : 11 94, 101, 171
8 : 20 149
9 : 4–10 150
9 : 10 174
9 : 15, 16 152
9 : 19, 20, 22 152
9 : 23, 24 139
9 : 32–5 164
9 : 32, 33 152
10 : 1 139
10 : 3, 8, 12, 13,
    14 139
10 : 18, 19 148
11 : 2, 3 145, 149
11 : 7–11 147, 149
11 : 7–9 149, 174
11 : 14–20 149
12 : 7–9 95
12 : 10–25 139
12 : 13–23 149
13 : 3, 4 153
14 : 17 139
15 : 1–16, 17–35 151
15 : 2 145
15 : 7, 8 90
15 : 7–9 91
15 : 17, 18 93
15 : 17–35 149
15 : 27–33 140
16 : 21 152, 164
18 : 2, 5–21 150
18 : 5–21 149
19 : 17 139
20 : 1–3, 4–29 151
20 : 3 145
20 : 4, 5 166
20 : 4–29 149

20 : 15, 19–21 140
21 : 7–15 139
21 : 27–34 140
22 : 4, 5, 29 149
22 : 5 145
23 : 3–5 152
23 : 6 145
24 : 2, 3, 9, 4, 12 138
25 : 2–6 149
26 : 12 66
27 : 5, 6 145
27 : 7–23 149
27 : 16 140
28 : 9–12, 23, 24 175
28 : 23–8 66
29 : 2–10, 21, 22, 24,
    25, 16, 17 140
30 : 1, 9–11, 15, 19 141
30 : 17, 18, 30 139
30 : 20 152
31 : 1–23, 31, 32 140
31 : 5–40 143
31 : 13–15 172
31 : 35, 36 33
31 : 35, 37, 40 143
32–7 143, 159
32 : 2, 3 159
32 : 8 160
33 : 3, 4 160
33 : 5–7 160
33 : 8–12 143
33 : 12 162
33 : 15–25 162
33 : 26–30 162
33 : 31–3 66
33 : 32 160
34 : 4 159
34 : 5–9 143
34 : 7–9, 37 143
34 : 7 143
34 : 10, 11 161
34 : 13–15 160
34 : 17–19 161
34 : 17 138
34 : 21, 22 19, 79
34 : 24 162
34 : 25, 26 161
34 : 37 143
35 : 2–4 143
35 : 8 162
35 : 10, 11 160
35 : 14 143
35 : 16 143

Job (cont.):
36 : 3   143
36 : 3, 4   159
36 : 5, 6   161
36 : 15   162
36 : 22   161
36 : 24–6   162
36 : 26   152
36 : 27, 28, 31   161
37 : 5–8   161
37 : 11–13   161
37 : 14–18   174
37 : 16   66
37 : 19, 21–4   163
37 : 20   162
37 : 23   147
38 : 1   144
38 : 1–41 : 6   151
38 : 1–41 : 34   174
38 : 2–5, 12, 18,
      33   144
38 : 3   61
38 : 4, 5   144
38 : 33   174
38 : 36, 37   66
39 : 13–18   142
40 : 6–34   151
40 : 15–24   142
41 : 1–34   142
42 : 2, 3, 5, 6   143, 151
42 : 7–17   151

Psalms
1   166
2   185
8   177
10   166, 185
14   166
16 : 11   162
17 : 15   162
18   185
20   185
33   177
33 : 13–15   79
34   166
34 : 8   166
37   166
37 : 11, 22, 29, 34   108
37 : 25   163, 167
40 : 6–8   96
44   185
45   185
46   110

46 : 4   109
48   110
49   166
50 : 7–15, 23   96
51 : 15–17   96
53   166
58 : 5   65
62 : 11, 12   88
72   185
73   166
73 : 4, 7, 8, 11, 16,
      17   167
73 : 21–3, 25   167
73 : 23–8   162
80 : 1   110
89   185
102 : 18   37
104   89, 177
104 : 1–4   103
104 : 24   57, 66
107 : 26, 27   65
111 : 10   83
112   166
112 : 1   166
117   103
127 : 5   166
132   185
132 : 13, 14   109
137 : 9   120
139 : 1–4   79
141 : 5   120
144   185
147   177
148   89, 177
148 : 1–13   144

Proverbs
1 : 1–9 : 18   87
1 : 1–6   67, 107
1 : 1   131
1 : 7   83
1 : 8   106
1 : 9   107
2 : 1   106
2 : 19   107
2 : 21   108
3 : 1   106
3 : 1, 4   78
3 : 3   107
3 : 5   68
3 : 7   95
3 : 13–18   107
3 : 13   166

3 : 19–20   66
3 : 32   106
4 : 1–4, 10–13   106
4 : 1, 2   86
4 : 6, 8   78
5 : 6   107
5 : 13   42, 66
5 : 14   42, 78
5 : 21   78
6 : 1–5   73
6 : 6   95
6 : 16–19   88
6 : 20–35   69
6 : 20–3   106
6 : 20–2   107
6 : 23   107
6 : 27–9   94, 171
6 : 27, 28   101
6 : 32–5   78
7 : 1–3   107
7 : 2   106
7 : 6–27   69
7 : 6–23   121
8 : 1–11   90
8 : 12–21   90
8 : 22–31   68, 90
8 : 32   166
8 : 33   66
9 : 9   66
9 : 10   83
9 : 13–18   69
10 : 1   131
10 : 3   82, 149
10 : 7, 24   82
10 : 11   82, 107
10 : 15   73
10 : 17   107
10 : 19   80
10 : 28   82
10 : 30   108, 163
11 : 1   68, 106
11 : 5   82
11 : 10, 11   82
11 : 13   79
11 : 15   73
11 : 20   106
11 : 21   163
12 : 9   85
12 : 10   82
112 : 15   81
12 : 16   79, 80, 119
12 : 21   163
12 : 22   106

12 : 23 79, 123
12 : 25 71
13 : 3 80
13 : 11 72
13 : 12 71
13 : 16 79, 81, 123
13 : 21, 25 163
14 : 2 83
14 : 4 84
14 : 8, 15, 8 123
14 : 10 71
14 : 11 82, 163
14 : 13 71
14 : 17, 29 80
14 : 20 77
14 : 21 75
14 : 23 84
14 : 30 71
14 : 31 68, 75, 172
14 : 35 67
15 : 2 81
15 : 3 78
15 : 8 68, 96, 106, 179
15 : 9, 26 106
15 : 11 78
15 : 13, 30 71
15 : 20 76
15 : 22 83
15 : 24 107
15 : 25 75, 149
15 : 29 68
15 : 33 68, 83
16 : 1, 9, 33 83
16 : 2, 11 68
16 : 3, 6, 20 68, 83
16 : 5 106
16 : 6 83
16 : 9 53, 118
16 : 10, 12–15 67
16 : 23 42
16 : 24 71
16 : 27, 28 79
16 : 28 77
16 : 32 80
16 : 33 68
17 : 3 68
17 : 5 68, 75, 172
17 : 15 106
17 : 18 73
17 : 22 71
17 : 27 80
18 : 2 81
18 : 8 79

18 : 11 73
18 : 12 68
18 : 14 71
18 : 16 67
18 : 20, 21 42
19 : 4, 6, 7 77
19 : 12 67
19 : 13 76
19 : 17 75
19 : 20 66
19 : 21 48, 53, 68, 83, 94, 118, 176
19 : 26 76
20 : 1 70
20 : 2, 8, 26, 28 67
20 : 3 80
20 : 6 77
20 : 9, 10, 23 68
20 : 10, 23 106
20 : 16 73
20 : 17 84
20 : 19 79
20 : 21 72, 98
20 : 22 77
20 : 24 53, 68, 83, 118
20 : 25 68
20 : 27 78
21 : 1 67
21 : 2 68
21 : 3 68, 96
21 : 27 68
21 : 6 98
21 : 9, 19 76
21 : 13 75
21 : 20 73
21 : 23 79
21 : 25, 26 82
21 : 27 96, 106
21 : 30 83
21 : 31 53, 83
22 : 1 78
22 : 2 172
22 : 3 79, 123
22 : 9 75, 114
22 : 17–24 : 22 87
22 : 17–23 : 14 51
22 : 17 42, 66
22 : 18 42
22 : 19 68
22 : 22, 23, 28 75
22 : 26, 27 73
22 : 28 50
22 : 29 51

23 : 1–3 72
23 : 4, 5 72
23 : 9 81
23 : 10, 11 75
23 : 13, 14 120
23 : 19–21 70
23 : 22, 25 76
23 : 26–8 69
23 : 29–35 71
24 : 3, 4 73
24 : 7 42
24 : 11, 12 75
24 : 12 78
24 : 17 77, 120
24 : 18 77
24 : 29 19, 77
25 : 1 38, 66, 131
25 : 4, 5, 15 67
25 : 6, 7 67
25 : 8–10 79
25 : 13 84
25 : 15 84
25 : 19 83
25 : 21, 22 77
25 : 23 84
25 : 24 76
25 : 25 84
26 : 4, 5 86
26 : 7 81
26 : 12 95
26 : 20–2 77
26 : 20 84
26 : 23 84
26 : 27 85
27 : 1 48, 175
27 : 7 84
27 : 12 123
27 : 15 76
27 : 22, 25–7 73
28 : 9 68
28 : 12, 28 82
28 : 14 166
28 : 20 72
28 : 27 114
29 : 2 82
29 : 3 69
29 : 4, 14 67
29 : 7 82
29 : 11 80
29 : 13 172
29 : 16 82
29 : 25 68
29 : 26 53, 68

Proverbs (*cont.*):
30 : 1–4 144
30 : 4 101
30 : 15, 16, 18, 19,
    21–3, 29–31 88
30 : 17 76
30 : 18, 19 85
30 : 20 69
30 : 24–8 88, 95
31 : 4, 5 70
31 : 4–9 87
31 : 8, 9 75
31 : 10–31 76

Ecclesiastes
1 : 1, 12, 13, 16 66, 131
1 : 2 153
1 : 5–8 154
1 : 8 154
1 : 12–2 : 26 154
1 : 13 155
2 : 1–11 153
2 : 12–17 153
2 : 12–16 155
2 : 17 154
2 : 20–3 153
2 : 24, 25 156
3 : 1–8 155
3 : 12, 13 156
3 : 19–20 153, 155
4 : 1 157
· 4 : 4 153, 155
4 : 7, 8 153
4 : 15 155
5 : 1, 2 155
5 : 8 157
5 : 10 153, 155
5 : 11 153
5 : 18–20 156
6 : 7 155
6 : 10 157
6 : 12 157, 175
7 : 2 155
7 : 14 157
7 : 15 153
7 : 23–5 175
7 : 24 157
7 : 25 155, 157
8 : 8 155
8 : 9 155
8 : 14 153, 156
8 : 15 156
8 : 16, 17 157, 175

9 : 1 157
9 : 3 153, 155
9 : 7–9 156
9 : 11, 12 156
9 : 13–16 155
10 : 14 157, 175
11 : 8, 9 156
11 : 15 157
12 : 8 153
12 : 9–11 154
12 : 9, 10 84

The Song of Songs
1 : 1 66, 131
1 : 4, 12 132
2 : 1–6 63
2 : 5 63
2 : 9 63
2 : 10–13 133
3 : 4 63
4 : 1–7 134
4 : 1–5 135
4 : 9–12 63
4 : 9, 13, 14, 12 134
4 : 12–5 : 1 62
5 : 1 63
5 : 2–7 63
5 : 8 63
5 : 10–16 134, 136
5 : 11, 14 63
6 : 2, 3 134
6 : 2, 3, 11, 12 62
6 : 4–7 134
6 : 8, 9 132
6 : 10 63
6 : 11, 12 134
7 : 1–7 134
7 : 3 63
7 : 10–13 133
8 : 1, 2 63
8 : 7 64
8 : 11, 12 132
8 : 14 63

Isaiah
1–12 93
1 : 2, 3 95
1 : 2,–9, 10–17, 18–20,
    21–6 111
1 : 10 106
1 : 10–17 96, 98
2 : 12–17 95

3 : 1–5 99
3 : 16, 17 95
3 : 16–4 : 1 98
5 : 11–17, 22 98
5 : 19 19, 98
5 : 20 98
5 : 21 3, 95, 98
5 : 24 106
7 : 3–9 95
7 : 4, 9 95
8 : 5–8 95
8 : 16, 20 106
9 : 8–10 95
9 : 9–10 98
10 : 12–14 95
10 : 15 95
13–23 93
14 : 24 94
14 : 27 94
14 : 32 110
16 : 13, 14 39
18 : 4–6 95
19 : 11 2, 91
19 : 12 2
20 : 1–6 95
20 : 4 123
22 : 8b–14 95, 111
22 : 12–14 98
22 : 15–19 95, 98
24–35 93
28 : 1–13 98
28 : 14–22 95, 111
28 : 16 95
28 : 23–9 94
28 : 24–6 94
28 : 29 94
29 : 11, 12 33
29 : 14 3
29 : 15 19, 98, 172
29 : 16 95, 98, 104,
    172
30 : 1–5 95
30 : 1, 2 35
30 : 9 106
30 : 15 95
31 : 1–3 95
31 : 1 35
31 : 4, 5 110
32 :,9–14 98
40–55 103
40 : 12–31 103
40 : 12–17, 18–26,
    27–31 104

40 : 12–14 104
40 : 12 61
40 : 13, 14, 28 66
40 : 20 65
41 : 1–5, 21–9 103
41 : 8–13, 14–16 103
42 : 5, 10–13 103
43 : 1–4, 5–7 103
43 : 8–13 103
43 : 22–4 96
44 : 1–5 103
44 : 9 105
44 : 18–20 105
44 : 23 103
45 : 9–13 104
45 : 18, 19 103
45 : 20–5 103
49 : 13 103
55 : 8–11 103, 104

Jeremiah
1 : 1–25 : 14 93
1 : 6 43
2 : 32 94, 171
3 : 2–5 102
5 : 7–9 102
5 : 23–5 171
5 : 30, 31 102
6 : 19–21 96
6 : 19 106
7 : 1–15 102
7 : 1–8 : 3 103
7 : 6 114
7 : 21–3 96
8 : 4 94
8 : 7 95
8 : 8 3
8 : 10, 11 102
9 : 3 102
9 : 5, 6 102
9 : 12–16 103
9 : 23 3
10 : 9 65
10 : 12 66
11 : 1–14 103
11 : 15 96
11 : 18–12 : 6 101
11 : 21–3 103
12 : 1 164
13 : 23 94, 171
14 : 11–16 103
15 : 10–21 101
16 : 1–18 103

17 : 7–8 166
17 : 14–18 101
17 : 19–27 103
18 : 1–6 104
18 : 13–16 99
18 : 14 94
18 : 18–23 101
18 : 18 3
19 : 1–20 : 6 103
20 : 7–11, 14–18 101
20 : 7–9 101
21 : 1–10 177
22 : 3 114
22 : 8, 9 103
22 : 13–16 102
23 : 9–14 102
24 : 1–10 103
25 : 15–38 93
26–35 93
26 : 1–24 103
26 : 24 103
29 : 1–32 103
31 : 29, 30 165
31 : 31–4 112
36 : 1–32 103
36 : 22, 23 36
36 : 32 36
37 : 1–10 177
37 : 11–21 103
38 : 1–13 103
38 : 14–23 103
39 : 11–14 103
40 : 1–6 103, 119
42 : 1–22 177
45 : 1–5 103
46–51 93
50 : 35 2
51 : 15 66
51 : 57 2
51 : 60–4 33

Lamentations
5 : 7 165

Ezekiel
1–24 93
8 : 12 164
9 : 9 164
18 : 1–32 165
18 : 2 165
18 : 4 165
18 : 7, 8 165
18 : 25, 29 165

25–32 93
27 : 8, 9 65
33–48 93
33 : 17–20 165
37 : 15–20 33

Daniel
1 : 4 115
2 119

Hosea
1 : 7 101
2 : 11 96
4 : 2, 6 101
4 : 15 101
5 : 6 96
6 : 6 96
6 : 11 101
7 : 11 35
8 : 1, 12 101
8 : 13 35, 96
9 : 3–6 35
11 : 12 101
12 : 2 101
14 : 9 101

Amos
1 : 6–2 : 16 100
1 : 13 100
2 : 1 100
3 : 1–8 101
3 : 2 110
4 : 1, 2 100
4 : 4, 5 96
5 : 21–4 96, 97
6 : 12 99, 101, 171
7 : 1–9 100
7 : 8 101
7 : 14, 15 100
8 : 1, 2 101
8 : 1–3 100

Micah
3 : 9–12 111
3 : 12 96
6 : 6–8 96, 112

Nahum
3 : 5 123

Habakkuk
1 : 2, 13 164
2 : 2 33

Zephaniah
1 : 12 19, 164

Malachi
2 : 17 164

APOCRYPHA

Tobit
1 : 21, 22 120
2 : 10 120
11 : 18 120
14 : 10 120

Judith
9 : 5 94

Wisdom of Solomon
16 : 24 169

Ecclesiasticus
1 : 11–20 83
1 : 23, 24 20
1 : 26 16
1 : 30 78
2 : 1–5 151
2 : 10–14 18
2 : 10 68, 168
2 : 15–18 68
3 : 2, 3 76
3 : 17–24 175
3 : 21–4 18, 20
3 : 21, 22 175
4 : 1, 4–6 75
4 : 23, 24 11
4 : 24 42
4 : 26 120
4 : 30 14
5 : 1–6 19
5 : 3, 4 168
5 : 10–13 12
5 : 13 78
5 : 14 79
6 : 2 80
6 : 7–17 77
6 : 7 52, 79
6 : 9 78
6 : 11 14
6 : 23, 24 86
6 : 32, 33 9
7 : 7 16
7 : 11 75
7 : 15 14, 73
7 : 19, 27, 28 76

7 : 20, 21 77
7 : 32 75
8 : 8, 9 9
8 : 11 80
8 : 16 80
8 : 19 13
9 : 3–9 69
9 : 8 11, 120
9 : 14, 15 17
9 : 17 73
9 : 18 13, 79
10 : 4 20
10 : 4, 5 68
10 : 26 15
11 : 1 78
11 : 4 14
11 : 9 79
11 : 10 73
11 : 12, 13 78
11 : 19 48
11 : 20, 21 14
11 : 23, 24 19
11 : 34 18
13 : 1 84
13 : 2 15
13 : 9–11 15, 47, 72
13 : 25 71
13 : 26 84
14 : 11–15 74
14 : 20 8
15 : 1 17
15 : 5 11, 42, 78
15 : 6 78
15 : 11, 12 19
15 : 14–16 173
15 : 14 170
15 : 16 21
15 : 18 79
15 : 19 19, 79
16 : 5 10
16 : 12, 13 168
16 : 17–23 19
16 : 20, 21 157, 175
16 : 22 168
16 : 23 8
16 : 24–30 68
16 : 24–17 : 14 20, 173, 174
17 : 1–7 8
17 : 1, 3, 6, 7 169
17 : 8, 10 177
17 : 15–20 19, 79
17 : 30 175

18 : 1–7 176
18 : 19 14
18 : 29 11, 84
18 : 32 74
19 : 2 70
19 : 2, 3 69
19 : 4 8
19 : 5–17 79
19 : 6–12 13
19 : 12 84
19 : 23–5 83
19 : 24 17
19 : 29, 30 10
20 : 5 85
20 : 6 13
20 : 7 13, 20, 79
20 : 13, 20 81
20 : 18 12
20 : 19 13
20 : 20 13
20 : 22, 26 78
21 : 11 17
21 : 13, 14 81
21 : 15 84
21 : 16 81
21 : 17 42
21 : 18 85
21 : 20, 22, 23 14
21 : 26 13
21 : 28 13, 79
22 : 7, 8 81
22 : 15 85
22 : 17 8
22 : 19–26 77
22 : 27–23 : 6 68
22 : 27–23 : 1 12
23 : 3 78
23 : 16–27 69
23 : 16–18 88
23 : 18 19
23 : 19 79
23 : 22, 23 17
23 : 24 43
24 : 1–6 90
24 : 23 17
25 : 1 76, 88
25 : 2 68, 88
25 : 7–11 88
25 : 9 11
26 : 1–4, 13–18 76
26 : 5–8, 28 88
26 : 9 10
26 : 16–18 136

26 : 16, 17 11
26 : 19–27 69
26 : 29–27 : 2 73
27 : 4–7 86
27 : 4, 5 12
27 : 16, 17 77
28 : 8 80
28 : 13–26 79
28 : 17 84
28 : 24–6 14
29 : 8, 9 75
29 : 20 79
29 : 23–7 15
30 : 3 16
30 : 23 74
31 : 1, 2 71
31 : 12–32 : 13 15
31 : 12–21 72
31 : 25–9 70
31 : 31 78
32 : 4–6 136
32 : 4 13
32 : 8 80
32 : 23 18
33 : 3 16
33 : 5 81
33 : 7–15 22
33 : 10–13 68
33 : 13 51
33 : 15 20
33 : 16 9
33 : 19–23 14
33 : 30, 31 14
34 : 1–5 9
34 : 9–12 10
34 : 13–17 68
34 : 19 96
34 : 20 85, 96
35 : 14–16 75
35 : 17 179
36 : 1–17 18
36 : 21–6 76
37 : 1–6 77
37 : 12–15 18
38 : 1–15 14
38 : 1–8 88
38 : 3 78
38 : 6–8 169
38 : 24–34 14, 55

38 : 31, 33 43
39 : 1–4 10
39 : 2, 3 67
39 : 12–21 68
39 : 15–35 174
39 : 15, 16 177
39 : 16–35 20
39 : 16–21 20
39 : 17 20, 154
39 : 19 19
39 : 21, 34 154
39 : 25–7 169
39 : 26, 27 22
39 : 28–31 169
39 : 32–4 168
40 : 18 14
40 : 22 11
41 : 1–4 22
41 : 8 18
41 : 14–42 : 8 78
41 : 18 43
42 : 8 78
42 : 9, 10 71
42 : 11 78
42 : 15–43 : 33 20, 89, 174
42 : 22 11
42 : 23–5 20
43 : 1–26 144
43 : 11, 17, 18 11
43 : 27–32 177
43 : 27 23
44 : 19 16
45 : 1 16
45 : 6–14 10
47 : 14–17 66
47 : 23 8
50 : 5–10 136
50 : 25, 26 88
50 : 27–9 6
51 : 23 1

Song of the Three
35–60 144

1 Maccabees
2 : 49–68 18
14 : 32 1

2 Maccabees
2 : 3 188
2 : 13, 14 37
2 : 23–6 188
15 : 9 40

NEW TESTAMENT
Matthew
5 : 17 40
5 : 44–8 181
6 : 34 48
7 : 11 181
7 : 12 40
25 : 40 75

Mark
10 : 1–9 181

Luke
12 : 57–9 181
16 : 1–8 74

John
1 : 1–14 91

Acts
13 : 15 40

Romans
1 : 19, 20 181
2 : 14, 15 181
9 : 21 51

1 Corinthians
1 : 24, 30 91

Colossians
1 : 15–17 91
2 : 3 91

Hebrews
1 : 3 91

Revelation
3 : 18 123
4 : 11 91
22 : 13 91

INDEX OF SUBJECTS

abomination 106, 118
Abraham 16, 119, 166
Absalom 126–8, 130
Achilles 127
acrostic poem 76, 141, 166
Adam and Eve 122–3
Adonijah 126
aesthetic appreciation 10–11
agriculture, see farming
Agur, Sayings of 144 n.
Ahimaaz 127, 130
Ahikar, Story of 119–20
Ahithophel 128–9
Akhenaten 57
Akkadian 26, 28
alcohol 70–1, 87
allegorical interpretation 132–3
'all-seeing' God 20, 78–9
Amarna Letters 28
Amasa 126
Amenemhet I 55, 57, 60
Amnon 126, 130
Amos 38, 99–101
Amun 35, 59, 124–5
Anaximander 21, 22 n.
ankh emblem 122
Antiochus Epiphanes 18
Aramaic 34, 119
aretalogy 17, 89–91
Ashurbanipal 27, 38
Assyrian army 34
Assyrian proverb 12

Babylonian literature:
  Babylonian Chronicle 27
  Babylonian Theodicy 27, 141–2,
    146–7
  Counsels of Wisdom 12 n.
  Creation Epic 27
  Epic of Gilgamesh 27
  Poem of the Righteous Sufferer 141,
    146, 164

banquets 15, 47, 71–2, 131–2, 136
Baruch 36
Barzillai 127
Bata 116
Bathsheba 126, 129
beauty 10–11, 115 n., 128, 134–6
Benjamin 115, 118
Ben Sira 6–23, 38, 43, 52 n., 67–92,
    167–170, 175–7
Bildad 149–50
Boaz 120–1
bureaucracy 13, 28–9, 99 n.
Byblos, prince of 35, 59, 63

Canaanite culture 109, 179
canon of scripture 40–1
caution 15, 49, 52, 55–6, 72, 77,
    79–80, 155
Chosen People:
  Holy Land 107–8
  holy war 108–9, 125–6
  Zionism 110–12
  see also covenant
christology 91
Chronicler, work of 37, 126, 165,
    184–5
colophon 6, 154
'Comforters', see Job
commerce 73
common sense 170–1
'counsel' of God 94–5
covenant 110–12, 187
creation:
  of man 8, 50, 75, 122, 160, 169–70,
    172, 174 n., 189
  of the universe 19–21, 56–7, 61,
    65–6, 68, 88–91, 103–4, 144, 169,
    173–5, 189
  see also nature and order; *onomastica*
cult 5, 96–8, 112, 177, 184
cuneiform 24–5
Cyrus 104

Daniel, book of 18, 41, 60, 119
David 37
  and Goliath 58
  story of 126–31
Dead Sea scrolls 37
death 22, 49, 155–6
Deir el-Medina 29
Deuteronomic literature 105–14
  demythologizing 108–10
  edition of Jeremiah 103
  reinterpretation of law 113
dialogue 118, 120
divination 8–9, 111
divine intervention 150, 160–4, 168–9,
  170 n., 179, 189
  see also retribution; theodicy
documents, storage of 37
dramatic irony 129–31
dreams 8–9

Ebla 24–5
Ecclesiastes 4, 80, 153–8, 164
Ecclesiasticus, Greek translation of 7
  see also Ben Sira
Eden 62, 122
editing 38–40, 85–6, 93–4, 142–4,
  151, 187–9
Edom, king of 100
education, see schools
Egypt:
  schools 28–30
  imperial policy 34–5
  see also Egyptian literature; morality
Egyptian literature:
  Admonitions of an Egyptian Sage
    99 n., 138 n., 141, 148 n.
  Book of the Dead 143
  Hymn to the Aten 56–7
  Hymn to the Nile 55–6
  Instruction of Ani 13, 19 n., 29, 35,
    49, 70, 76, 121–2
  Instruction of Amenemhet 55,
    126 n., 171 n.
  Instruction of Amen-em-opet 6,
    19 n., 48 n., 50–2, 53 n., 72,
    74, 77, 80, 106 n., 117, 166 n.
  Instruction for Merikare 9, 42, 68 n.,
    74, 96, 174 n.
  Instruction of Onchsheshonqy 52–4
  Instruction of Ptahhotep 9 n., 12,
    42, 46–8, 53 n., 69, 72, 80 n.,
    118 n.
  Kemyt 54

Lamentations of Khakheperre-sonbe
  81 n.
Love Songs 62–4
Man who was Tired of Life 147–8
Onomasticon of Amenope 89
Papyrus Anasti 96 n.
Papyrus Insinger 52 n.
Prophecy of Neferti 42, 60,
  99n., 126 n.
Satire on the Trades 14, 54–5, 81
Satirical Letter of Hori 60–1, 124,
  144–5
Story of Sinuhe 57–9, 115–16,
  126 n.
Story of Wenamun 59–60, 63
Tale of the Eloquent Peasant 48, 128
Tale of the Two Brothers 116
Elephantine 119
Elihu 143–4, 159–63
  see also Job
Eliphaz 150–1
enemies, love of 76–7
entertainment 62–3, 127, 131–6, 188
Epicureans 19
Esther, book of 119
examinations 26, 61, 144
exegesis, 'inner-biblical' 39
Exile in Babylon 119
Exodus from Egypt 124–5
Ezekiel, book of 33, 93, 165
Ezra 41, 185

family life, see marriage
farming 14, 73
festivals 114
finitude of man 158, 174–6, 180
fool, the 80–1
foreign travel 10

gardens 62, 122, 134
Genesis, book of 121–3
Gentiles 181
God's action, see divine intervention
goodness 102, 147, 157–8, 164, 168,
  177–9
  see also theodicy
Greece 41–4, 92
  see also Hellenism

Habakkuk 33
Hellenism 18–23
Heraclitus 21
Hezekiah 34

high priest 136 n.
Hiram, worker in bronze 65
historiography 124–6
Holy Land, *see* Chosen People
Holy Scripture, canon of 40–1
holy war, *see* Chosen People
homicide, law of 113
Hosea 101 n.
'House of Life' 37, 89
Hushai 128–9

idols 105
ignorance of man 48, 144, 157, 162–3, 175
Iliad and *Odyssey* 32
individualism 77, 155, 158, 165
instruction (literary genre) 45–6, 86–8, 154
    see also Egyptian literature
interior life 71
Isaac 121
Isaiah 32–3, 35, 39, 93–9
Isis 17, 89–91
Isocrates 30, 43–4

Jacob 121
Jashar, book of 37
Jason, books of 188
Jehoiachin 119
Jehudi 36
Jeremiah 33, 35–6, 93, 101–3, 119
Jerusalem, schools in 6–18, 35–6, 101
Jesus, teaching of 181
Joab 126, 129
Job 4, 61, 138–53
    'Comforters' 149–51
    editing of book 142–4, 151
    see also theodicy
Jonadab 127
Jonathan 37
Joseph, story of 58–9, 115–19, 120–1
Joshua, book of 105
Joshiah, reform of 109, 165
Judas Maccabaeus 37, 188
Judges, book of 105
Judith, book of 94, 119
justice, *see* morality
justice of God, *see* theodicy

Kings, books of 105
Kish 25
Kuntilat-Ajrud, ostraca from 31

Lachish 35
Lachish Letters 32
languages 25, 28, 34, 59
law-courts 187
Law of Moses 16–18, 185–8
'Law and the Prophets' 40
leather 30–1
Lemuel of Massa 87
Levites 41, 184–5
Leviticus, book of 185
libraries 27–8, 36–8, 187
literacy 27, 29, 31–4
    see also writing
love, bond of covenant 111 n.
love poems, *see* Egyptian literature;
    Song of Songs
Luke, St 74

Manasseh 165
'Man proposes, God disposes' 48, 52–3, 58–9, 83, 117–18, 176
manual work 14, 54–5, 73
Mari 27–8
marriage and family life 75–6, 121–2
Masada 7
mathematics 25, 29
Mattathias 18
Matthew, St 75
meat-eating 109
medical profession 87–8
Memphis 54
Mephibosheth 127
messengers 129
Messianic prophecy 60
Micah, book of 112
Moab 100
morality 50, 68–83
    see also creation, of man; goodness;
    marriage and family life; nature
    and order; poor; sexuality; and
    theodicy
Moses 16, 124–5

'Name' of God 109–10
Naomi 120
narrative art 56, 58–60, 122, 126–31
nationalism 6, 107–9
    see also Chosen People
nature and order 11, 20–2, 91, 94–6, 98–100, 144, 160–1, 171–2, 178–9
    New Testament teaching 180–2
    see also Noachian precepts

negative confession 143, 172
Nehemiah, memoirs of 37
New Kingdom in Egypt 48, 59, 62, 191
Nineveh 38
Noachian precepts 171–2 n.
nouveaux riches 140–2
novel 71, 115
Numbers, book of 124, 185
numerical saying 88

Odysseus 127
onomastica 88–9, 122–3, 144, 173–4
'opposites', theory of 20–2
ostraca 28, 31–2, 45, 54
Oxyrhynchus Papyri 17

papyrus 30–1, 45
parables 10, 67, 94
pastoral life 73
Paul, St 181
Pentateuch 123–4
piety 18, 49–50, 68, 167
   see also quietism
Plato 19
platitudes 91, 182
poor 74–5, 87, 102, 111, 113, 138,
   156–7
Potiphar's wife 116
potter, symbol for Creator 21, 51, 104,
   122, 172
prayer 49, 68 n., 109–10, 179–80, 184
priesthood 184–6
prophets 93–105, 177–8
   see also Amos; Hosea; Isaiah;
   Jeremiah; Micah; and Second
   Isaiah
Proverbs, book of 4, 51–2, 66–92
proverbs 11, 67
   authority of 170
   colloquial 53–4, 84–5
   didactic sayings 83–6
Providence 121
   action of God and action of man 95,
   117–18
   see also 'Man proposes, God
   disposes'; nature and order
psalmists 57, 166–7, 185
psychosomatic factors 71
Pythagoreans 21

Qadesh, battle of 124–5
Qadesh-Barnea, ostraca from 31–2
Queen of Sheba 131–2

questions, rhetorical 94–5, 99, 101,
   144 n., 171
quietism 47–8, 50, 95, 121
Qumran 7

rabbinic interpreters 187
Ras Shamra, see Ugarit
Rachel 121
reading and writing 24–33
Rebecca 121
religious instruction 82–3
reputation 15–16, 77–8, 107–9
retribution 146–7, 149–50, 152, 156,
   161–8
righteous and wicked 81–2
royal officials 33–4, 36, 66–7
royal propaganda 55, 60, 126, 154
Ruth 41, 120–1

sacrifice, see cult
Samuel, books of 105
Sarah 119
Satan 151
Saul 37
schools 1–6, 24–32, 92, 101
scribal profession 27, 30, 32, 49, 55,
   81, 116–17
'Scripture' 40–1, 187–9
Second Isaiah 61, 103–5
seminary in Jerusalem 41, 185–8
Sennacherib 119
Seraiah 33
Sermon on the Mount 48
Sesostris I 55, 58
sexuality:
   love poems 132–6
   nakedness, shame of 123
   promiscuity 68–70
   stories about sex 121–3, 129
   see also marriage and family life
Shallum 102
shame culture 15–16, 77–9, 123, 129
Shaphan 36
Sheba 126
Shema 107
Shimei 126–7
silence 13, 49
Siloam inscription 32
Sippar 27
slaves 76–7, 113–14
social order 13–15, 98–9, 139–42,
   147–8
Sodom and Gomorrah 165–6

Solomon 35, 126, 186
  patron of schoolmen 66, 131, 154
  reputation 131–2
Song of Songs 41, 62, 132–6
songs 63, 136
speaking, skill in 11–13, 30, 41–4,
  79–80, 81 n., 128–9
Stoicism 23, 172 n.
stories (Egyptian), see Egyptian
  literature
stories (Old Testament) 15, 115–32
Sumerian 25–6

Tamar 121, 126–7, 130
teaching 105–14
  see also schools
Tell Mardikh 24–5
temple, understanding of 109–10, 184
Theban tomb paintings 122, 134
theodicy 19–22, 138–9, 146–8, 151–2,
  164–70
Theodore of Mopsuestia 132–3
Theognis 23
Thomas à Kempis 117–18
  see also 'Man proposes, God disposes'
Thot 89, 116–17
tithing 109
Tobit, book of 41, 119–20
torah 106
transcendence of God 19, 48–9, 149,
  151–2, 157–8, 162–3, 173, 175–7
transmission of literature 4, 6, 36–9,
  103, 177

Ugarit 28, 185
Unjust Steward, parable of 74
Uriah 129

wasf 134–6
weak, care for 113–14
Wenamun 35
  see also Egyptian literature
widows, care for 74–5
wisdom:
  academic hypotheses 2–4, 183–4
  as craftsmanship 65–6
  in creation 65–6, 89–91
  as instruction 66–7
  as 'know-how' 65–6
  and Law 17, 107
  personified 17, 89–91
  proverbial 67
  transcendent 174–5
  see also creation
Wisdom of Solomon (book) 169
women, status of 75–6
  see also marriage and family life
writing 25–6, 29 n., 32–3

Yahwist 123–4, 189
Yin and Yang 20

Zionist theology 110–12
Zophar 149